THROUGH INDIAN EYES

The Living Tradition

About the Authors

Leon E. Clark, the author of *Through African Eyes,* is the general editor of the CITE World Cultures Series. He received his B.A. and M.A. from Yale University and his doctorate in International Education from the University of Massachusetts. He has lived in India on three separate occasions, teaching in a government college in Karnataka and conducting research at the Educational Resources Center in New Delhi. For seventeen years he directed the International Training and Education Program at American University, where he is now professor emeritus of sociology.

Donald J. Johnson is professor of International Education and Asian Studies at New York University, where he teaches courses on Hinduism, Indian History, World History, and Comparative Cultures. He is co-author of *God and Gods in Hinduism, Emperor Ashoka of India: What Makes a Ruler Legitimate?* and *Mao and Gandhi: Two Paths to National Independence and Development,* as well as numerous articles and teaching materials on Asia and world history. He has served as director of Asian Studies at New York University and conducted study programs in India and China. He serves as a consultant to the Asia Society.

Jean E. Johnson taught history for twenty years at Friends Seminary in New York City and teaches World History and Social Studies methods at New York University. She has also taught in Turkey and worked in India developing curriculum materials about South Asia for American students. She has served as director of TeachAsia, a staff development program sponsored by the Asia Society. She was Klingenstein Fellow at Columbia Teachers College and participated in the Woodrow Wilson TORCH program as a teacher-educator on world history. Co-author of *God and Gods in Hinduism, Emperor Ashoka of India,* and *Mao and Gandhi,* she and her husband Don are currently writing a world history textbook for secondary students.

THROUGH INDIAN EYES

The Living Tradition

Donald J. Johnson

Jean E. Johnson

Leon E. Clark

A CITE BOOK

New York • London

CITE Books are distributed by
The Apex Press, 777 United Nations Plaza, Suite 3C
New York, NY 10017 (800-316-2731)
and Central Books, 99 Wallis Road, London E9 5LN, U.K.
(081-986-4854)

CITE (Center for International Training and Education)
is a program of the Council on International and Public Affairs.
The Apex Press is an imprint of the Council.

Library of Congress Cataloging-in-Publication Data

Through Indian Eyes : the living tradition / Donald J.
Johnson, Jean E. Johnson, Leon E. Clark. Fourth rev. ed.
    p.   cm.
    "A CITE book."
    Includes bibliographical references and index.
    Summary: Uses selections from a variety of sources, including
traditional and modern literature, speeches, and historical docu-
ments to present a picture of life in India.
    1. India—literature.   [1. India.]   I. Johnson, Donald J.
II. Johnson, Jean E.   III. Clark, Leon E.
Library of Congress data in earlier edition of this title:
DS407.T49   1992   92-16595
954—dc20   CIP

ISBN 0-938960-47-4
ISBN 0-938960-46-6 (pbk.)

Cover design by Warren Hurley; photos by Donald Johnson
Typeset and printed in the United States of America

Contents

Preface

People—and nations—have a tendency to look at the outside world from their own perspectives. This is natural and perhaps necessary, for we are all prisoners of a particular space and time. But how limiting and boring one perspective can be! And how faulty and biased our information can be if we listen only to ourselves!

The main goal of *Through Indian Eyes* is to broaden our perspective by presenting a largely Indian view of India and the world. The hope is that by looking at India from "inside" we will add balance to our predominantly "outside" (and therefore lopsided) view of the Indian sub-continent. In short, the hope is that looking through Indian eyes will mitigate the negative effects of our ethnocentrism.

A majority of the selections in this book, then, have been written by Indians, and they come from a variety of sources: autobiographies, fiction, poetry, religious texts, historical documents, letters, speeches, and newspaper and magazine articles. When "just the right" Indian source did not exist, or when numerous sources had to be brought together to make a coherent whole, we have taken the liberty of writing selections ourselves. However, whenever possible, we have quoted Indian sources extensively and at times have simply adapted Indian material. (The sources for all selections are made clear at the end of the book.) Our goal throughout has been to represent an Indian perspective, except for those few instances when an outside view, say, that of the colonial British, is called for.

Unlike traditional surveys or histories, *Through Indian Eyes* does not try to "cover" all of India or to offer "expert" analysis by outside observers. Instead, it focuses on a few major themes, presenting material that re-creates, as authentically and concretely as possible, the reality of Indian life. Interpretation is left to the reader. In effect, this book has two major goals: to let Indians speak for themselves and to let readers think for themselves.

This does not mean, however, that scholarship has been relegated to a secondary position. Basic concepts and insights from history and the social sciences have been applied thoughout in the selection of material. And the Introduction preceding each reading attempts to put the reading in historical and cultural context, referring, where relevant, to academic attitudes and debates surrounding the issues at hand. In addition, Postscript commentaries and selections written especially for this book fill in gaps where they may exist between readings. But the overriding concern has been to *show* India rather than to *explain* it, to present the concreteness of experience rather than the abstractness of detached analysis.

Earlier editions of *Through Indian Eyes* consisted of two volumes, with Volume 1, "The Wheel of Life," focusing on cultural and social aspects of everday life, and Volume 2, "Forging a Nation," concentrating on "larger" issues, such as politics, economics, and national unity. This new edition of *Through Indian Eyes*—issued as one volume but containing 30 percent more material than the two earlier combined—is in some ways a different book and in other ways similar to its namesake. Divided into three sections, this new edition begins in Part One: The Hindu Cycle of Life with an intimate view of Indian family life, moving from birth, to growing up, to marriage, parenthood, and finally to death, all the while integrating Hindu beliefs and attitudes toward human relations, social institutions, and the ultimate meaning of life, including a look at the caste system and the role of women in Hindu society.

Part Two: The Historic Tradition traces the highlights of India's 4,000-year history beginning with the Indus Valley city of Mohenjo-daro and moving through the Mauryan Dynasty, the Gupta Empire, the coming of the Muslims, the establishment of the Moghul Empire, its supplanting by the British, and finally the rise of the nationalist movement, headed by Gandhi and Nehru, that led to independence. Old enmities between Hindus and Muslims are revisited here by examining current conflicts over land, temples, politics, and Kashmir— all issues with strident religious overtones that threaten the stability of India's secular state.

Part Three: An Old Civilization Builds a New Nation is almost entirely new. After uncovering the basic roots of Indian democracy, this last third of the book examines the recent political, economic, and social challenges that India has had to face: ethnic and linguistic conflicts; separatist movements; the assassination of Prime Minister Indira Gandhi following the army's assault on the Sikh Golden Temple; the subsequent assassination of Mrs. Gandhi's son, Prime Minister Rajiv Gandhi; and the ever-present, ever-growing pressure of India's 987 million people for improved standards of living. The book ends with a look at the dramatic turnabout in Indian economic policies that promise a shift from a highly centralized system to one more open to market forces and private investment.

In some ways, perhaps in many ways, India may seem different from the West, and indeed it is. But in many more ways, the Indians as people are similar to people anywhere in the world. Human beings, after all, no matter where they live, face the same basic needs: to eat, to work, to love, to play, to get along with other people and with their environments. Learning how Indians respond to these needs may teach us something useful for our own lives.

More important, getting to know Indians as people—sharing in their thoughts and feelings, their beliefs and aspirations—should help us to develop a sense of empathy, a feeling of identity, with human beings everywhere. In the end, we should know more about ourselves—indeed, we should have an expanded definition of who we are—because we will know more about the common humanity that all people share. Self-knowledge is perhaps the ultimate justification for studying about other people.

Washington, D.C.   Leon E. Clark
July 1999

Acknowledgments

The authors would like to thank Ward Morehouse, president of the Council on International and Public Affairs, for his support over the years. Not only has he provided the opportunity for all of us to work at the Educational Resources Center in New Delhi, but he has also arranged to have this book reissued and has generously shared his expertise on India throughout the process of revision.

We would also like to express our appreciation to Cynthia Morehouse for her careful and at times painstaking editing of the new manuscript. She has shown patience and flexibility above and beyond the call of duty.

And finally, we would like to thank Carol Grabauskas and Brinnie Ramsey for their help with proofreading, tracking down photographs, and in general for serving as insightful and honest critics.

PART ONE

THE HINDU CYCLE
OF LIFE

Introduction

"What *is* India?" the teacher asked.

Hands went up all around the room. "It's in Asia," one student offered.

"Is it?" the teacher replied.

"It's a subcontinent in Asia, bounded by the Himalayas, the Indian Ocean, and the Bay of something."

"No, not that," the teacher said.

"It's a country where people are segregated into castes and can't eat together or choose who they'll marry."

"No."

"It's a land where most of the people are Hindus and their prime minister is a woman."

"No, that's not India."

Fewer hands now. "I think it's a poor country where the people live in villages and die a lot."

"No," smiled the teacher. "Not that."

"Isn't it an Asian country where the people are either very rich or very poor?"

"Ahhh," moaned one boy in the back. "He's going to say, 'No, not that.' I know what the answer is. There is no India!"

In reply, the teacher said, "Let me tell you an old Indian story. There was once a King who tried to explain what a chariot was to an old man. 'Is it the wheels?' asked the old man. 'No,' said the King. 'Is it the axle? the yoke? the reins? the chariot-body?' Each time the King answered 'No.' 'Then,' said the old man, 'king though you are, you are lying to me. There is no chariot.'"

17

"The King wasn't really lying, of course, because the chariot was more than any one of its parts—or a collection of them. So too with India. We shall be trying to understand what India is, but India will always be more than the parts we choose to study."

As the late Prime Minister Nehru once said, "India contains all that is disgusting and all that is noble. You take your choice." We must choose what to study about this country, which is as complex as any continent, with almost three times as many people as the United States, 3,000 "ethnic" groups, sixteen official languages, all the major world religions, and a history that goes back 4,500 years. Anything we choose to study about India will be only part of the story of this complex nation.

India is a nation of many nations, for the states in India are like countries in Europe. Despite great diversity in culture, language, and life-style, India is *one* nation. It is like a vast garden with many species of flowers. The late Prime Minister Indira Gandhi has said:

> Many crises and dangers from within and without have obstructed our path but we have taken them in our stride. . . . What holds people together is not religion, not race, not language, not even a commitment to an economic system. It is shared experience and involvement in the conscious and continuous effort at resolving internal differences through political means. It is a sense of "Indian-ness" which unites our people despite ethnic, linguistic, and religious diversity.[1]

What is this "Indian-ness"? Perhaps it lies in a shared mythological past. Indians know their own nation as *Bharat*, after a hero of the great epic the *Mahabharata*. When Mahatma Gandhi talked about re-establishing *Ram-rajya*, Indians knew he meant a society like the one Rama ruled in the epic *Ramayana*. Hindus travel all over India on religious pilgrimages. An illustration accompanying a magazine article proposing a mammoth development plan to link up the major rivers in India has a picture of Shiva in the corner; every Indian knows that this refers to the story of that great god's catching the sacred Ganges River in his hair. Even Muslims share this past. "They are Indians," one hears Hindus say. "They are the same as us, but they were converted."

Hinduism is one of the major threads which has given unity to India for thousands of years. It is the major religion of more than 80 percent of Indians and has influenced the other faiths of India as well. Hinduism, like most religions, offers its believers a wide array of rules, ideals, and expectations, all within an ultimate world view. Writings about these moral values and ideals are often called by social scientists "prescriptive literature." Most humans cannot possibly live up to all the ideals taught by their religions, yet religious ideals and values provide members of most societies with something to strive for and a sort of script or playbook which guides one's life.

Descriptions of the life people actually live is termed "descriptive literature." As we go about our daily round of life, often thinking about survival, finding work, getting educated and married, the larger moral values we are supposed to live by sometimes get pushed to the background of our concerns. Indians are no different than we are, and like most of us their lives are often caught between moral expectations and the pressures of daily life. The tension between "prescriptive," what we ought to do, and "descriptive," or what we actually do, provides the framework for the first section on the Hindu way of life.

The sources which describe the Hindu expectations and rules, called *dharmas*, are woven in and around readings which portray a more realistic and human life for the majority of Hindus. Most of the selections in Part One have been chosen to provide the reader with both a sense of what the highest ideals of Hinduism say people should do and the round of life that most Hindus find themselves really living. This mixture of readings will, we hope, offer insight into both Hinduism's unique view of the world and how real Indian human beings struggle to live their lives according to the values of their religion, but often, like all but a saintly few of us, fall quite short of these ideals.

Hinduism, unlike Judaism and Christianity, does not expect everyone to follow the same moral rules. Each Hindu, the scriptures teach, is different in several ways. As they grow in age, Hindus have different expectations and should perform different roles or *dharmas*. Similarly, men and women follow different paths of *dharma* and there are different roles for each social group or caste in the society. Finally, each of us, Hinduism teaches, has a different combination of qualities or *gunas* and therefore all of us are uniquely equipped to carry out our own personal *dharma*.

Families in India

❧Introduction: "In India you have got to be connected," an Indian remarked. The most important connection, at birth and throughout life, is an individual's family, and so our story of India begins with the family. The following joyous mother's song suggests how many people are involved in an Indian child's birth.

> Husband, call the midwife quickly,
> Let my child be delivered.
>
> Husband, call the barber's wife quickly,
> Get the four-wick lamp lighted in my palace.
>
> Husband, call my mother-in-law soon,
> Beat the golden plate in my palace....
>
> Husband, give sister-in-law lovingly what's due to her,
> And fulfill all customs with double measure.[2]

How does an Indian family differ from an American family? The novelist Santha Rama Rau suggests some answers in this first selection.[3]❧

So often in the years I have lived in America, I have heard the pleasant inquiry, "How is your family?" It makes me realize that it is virtually impossible to translate the question into my native language, Hindi. In India, you would ask, "Is everyone well in your house?"

The point is that almost never do we, in India, use the word "family" in the American way, meaning, perhaps, only a husband and wife and their children. In India, a family

21

would mean something much closer to a clan, including numerous near and distant relatives. This odd fact of language illustrates the profound difference in the family life of the two countries. In the Indian household, with all its diverse relationships, you learn to become a part of the world that surrounds you.

I once quoted to an American friend a familiar Indian saying, "Every Hindu girl's ambition is to be a mother-in-law." My friend looked puzzled. "Why a mother-in-law?" she asked. Whatever rights may be denied a Hindu woman by society, in the intricate and all-embracing domain of her home, she is supreme. Living with a husband and wife often will be all their sons and daughters-in-law, all their grandchildren, and possibly, if the grandsons are old enough to be married, there will be great-grandchildren as well. The senior woman in the home, the mother-in-law, controls this empire—which requires all her skill, tact, and administrative competence.

Besides the immediate members of the family, there will also be distant relatives who, for one reason or another, have a right to be part of this large family organization—a widowed cousin, an uncle without a family of his own, or a maiden aunt. Relatives from near and far have the right to come and "visit" for a week, six months, the rest of their lives, and nobody will question their presence. After all, what is a family for?

I can remember from my grandmother's household an elderly cousin who used to visit us daily. He came to our house, not to share our company, but because he was too stingy to buy his own newspaper. At six every evening, a chair would be set out for him in our garden, our newspaper on it, weighted down with a stone to keep the rising night breeze from disarranging it. He would arrive, settle himself comfortably, enjoy the lovely colors of the Indian evening, read the paper, and then leave. Often, he would not exchange a word with any member of the household. Why should he? In the Indian view, the horizons of a family should be wide. No one in the family, and certainly not an older member, is ever thrown on the discard heap. All remain cherished and

Life in the South Indian courtyard is never dull. Here a visiting nurse talks with family members. (United Nations)

respected members.

When I first returned to India after four years at Wellesley College, my family was bursting with curiosity about my exotic adventures in that "new" country, America. The question that interested me most came from a very old relative, a lady who was partly deaf and nearly blind. "Tell me," she said, "is it really true that some old women in America live alone?"

"Yes," I admitted. "There isn't always room for old people in the household of a newly married couple."

"Oh," she said, "how very sad!"

"But the old people often prefer to have a place of their own."

"I wasn't talking about the *old*," she told me in a sharply impatient voice. "I meant, how very sad for the *young.*"

No wonder there is no true equivalent in India for the word "family" in the American sense. In every Asian family, there is not only space but necessity for all these many relationships and their diverse contributions. The Indian household encompasses a consideration of a world of people that may not be to every member's taste—but all of whom deserve equal consideration.

JOINT, NUCLEAR, OR SINGLE

☞INTRODUCTION: The Indian joint family, even a modern one like Santha Rama Rau's, is large and complex. Within the family, each member has a different role, and the lines of authority are clear. The oldest man in the family has the greatest status and power. His wife supervises the activities within the household. Ideally the sons and their wives all live in the same compound. In the home, a wife is subject to the power and authority of her husband's mother, which explains why most Indian women look forward to becoming mothers-in-law. The children tend to look upon each other as brothers and sisters rather than as cousins. Their differences in age are more important distinctions than their actual blood relationship. The children also tend to regard all older women as mothers and older men as fathers.

A diagram of an extended family might look like the one below. The age of each family member is listed below the symbol that indicates his or her sex. In this family, there are four sons who have a total of thirteen children. As the seven granddaughters marry, they will join their husbands in other joint families. The six grandsons will add their wives to this family.

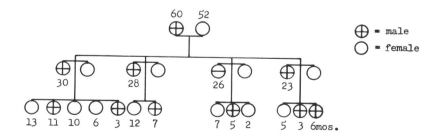

The following reading, taken from the August 1988 centennial edition of the *Times of India,* illustrates both the changing nature of the extended family and the tenacity of the tradition.[4]⁊

Like a chameleon which changes colour to adapt to its natural environment, family life in India, especially in metropolitan cities, has been undergoing a change with increasing modernisation and urbanisation. Joint families have given way to nuclear families, which in turn have submitted to single parent families, while there are still others who prefer to stay single. Family being the basic unit of organisation in society, it is but natural that it will reflect the changes taking place in it.

Joint families in India once used to be a common phenomenon. The traditional joint family may be characterised as a group of people related to one another and residing in the same dwelling, having a common hearth, religion and property and who have a set of rights and obligations. And more importantly the spending money comes from a common source, whether it be the family business or funds pooled.

Swraj Paul's family could be taken as a typical example of a joint family. A business family with 19 members, it consists of four brothers—Stya, Jit, Swraj and Surrendra. Stya is married to Rajeshwari and has a daughter. Jit is unmarried. Swraj is married to Aruna and they have three sons—Akash, Amber and Anhad. Akash and Amber too are married, with a son each. Surrendra Paul is married to Shirin. They have two daughters and two sons.

The brothers used to stay together in Jalandhar. Later on, three of the brothers came to Calcutta and shared the same roof for 25 years. Although now business demands compel the four brothers to stay apart, during vacations all of them come to Calcutta and spend time together. They have a common kitchen and they even try to share the same social life. Insists Jit Paul, "For me, joint family is the only way of good living, as you not only gain materially, but psychologically also. There is good scope for all-round development in a joint family."

One of the predominant aspects of a joint family is that

authority rests with the eldest male member and relations are based more on bonds between adult males than on conjugal ones. Said Dr. Promilla Kapur, prominent sociologist and director of Integrated Human Development Services Foundation, "In a joint family all your emotional needs are looked after and distributed among several people; consequently the husband and wife don't look to each other for fulfillment of all their emotional needs. Frictions between a couple are also subdued due to the presence of other families." This was corroborated by Jit Paul who said, "In a joint family one hardly faces strains at all because there is always someone who is acting as a cushion for you." This cushioning is absent in a nuclear family. Giving instances, Dr. Kapur said, "Conflict of interests between husband and wife often causes tension."

Sociologists have held different opinions on the influence of joint families on children. Some say that staying in an extended family makes a child share, socialize and adapt better than one in a nuclear family. However, Dr. Kapur said that this was not always true. In some cases, children in joint families are not motivated to do anything as they know their fathers and uncles will anyway support them if worst comes to the worst. She said, "Personalities can get curbed due to the authority of elders and a child can lose initiative."

Richard Sennett in his book *Families Against the City* [Cambridge, MA: Harvard University Press, 1970] said that unlike children in nuclear families, those in joint families were found to be more economically mobile. This was because in families, especially those in business, work was often discussed at home among the male adults and children often benefited by listening to the elders.

Generally women in joint families don't have much authority except in domestic matters. Exceptions of course are always there. Said Shirin Paul, "Our family is very flexible. There are no rigid laws. I have often been consulted in business matters and have a say in decision-making." For a working woman, living in a joint family has an added advantage.

The married ones are assured that there will always be someone at home to whom she can entrust her children. Unlike her counterpart in a nuclear family, she is not plagued by a sense of guilt at not being able to pay enough attention to her kids. Young working couples are realising the importance of living in joint families, and perhaps this could account for the small percentage of people reverting back to extended families. However, the joint family is not without its drawbacks. Tensions between various families under the same roof might be simmering below the surface, but are often held in curb, leading in some cases to deep-rooted resentment and a desire to set up one's own household. Jit Paul very rightly said, "In a joint family there must be some individual independence. It should be an open-house system. The elders should be adjustable if they want to hold the family together."

Disintegration of joint families is directly related to the modernisation sweeping our country. Emigration from places of one's birth to those providing better employment opportunities, the spiralling cost of living and pressures on living space are some of the factors responsible for break-ups. Nuclear families have indeed become a way of life. However, nuclear families do not live in isolation. In times of crisis, during festive and other such occasions, the link with the joint family is reinforced. Said Dr. Kapur, "At the emotional level, we are still integrated."

Twigs Are Bent Differently

&INTRODUCTION: The setting for most of the family's activities is the roofless courtyard in the center of the house. Many homes in India should really be called enclosures, for they encircle a bit of earth and sky rather than shutting them out. The courtyard is open to the heavens. The rooms surrounding it provide privacy and storage space; they are seldom used as areas to live in.

What about the quality of life "inside the courtyard?" How does it compare with life in an American home, where typically only mother, father, and children live? The following selection is an attempt to compare some of the experiences of an eight-year-old American boy and a six-year-old Indian boy, named Babu. The selection was written by the American's father after he and his family had visited Babu's joint family in a North Indian village.[5]&

An American child and his nuclear family stand out in bold relief when seen in the midst of an Indian joint family going about its daily round in the courtyard. It is easy to tell who the American boy's mother and father are. Babu, the Indian boy, one of thirteen children in the courtyard, is surrounded by four women. Judging from his attitude toward them and their attitudes toward him, any one of them could be his mother.

In fact, however, Babu's mother is not even in the courtyard. She is visiting her family in another village. Babu has chosen to stay with his aunts, who share in his care. At various times one of them may give him water, another feed him, another pick him up after a fall, and still another make room for him on her *charpoy* (string cot) at night.

The American boy, although only eight years old, has a

clear sense of "mine," by which he means things that belong to him and to him alone. You may borrow his pencil or matchbox cars, but you must ask first and must be sure to return them. Even space is included in his possessions. At night, when the *charpoys* are put out, the American assumes that he'll have "his" bed, or at least share Daddy's.

For Babu, in contrast, the bed and all other possessions in the courtyard belong to everyone. Toys bought at a fair are passed from cousin to cousin, brother to brother. As they disintegrate, their pieces are also shared. At one such fair, Babu had been given money to buy a few sweets, which he was eating with evident relish. A younger cousin climbed off his mother's lap, swept the sweets out of Babu's hand, and returned with them to his mother. Babu made no protest. He simply followed the younger child and started eating the sweets from his hand. He did not complain, nor did any aunt scold the younger child for taking what "wasn't his."

Babu is learning that "mine" means what belongs to the family and no one else. "Mine" extends to the limit of the courtyard, which his mother and aunts seldom leave. He learns from his grandmother's attitude that no one is to come into the courtyard or take anything out of it unless he is a family member. He hears the family justify the exploits of a young uncle, which include stealing a bicycle and some jewelry; the blame is put on someone outside the family. He realizes that his aunts will feed any member of the family but no one else unless it's a special feast day. For Babu, "me" and "mine" mean family.

Individuality is another thing that is different in the courtyard. The American boy tries to learn the names of Babu's aunts and discovers that they are all called Bahu, which means "daughter-in-law." One is "oldest daughter-in-law"; one is "middle daughter-in-law"; one "next to youngest"; another "youngest." Babu similarly refers to other children in the courtyard as "oldest brother" or "middle brother." Individuality does not seem to be as important as position in the family. Each member seems to know his place and over

South Indian children help their mother thresh rice in the family courtyard.
(United Nations)

whom he has authority.

The American boy has a vivid sense of time. How often he hears, "It's time to go to bed" or "Wash up, it's time to eat." He has learned to ask, "Mommy, is it time for dinner?" All his life he has done things on time. There is a time for watching *Sesame Street*, a time for school, a time for play, and a time for bed.

In the courtyard, the American boy realizes, each person goes to bed when he is tired, even the very young. For Babu, the only time is the time it happens to be. There are far more important motivations than Daddy's watch. Chances are there isn't even a watch in the courtyard. Babu's stomach tells him when it is time to eat, and he is served a meal. Babu's heavy eyelids tell him when it is time for sleep, and he crawls into the nearest *charpoy*. He is welcomed by whomever is already there, and he will probably make room for others as the night progresses.

Another thing the American boy notices is the lack of distinction between work and play. They seem to run together in the courtyard, and the result causes him to remark, "I like it here; there is always something to do." He is used to hearing, "Finish your work and then you can go out and play." Or, more likely, "Finish your work or you can't play."

For Babu, however, life is more flowing. He watches cousins pounding the wheat and waits eagerly for a turn with the heavy wooden pounding rod. He goes out to gather dung for the fuel cakes because it's something to do. Happily, he follows his father and uncles to the fields to glean after the harvest, thus beginning his apprenticeship as a farmer. He learns, without knowing he is receiving a lesson, from the actions of the older children and the older men. He is not told; he watches and copies.

The American boy, on the other hand, is constantly being told how to act. "Be good." "Don't forget to say thank you." "Help with the work." He had been hearing this sort of advice as long as he can remember. He senses somehow that he could always be a little better, work a little harder. There seems to be an abstract image for him and him alone that he has to live up to but which is never quite defined. His actions somehow reflect on his parents, and they are anxious that he should "measure up."

"Measure up to what?" Babu might ask. Babu does not know this tension between parent and child. For Babu, there is no talk of what he is to be when he grows up. He will be a farmer. If the family wants him to be something else—say, a tube-well operator, or a tractor driver—he will do that. But those decisions will come later and will be made by the family. He is not reminded of the future, of *becoming*. He *is*.

Babu is also saved from competition for parental love. When there is just a father and a mother, the American boy finds that he must jealously fight for his position in their affections. Babu has the attention of at least five adult women in the courtyard, and one of them is bound to think that what he has done is wonderful. Someone will notice his mood. One morning his grandmother observed that he was out of sorts. Without a word she filled his shirt front with grain, which he exchanged for popcorn balls with the local grin parcher. He returned to the courtyard with his sweets and a broad grin. "Too permissive," we would have said if it had happened to our son. "Don't spoil the child. He shouldn't be rewarded for surliness, and anyway he's *my* son. Grandmother shouldn't interfere with his training." Abstract standards again. Babu's life has more of a flow to it.

A wise Indian once said that a child's life is largely dream play and fantasy; it must not be disturbed too much by what we consider reality or the child will not develop into the next stage. The American's development is not fantasy; it's Dr. Spock and Dr. Gesell. If a child is one year old, he walks; if he is two, he must be toilet-trained and should be talking. The parents, and through them the child, are hard put to meet the deadlines. Babu walked when he could and nursed as long as there was milk and the urge remained. Very gradually he learned to imitate the men who went outside the courtyard to relieve themselves. From the very beginning, there was no abstract standard for becoming. Babu was allowed to be.

Babu's life seems to have great freedom compared to the American boy's. No parent hovers over Babu to make sure he is good. There are no abstract standards of success set before him, either in the courtyard or in school. No one checks his actions, outside of an occasional head count to make sure he is still around. He seems to have fewer pressures, no worry about learning the tables or the reading of words, no concern about his future success. Within the limits of the family and the village, Babu's life is filled with freedom.

Yet the limits of the village and family are real, and they impose restrictions on Babu that his American counterpart will never know. Babu is being trained to imitate, to submit to the decisions of the family, especially the elders. He has seen family member after family member follow the decisions of the head of the courtyard. One son gave up an important meeting to take a family member's ashes to the Ganges River.

Another son first went for training in the Punjab and then, with equal acceptance, returned to life in the village when directed to do so by his family. Sons and daughters have accepted the spouses chosen for them. Babu is learning the lesson that family loyalty and obedience come first.

The American boy seems on the surface to have a much more restricted life; yet he is learning that it is his own decision-making that is important. He must think for himself, become something on his own. From the example of those around him and from his experience in places far from home, he is realizing that he has a worldwide range of choice.

The Banishment of Rama

🙥INTRODUCTION: In the previous reading, we saw how Babu was learning by example that his primary duty was to obey the *decisions* of his family. Another source of training is the stories told to the young. It is not uncommon to hear an Indian remark, "I learned more from my grandmother than from my school." Countless Indian children have listened as their grandmothers filled the evenings with stories from the ancient Hindu epics, some of which go back 3,000 years.

Many of the stories are about Rama, the hero of the epic *Ramayana*. Rama is held up as the ideal son because of some of the qualities he exhibits in the following episode. [6]🙥

Ayodhya lay north of the Ganges, where the land was rich and fertile. The roads around Ayodhya were broad and even, shaded by trees and dotted with wells. The people were ruled by a wise and just king, Dashratha, and their contentment was complete when, after many years, King Dashratha's wives were blessed with sons: Rama, Bharata, Lakshmana, and Satrughna.

All four brothers were trained in the arts of statecraft, archery, and warfare, and in the wisdom of the ancient books. Rama, the eldest, was the favorite of the people. If only we all had sons like Rama. Would that all fathers were so blessed.

And what a wife Rama had! Sita, as faithful as she was beautiful, was the ideal partner. All was at peace in the kingdom, and Dashratha summoned his advisers to him one day and said: "I am growing old. It is time I retire from worldly concerns and seek truth. Rama is loved by all. He is my firstborn son and should now assume the responsibilities of leadership."

The advisers agreed, and Rama was summoned. King Dashratha told him he was to be crowned and charged him: "Protect your subjects, fight your foes, and be always faithful to your duty." Rama's face was calm and serene as he received this news. He touched his father's feet and humbly accepted his decision. "I am in duty bound to do as you say," he said. Ayodhya went mad with joy. Their beloved prince was to be crowned. Halls were decorated, trumpets blared, flags flew from housetops. In the palace, everything was prepared for the coronation.

But later that night, all this changed. Bharata's mother, King Dashratha's second and favorite wife, desired that her own son be crowned and Rama banished. She recalled that once, years ago, the King had promised her any two wishes. At the time she had desired nothing. Now, reminding the King of his promise, she demanded that Bharata become king and Rama be banished. Dashratha was stunned; in vain he begged his pretty queen to ask for anything else. She could not be moved. A king must keep his word, so Dashratha had no choice but to grant her demands. Rama was summoned once more.

As Rama entered his stepmother's room, he saw his father lying motionless on the ground, too pained to speak. The Queen spoke for him: "Long ago your father offered me two boons. I want him to grant them now. Bharata is to be crowned in your place and you are to go into exile for fourteen years."

Rama received this order with the utmost calm. He looked steadily at the Queen and said, "Is that all? I shall indeed be happy if Bharata ascends the throne. He is the most noble of princes. As for going into exile, it is but a small thing for me, who am ready to lay down my life if need be to help my father discharge a sacred duty."

Calm and controlled, Rama left, after touching the feet of Dashratha and his Queen. Lakshmana, standing outside, had heard all. His eyes were red with anger as he followed Rama. Furiously, his fist clenched tightly around his bow, he

cried out, "As long as there is breath in this body, I shall fight
to see that Rama sits on the throne. I shall kill anyone who
stands in his way."

Rama answered calmly, "Lakshmana, do not get so heated.
You know very well that I shall obey my father to the last word.
It is my first and foremost duty. Let us therefore do what
father bids cheerfully and with a smile on our lips."

Lakshmana, however, was not to be pacified. He stormed

*This painting, circa 1780-1900, shows Rama, Lakshmana, and Sita in the
forest.* (Victoria & Albert Museum, London)

again. "What! Does the old King think of fulfilling his word to his Queen and not to the word given to his son? He has come under evil counsel. It is the *dharma* ["duty"] of a *Kshatriya* [a member of the warrior and ruler caste] to fight evil and establish good. My bow and arrow, sword, and broad shoulders are not for appearance only. Today the world shall see the might of Lakshmana's arm!"

Rama only soothed Lakshmana, saying, "So long as our parents are alive, it is our foremost duty to obey them. Let us not be swayed by emotion. Let us think clearly and follow the path of *dharma*."

"WE ARE *WE* . . ."

✦POSTSCRIPT: *Dharma* is a concept we will meet again and again in our study of India. It can be translated roughly as "duty" or "appropriate action." In Hindu thought, everyone and everything has a *dharma*. In the physical world, this is called an object's properties. In the world of social relations, it is one's duty. If you are a son, your *dharma* is to obey your elders, even if it means banishment. In the classical Hindu tradition, you must do your *dharma* no matter how you feel about it personally. Does anyone ask the rain whether it wants to fall? Can you imagine a lake acting like rain? In the words of the *Bhagavad Gita*, a sacred Hindu text:

> Better do your own task imperfectly
> Than do another's well
> Better die in your own duty.
> Another's task brings peril.

Rama, in the previous story, accepted and followed his dharma. He was as content to be banished as he was to be crowned. His only concern was to obey his father.

But Rama represents the ideal. Some Indian young people are trying to break away from the restrictions imposed by the ideals of dharma or traditional courtyard life. The following conversation among some young Indians and an English sociologist reflects the ideas of many urban students.[7]✦

Usha's party was quite special. Except for myself and her father, everybody was young. At my instigation the young had taken a look at themselves in . . . anticipation of [an] American

teach-in. The result had been most instructive. They felt that
the young Indians were angry, not because it is fashionable
to be angry ("John Osborne and all that!"), but because
things had improved.

In the past, the young had no place in society, they had
no entity; they were merely an extension of their parents, and
from the time of their birth to that of their death every
decision had been made for them. The decisions were made
by their parents, by the caste council, by the astrologers. As
one young architect put it, "We could not even decide what
to eat. We had to eat spinach on a particular festival; not at
any other time would spinach be cooked, for the taste, or the
vitamins. And the same was of course true of marriage, and
of jobs!"

Nisha, a beautiful teacher of English who had broken with
tradition by marrying outside her religion, chipped in: "We
are angry because for the first time . . . we have become
individuals instead of being links in a chain. For the first time
we are *we*, we are no longer *they*." Rohit, a manager in an
advertising agency, added: "We cannot afford to compromise;
to compromise would mean to get lost, to be swallowed back
by tradition."

The Student Stage of Life

❧INTRODUCTION: The informal education of the young through imitation, example, and story eventually gives way to more formal education. Traditionally, this was known as the first stage of life, the student stage. Precise rules were set down to govern the student's behavior, specifying, among other things, chastity and total devotion to his *guru*.

Ravi Shankar, the world-famous sitar player, learned his music from a *guru* named Baba. Baba believed that students should follow the traditional *dharma* and, according to Ravi Shankar, provided an excellent example.

> His own life has been one of rigorous self-imposed discipline, and he expects no less from his students. Baba's views on celibacy and especially on intoxication through alcohol or drugs are extremely rigid and severe. He strongly insists that the students follow *brahmacharya* [chastity]—for the disciple, a traditional Hindu way of life that includes only the absolute essentials of material needs. This way, with no thoughts of fine clothes, fancy foods, sex, complicated love affairs, or anything else that satisfies and encourages physical desires, the student can channel all of his powers and forces, both mental and physical, into the discipline of his music.[8]

In the following selection from his autobiography, Ravi Shankar describes the relationship between the student (*shishya*) and his *guru*.[9]❧

Guru, vinaya, sadhana—these three words form the heart of the musical tradition of India. *Guru*, as many people now know, means master, spiritual teacher, or preceptor. We give a very important place to the *guru*, for we consider him to be the representation of the divine. . . . The choice of the *guru*, to us, is even more important than choosing a husband or a

39

wife. A potential disciple cannot make a hasty decision to take just any teacher as his *guru*, nor should he break the bond between *guru* and *shishya*, once the *ganda or nara* ceremony, the initiation, which symbolically binds the two together for life, has taken place.

Vinaya means humility; it is the complete surrendering of the self on the part of the *shyshya* to the *guru*. The ideal disciple feels love, adoration, reverence, and even fear toward his guru, and he accepts equally praise or scoldings. Talent, sincerity, and the willingness to practice faithfully are essential qualities of the serious student. The *guru*, as the giver in this relationship, seems to be all-powerful. Often, he may be unreasonable, harsh, or haughty, though the ideal *guru* is none of these. Ideally, he should respond to the efforts of the disciple and love him almost as his own child.

In India, a Hindu child from his earliest years is taught to feel humble toward anyone older than he or superior in any way. From the simplest gesture of the *namaskar*, or greeting (putting the hands palm to palm in front of the forehead and bowing), or the *pranam* (a respectful greeting consisting of touching the greeted person's feet, then one's own eyes and forehead, with the hands held palm to palm) to the practice of *vinaya*, or humility tempered with a feeling of love and worship, the Hindu devotee's vanity and pretension are worn away.

Sadly, this feeling of *vinaya* is lacking today in many young people, in the East and West alike. The Western student especially seems to have an excessively casual attitude toward his teachers and toward the process of learning. The teacher-student association is no longer patterned after the old father-son relationship; . . . the two are encouraged by prevailing attitudes to act as friends and to consider each other of an equal level. This system, of course, has its benefits, but it is far from ideal for studying Indian music and understanding our traditions. The Indian teacher finds this casualness disturbing even in so small a thing as the position the student takes when he sits. Often the Western student will try to sit

Ravi Shankar playing his sitar. (Information Service of India, New York, N.Y.)

on the floor like an Indian, but since he is not accustomed
to this (poor thing!), sooner or later he stretches out his legs
and shows the soles of his feet to the *guru*. To us Indians, the
feet are . . . the most ignoble part of the body, and this position is one of extreme irreverence.

Among our legends, there is a story that illustrates very
well this quality of *vinaya*. Long ago, it is said, the great *rishi*
(saint-sage) Narada was convinced that he had gained complete mastery of the art of music, both in theory and performance. The wise Vishnu [God] decided to teach Narada a
lesson and shatter his pride, so he brought him to the dwelling place of the gods. . . . As they entered one building, they
saw many men and women with broken limbs, . . . weeping
over their condition. Vishnu . . . asked [them] what was the

matter, and they told him they were the spirits of *ragas* and
raginis [songs] created by Shiva. They said a certain *rishi*
named Narada, who could neither perform nor understand
music properly, had twisted and broken their limbs through
his singing. And they said that, unless some great and skilled
musician could sing them again correctly, they would never
regain their unmarred wholeness. When he heard this,
Narada was deeply ashamed and, in all humility, knelt before
Vishnu and begged forgiveness.

The third principal term associated with our music is *sadhana*, which means practice and discipline, eventually leading
to self-realization. It means practicing with a fanatic zeal and
ardent dedication to the *guru* and the music. If the student
is talented, sincere, faithful to his *guru*, and devoted in his
practicing, and if the *guru* is teaching with utmost dedication
and not being miserly with his knowledge, there is a distinct
pattern for learning Indian music. The student must begin by
acquiring the most basic techniques of the voice or instrument. . . .

This elementary training, for a talented and persevering
student, should last not less than five years, very much like
the elementary training for any Western musical discipline
. . . . The student should practice every day for at least eight
hours. In Western music, of course, the student has a visual
advantage. That is, much of his learning can be taken from
books, without the close supervision of a teacher. But with
Indian music, for the first five or six years the student relies
completely on the guidance of his *guru.* This is because the
guru teaches everything to the student individually and directly, according to our ancient oral traditions, for very rarely do
we use textbooks or manuals. Then, little by little, the student
learns to improvise, and he works at it until he feels free and
confident with a *raga.* . . .

Even after the student has become a fairly proficient per-
former and has created his own musical personality, he goes
back to his *guru* from time to time for an evaluation of his
development and to be inspired by new ideas. A true *guru*

never stops growing musically and spiritually himself and can be a constant source of inspiration and guidance to the loving disciple.

So, starting from the very beginning, I would estimate that it requires at least twenty years of constant work and practice to reach maturity and a high standard of achievement in our classical music.

Arranging a Marriage

☙INTRODUCTION: Childhood and the student stage of life end when the young man or woman is married. We say "is married" because most marriages in India are arranged. Just as childhood in India is usually set in the context of the joint family, marriage is a family affair as well, for the new couple has the responsibility of carrying on the family line. As we have noted, the young wife traditionally joins her husband's household. It is against this background that you must consider the arranged marriage.

An Indian once observed: "American young people go to college. There they choose from among the twenty or so possibilities they have met." Whether or not that observation is precisely correct, it is true that Americans generally choose a mate for themselves from among the relatively few people they happen to know.
The Indian system of arranged marriages offers a much wider range of choice. Some families even advertise for a partner for their son or daughter. A typical ad might read like one of these:

> Pretty girl for graduate, 36, getting Rupees 400/. No dowry. Caste no bar.

> Match: Educated virgin or widow for widower Brahmin, leading advocate, 40. No bars.

A more common, and usually more successful, practice is to ask family and friends to suggest a partner or to check on the suitability of a candidate. Even Americans are sometimes asked to help. The editors of this book, for example, received a letter from a friend in Delhi asking them to look up a young male student at one of the metropolitan New York colleges. The letter read in part: "This young man is shortly coming to India to get married and is still not engaged. If you find him alright, we shall, on hearing from you, send a proposal to his parents in Kanpur, in request of our daughter."

For some, marriage takes place in the natural flow of life. Since childhood, a girl has heard her mother correct her behavior and then add, "What will they say?"—the "they" referring to the family of her husband-to-be. Boys and girls in villages in the Punjab play together in groups, but as soon as boy and girl show the slightest signs of interest in each other, the villagers say, "Youth has come to your girl; it is time to have her asked." Engagement, known as "being asked," is arranged by the families, and the wedding follows within a year. Once engaged, the girl is considered a member of her future husband's family. It is they who will now avenge any insult directed to the bride-to-be.[10]

For the young urban Indian, who has been exposed to new ideas, such as love matches, the process of finding a mate is sometimes rather different. The following selection tells how an upperclass, well-educated family arranges the marriage of their eldest daughter, Promila (Pom for short).[11]

In the month of February, when we had been in Lahore almost four months, we heard through one of my father's friends about an eligible young dentist in Dehra Dun named Kakaji Mehrotra. As always in such cases, a thorough investigation followed, in which the young man and his family background were scrutinized. Even his friends were reviewed. Did they drink? With the precision of a lawyer, the liabilities and assets were carefully evaluated.

Even though her whole future happiness was at stake, sister Pom, who, as the eldest daughter, by tradition must be the first to marry, was given no hint of what was going on. For this there were several reasons: first, because when a girl reaches the age of marriage, many inquiries are made, and almost all the network of relations keeps on the lookout. Since the families are so large and remain in such close contact, there may be hundreds of people who, without being told, bear the eligible members of other families in mind. So there are many leads, all of which have to be carefully tracked down, and it is thought best not to worry the children with these steps. Then, too, since the parents ultimately make the decision, they deem it unnecessary to consult the child prior to . . . final arrangements.

As Kakaji was a more attractive prospect than any other leads, his parents were finally approached—for the initiative always rests with the girl's parents. Then his family follows the same intricate process of thorough investigation, often with the help of relatives on the spot. If they are favorably impressed, then the parents, sometimes with their son, come to view the girl in question. But because Dehra Dun was so far from Lahore, Kakaji came by himself.

He arrived in Lahore in the early part of March and casually dropped in for tea. I say "casually" because his manner was that; but with the . . . elaborate planning behind the event it was actually anything but casual. Sister Pom—she was now nineteen—was sent for and came with mother into the drawing room. Dressed in a soft, silver-bordered sari, she shyly served Kakaji tea while he continued to talk to other members of the family. During the tea, he addressed some remarks to sister Pom about her studies in college and the painting over the mantelpiece, and told her about his summer practice at a hill station.

(After this short interview, on which so much depends, if Kakaji is attracted to sister Pom and favorably impresses our family, the talk proceeds, but without sister Pom's presence. Kakaji judiciously keeps from committing himself until he has spoken to his parents. If he doesn't like her, the matter is dropped.)

Actually, four days later a note arrived from his mother asking if sister Pom could be betrothed to Kakaji. My father, with his Western attitudes, refrained from answering the letter until sister Pom was consulted. So, in the drawing room one night, Mother approached sister Pom as to what she thought of Kakaji. Before Pom said anything, sister Umi, amused by all the arrangements, remarked, "How do you expect her to know what her mind is when all they talked about was the furniture? Could she have fallen in love already?"

"Love, Urmil," my father answered, "means something very different from 'falling in love.' It is a process rather than an act, and only time can shape it. The best we can do is give it every opportunity to succeed, and I'll admit this is hard."

"But doesn't 'every opportunity' include knowing the person better?" sister Umi asked.

A North Indian bridegroom ready to ride to the wedding ceremony. (Wide World Photos)

"Yes, it should," Father replied; "but here the question is one of choosing. To know a person thoroughly might take years. We believe that knowing can come only through living together."

"Do you mean, then," said Umi, "that knowing and love are the same thing?"

"Not quite, but understanding and respect are essential to mature love, and this deep understanding cannot come from friendship alone. Even serious conversations can't fully reveal a person's character. That can come only through experience, through sharing each other's problems. No amount of talking will bring about full understanding. It is only when you consider each other's problems as one and the same that you can hope for true understanding."

"But, Father," said Nimi . . . the political rebel in the family, "look at the risk that's involved."

"We minimize the risk as far as possible," he explained. " We try to find a home that is most like ours. Take Kakaji. He's a dentist. His life will not be too different from mine. Now, if I were to marry Promila in the Brahmin [priestly] caste, I would be increasing the gamble. They might not eat meat; they would pray two or three times a day; and their professions would be on totally different lines. These things are small, perhaps, but they have far-reaching effects."

Nimi spoke again. "Then you are perpetuating a caste, because this presupposes that Pom would have to be married in the *Kshatriya* [warrior] caste of professional people. For myself, I'd willingly marry a *Bania* [merchant] shopkeeper or even a *Shudra* [worker] untouchable and help break down these barriers."

"That day might come. But you will admit, Nirmil, that you are increasing the gamble."

"But for a cause I believe in," said Nimi.

"Yes," he answered, "but that's another matter."

"You say," Umi broke in, "that understanding and respect are necessary for a happy marriage. I don't see why you would respect a person more because you lived with him and shared his problems."

"In our society," said Father, "we think of respect as coming only through sacrifice."

"Then," said Umi, "you're advocating the subservience of women. Because it's not Kakaji who will sacrifice but sister Pom. And why should that be? And how is it that sister Pom will respect Kakaji because she sacrificed for him?"

"No, Urmil, it is the other way around. It is he who will respect her for her sacrifice."

"Does that mean that sister Pom will respect Kakaji, though?"

"Not necessarily. But if Kakaji is moved by Promila's sacrifice, he will show more consideration and growing concern for her. I know in my own case I was moved to the depths to see your mother, Shanti, suffer so. It took me long enough—too long, I believe—to reach that understanding, perhaps because I had broken away from the old traditions and had given in to the Western influence. You can hope, then, for this respect to be reciprocal between Promila and Kakaji; and don't forget that all this time they are getting to understand each other better."

Umi persisted. "This may take years! Is sister Pom to be unhappy all this time?"

"Perhaps so. But she is striving for ultimate happiness and love. These are precious gifts which can only be cultivated in time."

"Hard only for Pom," sister Umi insisted. "Aren't you struck by the injustice of this? Shouldn't Kakaji sacrifice for their happiness, too?"

"There has to be a start. Remember, it's her life that's joined with his. She will forsake her past to build a new future, and you may call this a complete beginning of absolutely new experience. If both Promila and Kakaji were to be obstinate and wait to see who will take the first step, what hope do you have of their ever getting together?"

"That's evading my question, Father. Why shouldn't he take the initiative?"

"He would, perhaps, be expected to do so if Promila were working too and leading another life which would be equal to his. I suppose more than this I really can't say, and there may be some injustice at that."

"What is this happiness you speak of?" said sister Umi. "I only vaguely understand it."

"It is a uniting of ideals and purposes, making them blend into one. Love grows gradually. This is the tradition of our society, and these are the means we have adopted to make our marriages successful and beautiful. We must have faith in the goodness of the individuals and rely on the strength of this sacred bond. In the West they have solved the problem in a different way, because their conditions differ from ours. I cannot say if it has worked any better."

"But I love my independence," said sister Umi, "for that is my ideal."

"Remember always," said Father, "that the ideals must be resolved by placing values on every one of them, for you must choose among them."

Then to sister Pom he said, "I have done my best, and my responsibility for you is not over. I will always be there to help and will continue to find satisfaction in your happiness. I have lived and worked for these values."

"And I respect your values and your judgment," replied sister Pom. "I have faith in your choice. Even if I do suffer, I can hope that some day our marriage will be as happy as yours."

Viewing a Prospective Bride

❧INTRODUCTION: In the previous selection, we considered marriage from the point of view of the girl and her family. In this reading from a novel by R. K. Narayan, Chandran, a young newspaperman, is told that his mother has started the process of arranging Chandran's marriage. [12]❧

[O]ne evening, as Chandran was working in his office, his father paid him a visit. They made polite conversation for a while.]

And then the conversation lagged for some time. Father suddenly said: "I have come on a mission. I was sent by your mother."

"Mother?"

"Yes. She wants this thing to be made known to you. She is rather nervous to talk to you about it herself. So she has sent me."

"What is it, Father?"

"But I wish you to understand clearly that I have not done anything behind your back. I have had no hand in this. It is entirely your mother's work."

"What is it, Father?"

"You see, Mr. Jayarama Iyer, who is a leading lawyer in Talapur, sent his daughter's horoscope to us some time ago; and for courtesy's sake yours was sent to them in return. Yesterday they have written to say that the horoscopes match very well and asking if we have any objection to this alliance. I was for dropping the whole matter there, but your mother is very eager to make it known to you and to leave it to your decision. . . . "

Chandran sat looking at the floor. His father paused for a moment and said: "I hear that the girl is about fifteen. They have sent a photo. She is good-looking. You can have a look at the photo if you like. They have written that she is very fair. They are prepared to give a cash dowry of [Rs] 3,000 and other presents."

He waited for Chandran's answer. Chandran looked at him. There were drops of sweat on Father's brow, and his voice quivered slightly. Chandran felt a great pity for his father. What a strain this talk and the preparation for it must have been to him! Father sat silent for a moment and then said, rising: "I will be going now. I have to go to the club."

Chandran saw his father off at the door and watched his back as he swung his cane and walked down the road. Chandran suddenly realized that he hadn't said anything in reply and that his father might interpret silence for consent and live on false hope. What a dreadful thing. He called his office boy, who was squatting on the steps of a neighboring shop, asked him to remain in the office, took out his cycle, and pedalled in the direction his father had taken. Father hadn't gone far. Chandran caught up with him.

"You want me?"

"Yes, Father."

Father slowed down, and Chandran followed him, looking at the ground. "You have taken the trouble to come so far, Father, but I must tell you that I can't marry."

"It is all right, Chandran. Don't let that bother you."

Chandran followed him for a few yards and said: "Shall I go back to the office?"

"Yes."

As Chandran was about to mount his cycle, Father stopped him and said: "I saw in your office some papers and letters lying loose on your table. They are likely to be blown away by a wind. Remind me, I will give you some paperweights tomorrow."

[In spite of what he thought about the marriage plans], early in the morning, five days later, Chandran, with his mother was in a train going to Talapur. He was to look at the girl who had been proposed to him and then give his final word.

He said to his mother for the dozenth time: "If I don't like the girl, I hope they won't mind."

"Not at all. Before I married your father, some three or four persons came and looked at me and went away."

"Why did they not approve of you?" Chandran asked, looking at her.

"It is all a matter of fate," said Mother. "You can marry only the person whom you are destined to marry and at the appointed time. When the time comes, let her be the ugliest girl, she will look all right to the destined eye."

"None of that, Mother," Chandran protested. "I won't marry an ugly girl."

"Ugliness and beauty is all as it strikes one's eye. Everyone has his own vision. How do all the ugly girls in the world get married?"

Chandran became apprehensive. "Mother, are you suggesting that this girl is ugly?"

"Not at all, not at all. See her for yourself and decide. You have the photo."

"She is all right in the photo, but that may be only a trick of the camera."

"You will have to wait for only a few hours more. You can see her and then give your decision."

"But, Mother, to go all the way to their house and see the girl, and then to say we can't marry her. That won't be nice."

"What is there in it? It is the custom. When a girl is ready for marriage her horoscope will be sent in ten directions, and ten different persons will see her and approve or disapprove, or they might be disapproved by the girl herself; and after all, only one will marry her. A year before my marriage a certain doctor was eager for an alliance with our family; the horoscopes, too, matched; and his son came to look at me.

But I didn't like his appearance, and told my father that I wouldn't marry him. It was after that that your father was proposed, and he liked my appearance, and when my father asked me if I would marry him I didn't say no. It is all settled already, the husband of every girl and wife of every man. It is nobody's choice."

They reached Talapur at 4 p.m. . . . They were welcomed into the house by Mr. Jayarama Iyer and his wife, both of whom subjected Chandran to a covert examination just as he tried to make out something of his future relatives-in-law. He found Mr. Jayarama Iyer to be a middle-aged person with a graying crop and a sensitive face. He was rather dark, but Chandran noted that the mother looked quite fair and hoped that the girl would have a judicious mixture of the father's sensitive appearance and the mother's complexion.

To his immense satisfaction, he found that it was so when, about an hour later, she appeared before him. She had to be coaxed and cajoled by her parents to come to the hall. With her eyes fixed on the ground, she stepped from an inner room, a few inches into the hall, trembling and uncertain, ready to vanish in a moment.

Chandran's first impulse was to look away from the girl. He spent a few seconds looking at a picture on the wall, but then remembered that he simply could not afford to look at anything else now. With a sudden decision, he turned his head and stared at her. She was dressed in a blue sari. A few diamonds glittered in her earlobes and neck. His heart gave a wild beat and, as he thought, stopped. "Her figure is wonderful," some corner of his mind murmured. "Her face must also be wonderful, but I can't see it very well, she is looking at the ground." Could he shriek out to Mr. Jayarama Iyer, sitting in the chair on his right and uttering inanities at this holy moment: "Please ask your daughter to look up, sir. I can't see her face?"

Mr. Jayarama Iyer said to his daughter: "You mustn't be so shy, my girl. Come here, come here."

The girl was still hesitating and very nervous. Chandran

A Brahmin priest conducts a Hindu wedding ceremony around the sacred fire. (Government of India Tourist Office. New York, N.Y.)

felt a great sympathy for her. He pleaded: "Sir, please don't trouble her. Let her stay there."

"As you please," said Jayarama Iyer.

At this moment the girl raised her head slightly and stole a glance at Chandran. He saw her face now. It was divine; there was no doubt about it.

Jayarama Iyer said to his daughter: "Will you play a little song on the *veena*?" Chandran saw that she was still nervous and once again rushed to her succor. "Please don't trouble her, sir. I don't mind. She seems to be nervous."

"She is not nervous," said her father. "She plays very well

and also sings."

"I am happy to hear that, sir, but it must be very difficult for her to sing now. I hope to hear her music some other day."

Jayarama Iyer looked at him with amusement and said: "All right."

It was with a very heavy heart that Chandran allowed himself to be carried away in the car from the bungalow. He could have cried when he said goodbye to his future brother-in-law and the train moved out of Talapur station.

His mother asked him in the train: "Do you like the girl?"

"Yes, Mother," said Chandran with fervor. "Did you tell them that?"

"We can't tell them anything till they come and ask us."

Chandran made a gesture of despair and said: "Oh, these formalities. I loathe them. All this means unnecessary delay. Why shouldn't we send them a wire tomorrow?"

"Be patient. Be patient. All in its time, Chandran."

"But supposing they don't ask us?"

"They will. In two or three days they will come to us or write."

"I ought to have told Mr. Jayarama Iyer that I liked his girl," Chandran said regretfully.

Mother asked apprehensively: "I hope you have not done any such thing?"

"No, Mother."

"Patience, Chandran. You must allow things to be done in proper order."

Chandran leaned back, resigned himself to his fate, and sat looking out of the window. . . .

Selling the Bride

❧INTRODUCTION: Arranging a marriage includes agreeing on a dowry, the money or goods the bride's family gives to the groom's family and to the bride to take to her new marriage home. Nowadays dowries can be very expensive, and for families with several daughters, providing a dowry for each of them can become an almost unbearable burden, leading many families into deep debt. Moreover, the dowry system is officially illegal in India today. However, giving a dowry is an ancient tradition in India and it probably will not disappear anytime soon, for as we shall see, it serves some useful purposes. In the following selection, Ved Mehta, the author of the earlier reading "Arranging a Marriage," discusses the dowry his family arranged for his sister Pom.[13]❧

Originally in Vedic times [3,000 years ago], the bride was adorned simply and affectionately and the dowry consisted of no more than a few presents from the family at the wedding. I soon learned how different it was now. Sister Pom's dowry must include clothes, jewelry, bedding, a sewing machine, cooking utensils, and cutlery—in fact, everything for a home save a car and the house itself, which might have been included had it not been for the three younger sisters, whose dowry had to match sister Pom's. The splendor of this dowry might well determine the subsequent offers to my other three sisters, and my grandmother carefully canvassed many of our relatives as to the presents they would give to the bride, so that there might be no duplication.

Although a few of the relatives thought the number of twenty-two saris was rather few, most consented. Long days were spent by Mother and sister Pom going to crowded bazaars and choosing the saris, which had to differ in materials, colors, and borders. No two could be alike, and even though the expensive ones of Benares brocade cost hundreds of rupees, the wardrobe was supposed to be so rich in variety that the bride could have a sari for each and every occasion for many

A shy bride arrives in her new home with part of her dowry. (Mrs. Charlotte Wiser)

years to come. (Actually, saris are very practical garments. Always six yards in length, they fit every size of woman, be she short or tall, slender or stout, merely with a few subtle adjustments of the folds.)

Jewelry matching the saris had to be made to order. Because until recently the laws of inheritance in India favored the male members of the family at the expense of the widow, a woman's most valued possessions were her gold and diamonds. These jewels alone formed her *istri-dahan*, her inheritance, which could not be taken away from her after her husband's death, according to Manu, the great Hindu lawgiver. My mother had recited to me the law of Manu sometime before: "The ornaments which may have been worn by a woman during her husband's lifetime his heirs shall not divide. Those who divide them shall be outcasts."

A Wife's *Dharma*

&Introduction: When she is married, an Indian wife usually joins her husband's family. Within her new family she must follow the wife's *dharma*. According to the *Dharmashastras* (ancient Hindu texts for the ordering of social life) the ideal wife must perform numerous functions and is to refrain from many things as well:

> He who carefully guards his wife, preserves the purity of his offspring, virtuous conduct, his family, himself, and his means of acquiring merit . . . . Let the husband employ his wife in the collection and expenditure of his wealth, in keeping everything clean, in the fulfillment of religious duties, in the preparation of his food, and in looking after the household utensils. . . . Drinking spirituous liquor, associating with wicked people, separating from the husband, rambling abroad, sleeping at unseasonable hours, and dwelling in other men's houses, are the six causes of the ruin of women. [14]

At first, the young bride must try to fit into the pattern of her husband's extended household. She must transform her loyalty from her own family to a family she does not know. The most difficult part of this transition is trying to please her new mother-in-law, who may not want to share her son with a stranger. The mother-in-law may even try to keep the wife from spending time alone with her new husband. The one way a new wife can gain acceptance into the new family is to become a mother herself. Should she give birth to a son, the new wife's status rises dramatically.

To appreciate the position of the young woman as she starts her married life, it is important to understand the Hindu ideal for the perfect woman. The following selection by an Indian journalist analyzes the religious origin of the contemporary view of the woman's role and her source of power.[15]&

In the beginning, according to Indian mythology, was

Shakti, and *Shakti,* which means energy, has a feminine gender in Sanskrit. The cosmos was her creation, her child. Now this image of the beginning of the world is not only appealing in an idealistic sense, but it also approaches the story patched together by the discoveries of science. And what could be nobler than to see the Creator as a Mother? It is the mother, not the father, who comes to mind first whenever the word "creation" is mentioned. . . .

The most meaningful word the Hindus have for woman is *mata,* or "mother." Philosophers and poets alike have believed "mother love" to be the ideal love, the real love, a love utterly unselfish and boundless. From conception to death, she intuitively and naturally believes in giving with no thought of return. . . . All other loves, the loves of the betrothed, of married couples, of friends, of fathers for their sons, of brothers and sisters, are based on reciprocity and are forms of friendship; mother love alone can be one-sided, lavishing care and affection upon the prodigal as well as upon the perfect child. . . .

It is motherhood more than womanhood, then, that the Hindus glorify. Manu the law-giver [who wrote between the first century B.C. and the second century A.D.] took many occasions to say unlovely things about womanhood. Only once in his life, when he wrote that "the gods come down to play where women are worshiped," did he permit himself to pay women a compliment. But in his idolization of motherhood he is quite emphatic, and his code says: "A master exceedeth ten tutors in claim to honor; the father a hundred masters; but the mother a thousand fathers in right to reverence and in the function of teacher."

. . . the usual blessing offered the newlywed bride as she bows to her elders is: "Be the mother of a hundred sons!" Generally, the Hindu woman does not come into her own until she becomes a mother, preferably of a son. She then becomes the head of household affairs and is venerated.

Paying greater honor to motherhood than to womanhood implies an emphasis on creation rather than on recreation.

Shiva-Shakti, the male and female energies in the universe, pictured as a single being. (Archeological Survey of India, Government of India, New Delhi)

Accordingly, marriage becomes more work than play. It becomes a sanctioned and sacramental union of man and woman whose purpose is to carry on the sacred task of perpetuating the race.

. . . When motherhood is put before womanhood, romance dies a little. This does not mean that there are no flirtations or no elopements in India, for girls will be girls and boys will be boys the world over; but it does mean that romance cannot be the central theme of marriage. . . .

This Hindu preoccupation with motherhood in no way implies an inferior status for the Indian woman. . . . But the worship of motherhood in preference to womanhood had one great latent danger in it. It was capable of fostering the conception that woman was merely a means to an end rather than an end in herself. It is the materialization in Hindu society of this danger that has dismally marked Indian life ever since; . . . even Uma [consort of the great god Shiva] was quoted as saying to Shiva: "A woman should be beautiful and gentle, considering her husband as her God and serving him as such in fortune and misfortune, health and sickness, obedient even if commanded to unrighteous deeds or acts that may lead to her own destruction."

Motherhood means sacrifices and anonymity, a life of self-effacement and silent toil. No one will claim that the ideal of motherhood is not a noble ideal. But it is likely, in a society dominated by such a concept, that woman's needs and desires as a flesh-and-blood creature may be overlooked or even forgotten. That is exactly what has happened in India . . . . Although the Western preference of womanhood to motherhood can be equally harmful when carried too far, creating its own dire problems, it at least guarantees woman her own personality and her peculiar claims on the pleasures of life; it does not put her to scorn if she is barren or if she bears no sons.

Stories My Mother Told Me

🔖INTRODUCTION: One major area in which Indian women have had influence is the education of the young. We have already suggested in "The Banishment of Rama" (pp. 34-38), how the stories grandmother tells teach children to accept their *dharma*. In the last reading, you saw that the expectations for men and women may be quite different; the stories used to teach girls therefore will be different from the stories told to the boys. Just as Rama is held up as the ideal for young boys, Rama's wife, Sita, is offered as an example for girls. When Rama was banished to the forest, Sita insisted on going with him: "As it is your duty to obey your father's wish, so it is my duty, as your wife, to be at your side." Moreover, Sita insisted on her duty to serve Rama in all things: "I shall walk in front of you in the forest ways, and tread the thorns to make the ground smooth for your feet." During their forest exile, Sita was abducted and held captive by the demon-king of Lanka (Sri Lanka). After her rescue, she proved her purity and constancy throughout her captivity by submitting to an ordeal by fire. At no time did her absolute devotion to Rama waver. "Be as Sita," young wives are told.

In the following reading, an Indian girl describes to her brother how their mother used stories to educate her. The author, a well-known Bengali writer, recalls, "No two in our family were taught alike. It was an individualistic training, and these stories, some of them apparently so slight, were the means by which our mother presented truth to our young minds."[16]🔖

"To me, mother gave different instructions from yours, my brothers. I was taught only stories and songs of devotion. I do not know whether she had a premonition that I should become a widow at twenty-two, but . . . she taught me as if she felt certain of it, her sweet understanding firmly paving the road, so that it would be firmer under my feet at the bleak hour of calamity. And I believe that was why she had me taught English."

I expressed surprise at this, for my mother herself knew not how to read or write. My sister explained that Mother had said to her:

"I belong to the age when wisdom came to men's hearts naturally, but thou, my child, art born in a time when only printed words are considered true. Learn English, my daughter; it is the ruler's language and since thou canst not rule men without some cunning, the English tomes may help thee to hold thy place in this world."

"It did serve me in good stead after my husband's death," went on my sister. "But, thank God, I have forgotten all of that language now."

"Why?" I asked.

"Oh, it has so little wisdom and not much beauty. The last story I read in English was about a dead man's ghost who tells his son how he, his father, was murdered; then the young prince, an innocent dreamer, kills an old fool, whose daughter's heart he breaks, and fights her brother at her funeral. Later, the prince is killed by the brother, whom he kills as well. It has luscious words in it, for an innocent young man's sorrow tastes sweet to the reader; but how can it be a tale of wisdom which our mother would have had me learn? Can ghosts be so revengeful? Is it right to tell a mother that she is unchaste, and all because of the idle talkativeness of a good-for-nothing Spirit who should go to Heaven instead of walking about at night to poison his son's life with cruel thirst for vengeance? That tale destroyed all my ambition to know English. Thou dost know the language well; was I not right to give it up?"

"Yes, that wanton tale of beauty should discourage anybody." Thus I disposed of Prince Hamlet.

My sister resumed: "I took to learning from Mother all the stories . . . she taught me line after line of the story of Savitri and how she saved her husband from death. Next I

A dance pose. (Information Service of India, New York, N.Y.)

memorized the trial of Sita. When I grew to be a woman, I was made to fast twenty-four hours in seclusion with her, and in that seclusion she taught me Gita Govinda, the Song of Songs, and imparted the secret and wisdom of love to my heart." Suddenly, she stopped to ask me, "How do Western mothers teach their daughters the art of wisdom and love?"

"Am I a woman or a Westerner that thou shouldst ask me that?" I questioned.

"Men always insist on remaining ignorant," she retorted, and went on with her story. "I learned to cook, to serve dinner, how to dress for cooking, then how to dress for dinner after cooking. The garment of the kitchen may be worn only after an arduous bath and the cleansing of the body. Once the cooking is done, the garment of the kitchen must be put away and the garment of the feast donned. I was not allowed to rest in the afternoon in the dress of the feast. . . . Oh, there were a thousand little things that the woman-mind picks up as a miser gathers his pennies—there was the evening toilet, the meditation—all these things was I taught as well as the work of pleasing a husband."

The Householder's *Dharma*

🙪INTRODUCTION: With marriage, Indians enter the second phase of life, known as the householder stage. In this period of life, woman's power is mostly within the family circle, while the man is responsible for activities in the outside world. The man controls the family's economic position, makes the decisions involving relations with neighbors, and earns the family living according to the rules of his community. He expects unquestioning service and devotion from his wife and absolute obedience from his children.

The ancient texts teach that the householder's *dharma* is to seek *artha* (material wealth and power) and *kama* (physical pleasure, especially in sex). For most Indians, however, the householder stage is a daily struggle for existence, a never-ending battle to pay the bills and stay out of trouble. Renouncing the world and seeking God are not even options for this stage of life. That comes later.

The householder must follow an occupation. In the ancient Hindu system, occupation was determined by heredity. A carpenter's son was a carpenter. Each occupational group had specific duties to perform, duties that it alone could do. Crossing occupational lines was a violation of one's *dharma*. To do another's work was as inappropriate as if the moon were to burn instead of reflect. Each occupation was important for the functioning of the total society.

The tailor in the following selection has descended from a long line of tailors. He takes pride in his profession. The young man in the story is Ved Mehta. In an earlier selection, we read of the arrangement of his sister's marriage (pp. 44-50). This selection is taken from a travelogue he wrote about India.[17]🙪

The tailor sits on our veranda. He has been working for us for many years. In the days before we fled from Pakistan, he made my rompers and knee pants, and when I graduated to

68

wearing long pants he put them on me and slapped my behind three or four times to remind me of my manhood. "But," he added quickly, "Ved Sahib, you will always be a boy to me. . . ."

A low-income housing project near Bombay. (Information Service of India, New York, N.Y.)

Unlike many other Indian tailors, our tailor is never on the lookout for new clients. All his customers seem to be of twenty years' standing. . . .

Our tailor, though modest in appearance, claims he can change a man by changing the style of his clothes. He can transform babu into sahib, sahib into officer. . . . Nothing is beyond him. His confidence is unnerving, and the only thing that makes him real is his endless family saga. . . .

The tailor is the last of our old servants; the two house servants are new. I feel a bond with him because he has watched me through my changing years.

I can hear the slap of my bare feet when as a child I raced with forbidden street children, the old servants watching and scolding and flattering, the tailor among them shouting,

"Watch out for your clothes," and, in the same breath, "Don't stop, get on with you." They smiled whether I won or lost. This was loyalty. Sometimes my parents reproved me for being too close to the servants, but when they were out in offices and shops, parties and clubs, the servants remained home as companions and storytellers. The children next door moved away, their father transferred to another district. But the servants grew up with us. They never changed.

The tailor sits on the veranda of our new house, turning the wheel of his machine. I recline on the small lawn in front of the veranda and look at him from my wicker chair. I am thirsty. I get up and bring two glasses of water, one for the tailor and one for myself.

"Sahib, you should have asked me to get you some water. Don't you like me anymore?"

"What is the difference?" I ask.

I sit back in my chair and look at him. He is lean and frail with a chest clamped between round shoulders, a bald head and a yellowed beard rich with color of age. He stops turning the wheel, leaves his stool on the veranda, and comes and sits on the ground at my feet.

"Take this chair, take this chair," I say, nervously standing up. He puts both his gaunt hands on my knees and I drop back into the chair.

"Sahib, don't you like me anymore? It's little things about you that trouble me. You won't let me cut you a suit like your English one because you don't trust me. You don't let me get you a glass of water because you don't like me. What has England done to you?"

He won't remove his hands from my knees, and he stubbornly keeps his position on the ground.

"Look here, tailor, I don't want an English suit because I am comfortable in pajamas and kurta."

"Sahib, I don't understand the world. Why have people stopped wearing suits? Why have all the Indian gentlemen started wearing ugly black coats with buttoned-up collars? Why does everyone want to look like their poor tailor? What is going to happen to my profession? When I saw you in the beautiful English suit, my heart went out to you. . . . Won't you let me cut you another? Never mind the rest of my customers. I'll work for you, Sahib, day and night, and it will be the best suit made in Delhi this year."

"But, tailor," I say, "you don't understand. A new English suit is the last thing I need. And about the water—I can get it as well as you can."

"Ved Sahib, your old servant and friend though I am, I would rather have you kick me than bring me a glass of water."

I try to explain to the tailor that he and I should be able to get each other water without his being hurt. But he sits at my feet holding my knees and refuses to accept my explanation. He feels offended. I stand up and nervously motion him to sit down in the chair. He looks even more hurt and shakes his puzzled beard. "What has England done to you? I don't understand. I could never sit in that chair and you know it. I have never sat in a chair and I don't want to."

As in the old days, the understanding really comes from him. I sit down. "Maybe I'm just old," he says. "Maybe I'm just ancient. Many of these young servants would like nothing better than a soft chair; they would let this grass grow under their feet until they were buried in it. They wouldn't lift a hand to cut it. By their rebellion they dig their own graves, and Sahib, you aren't helping them learn their station by offering them chairs."

"Tailor, there is no station. Everyone must make his own station."

He points to his scarred forehead. "My station is written here." Then he points to my forehead. "Your station is written there. It is all in the books of *karma* and *dharma.* My *karma* says I must be a tailor and my *dharma* says I must do my duty by my sahibs."

"Tailor, these are old ideas."

"I am an old man," he says, and he runs a finger through his yellowed beard. "But, Sahib, I am wise. You can no more change my station than I can change yours. You will marry in your caste, and I will marry my son to a girl in our own caste. You will send your children to England to be educated, and I will teach my grandsons to be good tailors."

What Is Caste?

•INTRODUCTION: If you were to ask Ved Mehta's tailor, "What is your caste?" he would probably answer, "I am a tailor." Occupation is one definition of caste in India, but it is not the only one.

In Indian society there are four large classes, called *varnas*, that date back to 1000 B.C.: Brahmin (priest), Kshatriya (ruler), Vaishya (businessman), and Shudra (worker). Each *varna* has its *dharma*. The Laws of Manu (law books of Manu, mythical law giver and first king), written at least two hundred years before Christ, describe these four groups as follows:

> But for the sake of prosperity of the worlds, he created the Brāhmin, the Kshatriya, the Vaishya, and the Shūdra. . . .
>
> To Brāhmins he assigned teaching and studying (the Veda), sacrificing for their own benefit and for others, giving and accepting (of alms).
>
> The Kshatriya he commanded to protect the people, to bestow gifts, to offer sacrifices, to study (the Veda), and to abstain from attaching himself to sensual pleasures.
>
> The Vaishya to tent cattle, to bestow gifts, to offer sacrifices, to study (the Veda), to trade, to lend money, and to cultivate land.
>
> One occupation only the lord prescribed to the Shūdra, to serve meekly even these three (other) castes.[18]

But these categories have always been more theoretical than real.

India, from earliest times, has been divided into many small communities, known as *jati*. Today there are over three thousand *jati* in India. Each is distinct because it does not exchange food or intermarry with any other *jati*. But knowing these facts does not fully ex-

A Brahmin blows on his sacred conch
in preparation for reading from the
Ramayana.

(Photos by Donald and Jean
Johnson)

Above: A land recorder (Kshatriya) uses a charpoy (cot) as his office.
Below: An oil presser (Shudra) in a South Indian village.

plain how the caste system functions in Indian society. To understand the complexity of the caste system, consider the following imaginary conversation between an American teacher and an Indian businessman.[19]✒

AMERICAN: I appreciate your willingness to explain caste to me. Most Indians tell me I couldn't possibly understand it and can only see caste as a problem. But I want to understand. Is it true that caste began when the light-skinned Aryans came to India and subdued the darker-skinned Dravidians?

INDIAN: Yes and no.

AMERICAN: Do you mean yes or no?

INDIAN: I mean yes *and* no. The early Brahmins were probably Aryans, but many of the very strict Brahmins are in South India, and they are darker than some of the very low-caste people.

AMERICAN: Then caste is not based on color?

INDIAN: That's right. Some high castes are dark, some are light. Low castes also are both dark and light.

AMERICAN: Then race doesn't explain caste. What about rich and poor? Surely the high-caste Brahmins are richer than the low-caste workers—Shudra.

INDIAN: Again, yes and no. Many members of high castes are also well-born, with more education and better jobs, and would be considered "upper class" in your sense. Yet there are many poor Brahmins and rich Shudras. Apu's family in the movie "Pather Panchali" were very poor Brahmins. The night watchman in that office over there is Brahmin. But take the Nadars in South India. They were untouchables but are now among the most successful businessmen in the area.

AMERICAN: So caste isn't race or class. Would you agree that it is based on occupation?

INDIAN: You can guess my answer: yes and no. Occupation is an important feature of caste. Many names are occupational, like your Mr. Potter, Mr. Carpeter, Mr. Smith, Mr. Weaver, Mr. Taylor. Most of our craft groups are also caste groups.

Sons follow their fathers' occupations, and daughters marry boys who do the same work as their fathers.

But there are also exceptions. Most Brahmins are not priests. There are villages in North India where most of the farmers are Brahmins. The army is made up of hundreds of castes, and most of them are not from the Kshatriya or warrior group. In Kerala, the Nairs are the dominant caste, and they are not even in the top three *varnas*. Some of India's most important saints came from non-Brahmin castes. Gandhi became a saint, but he was of a commercial caste, and his name means grocer. It's like your John Smith who was a colonizer in America. Did he ever work as a blacksmith? So caste is not based just on occupation.

AMERICAN: It's easier to say what caste isn't than what it is. How about ethnic loyalty? Is caste membership like belonging to a Polish-American or an Italian-American group?

INDIAN: Yes and no. India does have thousands of different ethnic groups, many of which migrated here through the more than 4,000 years of Indian history. You probably know the Aryans, Muslims, and British. But there were also Bactrians, the Kushans, the Huns, the Parsees, the Afghans, and hundreds of others. Many groups have different physical appearances and claim different histories. How did the Coorgs of South India come here? The Chitpavan Brahmins of Maharastra have blue eyes. Did they come from the Middle East? Are the Jats of North India descendants of the white Huns? One of our great anthropologists, Professor Karve, claimed that all caste members were blood-related. She explained caste as an expanded kinship system.

AMERICAN: I give up. Let's say we just don't know why caste groups formed, how they came about, or why.

INDIAN: At last you've said something I can agree with.

AMERICAN: Can we at least learn how many castes there are in India?

INDIAN: That depends on whether you mean the large groupings like Brahmins, Jat, Nairs, etc., or the thousands of so-called subcastes.

AMERICAN: Don't tell me you can't answer this either. How many subcastes?

INDIAN: No one has ever counted them, but there are several thousand. There are 550 subcastes of untouchables alone. In the Delhi area, there are hundreds of Brahmin castes.

AMERICAN: This is really getting complicated. Let's forget numbers. Can you tell me how a caste acts—any caste?

INDIAN: Well, behavior, rituals, and taboos are different for each one. I'm a member of the Srivastava community.

AMERICAN: How does that affect your life?

INDIAN: Well, in spite of the fact I live in Delhi, my caste is always a part of my life. My wife, naturally, is a Srivastava. She comes from a family that has known my family for more years than we can remember. Because she is a Srivastava, she knows the food I like, the religious rituals I am used to, she tells our children stories from the *Ramayana*, the same ones I was told as a child. In a thousand unconscious ways, her behavior will echo mine because we are members of the same caste. Marriage almost always takes place within one caste for these reasons. Sometimes women marry into a higher caste, but men hardly ever.

Eating is another thing. My mother, sixty years old now, will not take food from a lower caste. My partner's a Brahmin. In his home I do not ask for food, although we eat in restaurants together. Perhaps this practice came about as a protection from disease. Maybe it's a way to preserve one's culture. You have that in America, don't you? Russian-Americans like their borscht; Italians prefer their spaghetti; not everyone likes soul food.

Then there's the matter of social life. Most of us prefer to be with members of our own group because we have more in common. We share a history, a tradition; we laugh at the same jokes. Don't you feel more at home with other northern Europeans like yourself? And don't answer by telling me,

"Some of my best friends are black."

Then there's the loyalty. If I'm in trouble I can always count on my family and my community. No matter where I travel in India, I know caste members will accept me. Even when I travel to your country, another Srivastava will take me in. It's good to know you are never alone. Being part of a community really matters; it gives meaning to life, although the community also imposes restrictions on its own members.

AMERICAN: How can you tell the difference between a high caste and a low one?

INDIAN: It has to do with ritual purity. A Kshatriya king may be powerful and a Vaishya trader may be rich, but their ritual status is lower than that of the poorest Brahmin.

AMERICAN: Well, either some castes are higher than others or they aren't.

INDIAN: Why must you Americans always insist on things being one way or another? Things aren't always black or white.

AMERICAN: We'll discuss philosophy another time. Now we're discussing sociology.

INDIAN: That might be one reason you have trouble understanding India, but, as you say, let's get back to the point. High and low castes have a lot to do with purity—ritual purity. We Hindus have divided everything into pure and impure. That's not the same as sanitary or unsanitary, I might add. For example, meat eating, especially beef, is polluting; alcohol is polluting to some, and so are occupations dealing with the body, like cutting hair. Animal skinning and garbage collecting are also polluting jobs. On the other hand, bathing is ritually purifying; fire can be purifying; the water of the Ganges is purifying. Generally, the more purified the daily life, the higher the caste. Less ritually pure behavior means lower caste, although there are exceptions.

AMERICAN: How does a low-caste person feel about this? Does he want to move up?

This untouchable woman has built a small temple next to her house. She is "reading" a book that consists of two words: "Sita-ram." (Donald and Jean Johnson)

INDIAN: Many lower-caste members probably think they are exactly where they should be; that it's a result of deeds done, good or bad, in past lives. Others may think moving up is a good thing. Let me give you one example. The Chamars, people who used to do mainly cow skinning, have a caste tradition that they used to be Brahmins, but long ago one of them was trying to help a cow out of the mud by pulling on its tail and the cow died just as some people were passing by. The Chamars were accused of killing the cow and were polluted by that and condemned to live in a low caste. Caste has never been as rigid as many think. In ancient times people moved up quite often. The scriptures and epics like the *Mahabharata* speak of this a lot. One of our great anthropologists, Professor Srinivas, has studied this moving up the scale by caste. He calls the process Sanskritization.

AMERICAN: What does that mean?

INDIAN: It is quite simple, actually. Sanskrit was and is the classical language of India. It is associated with high culture, often Brahmin culture. It's more than a language, really, it's a way

of life. Sanskrit culture means the highest culture. When
a lower caste imitates the behavior of an upper, often
Brahmin, caste, that's called "Sanskritization." It doesn't
mean that the lower caste learns to speak Sanskrit.

AMERICAN: I can understand moving up as a caste group, but
I don't quite understand that way of imitating upper-caste
behavior. I thought moving up the scale meant driving a
bigger car, getting invited to fancy parties, doing things
that were more fun.

INDIAN: Don't forget we're talking about India, not America.
The upper castes in India are associated with ritual purity.
So a caste that makes its move upward often imitates this
ritual purity of the Brahmins. If a low caste eats meat, it
might become vegetarian when it moves up; it might stop
drinking alcohol. It might even change its caste name in
the hope that other people will think it is a higher caste.

AMERICAN: But that's no fun. In America, going up the ladder
means you live better.

INDIAN: I told you, this is India. Not America. Remember the
Nadars I spoke of earlier—the untouchable caste that
moved up in South India? One of the ways they spent
their new money was on building temples. That's because
temple building is associated with the upper castes. By the
way, didn't your John D. Rockefeller build a cathedral in
New York?

AMERICAN: Yes, I guess he did.

INDIAN: There's one more thing. Here in India we hardly ever
refer to the "caste system" or to caste at all. "Caste" is a
Portuguese word. We speak of our *community* instead. Of
course, "community" doesn't mean to us what you mean
by the word. It means all the things we've been talking
about. And more.

AMERICAN: It's certainly complicated.

INDIAN: Yes and no. Yes, if you're looking at it from the outside; no, if you're a part of it.

"Let Every Caste Be Touchable"

❧INTRODUCTION: Many people confuse the caste system with untouchability. Traditionally, the untouchables, who were responsible for the unclean work of society, were outside the four major castes. They collected dead animals and skinned them, swept the streets and carried away the human waste, washed the clothes, and delivered the babies. These jobs were considered unclean, both ritually and literally. Because those who performed these tasks often carried diseases, people feared contact with them, so over the years they became "untouchable."

Quarantining diseased people is an accepted means of preventing infection in many societies. However, this practice became extremely rigid in India and evolved into the untouchable system, prohibiting all contact between untouchables and cast Hindus. In some areas of India, untouchables had to ring a bell to announce their approach so that not even their shadow would fall on one in the higher castes. Money that passed through their hands had to be rinsed off; food that they received in payment for work was tossed to them.

Untouchability was abolished by law in the Indian Constitution in 1949. Legally, all who had been untouchable were now "ex-untouchables." But eliminating the pain of thousands of years of untouchability—or the practice—is not accomplished merely be passing a law. Think of the legacy of racial segregation and the condition of African American's today. Have civil rights laws solved that problem? Like racial discrimination within the United States, caste discrimination and untouchability still exist all over India. However, the problem is less severe in cities, where all kinds of people travel side by side in city buses and eat together in restaurants. But even in the cities, former untouchables face many problems. Harold Isaacs, an American scholar, discussed some of these problems in the following excerpts from his book *India's Ex-Untouchables.*[20]❧

The [Indian] government, itself caught by so much ambivalence and conflict over the caste system, is committed to giving the ex-untouchables special help. It is doing this not only by helping them through school but by opening the way afterward to jobs. Since ex-untouchables cannot hope to find jobs in a society still dominated by caste-bound Hindus, the government has opened its own services and has set up quotas of reserved places for them to fill as they qualify.

This system of "reserved places" or "reservations" began well back in the British time, mainly for the benefit of the non-Brahmin lower castes, and came partly as a result of the non-Brahmin fight against Brahmin domination. It has been enormously expanded by the government of independent India. It is now the lifeline by which more and more people are pulling themselves—or are being pulled—out of the cesspools of untouchability.

[The problem with the compensatory policy of "reserved places" is that it accentuates one's former untouchability rather than working to eliminate it. Another "solution" is for untouchables to try to pass themselves off as members of another caste.]

Many of these who have moved up in life have naturally continued to find it easier to "pass" in many situations than not to, and. . . this often meant not falsifying your identity but not proclaiming it either. . . . Wherever it was needful or possible, you would pass, whether while traveling or even, in a more consistent way, at your place of work, where what other people did not know could never hurt you. The need to "pass" on a more consistent basis seemed to come most often out of the effort to get better housing.

But there are serious limits to how far and for how long an educated ex-untouchable can continue to pass successfully in India today. . . .

[As one informant explains:]

If a man conceals his caste, sooner or later it is discovered, and then he suffers a lot. There was a Mahar, a contractor who got rich. He told everybody he was a Mahratta. He lived in a caste Hindu community and never disclosed his caste. But then his daughter died. The custom is that your relatives must come to prepare the body, not yourself or a stranger. But nobody came. No Mahrattas came, of course. He had cut himself off from his relatives, so they didn't come. Some of his friends and neighbors came and said to him: "How is it nobody is here? Call your nearest relative now, right away!" In desperation he finally called on some of his old people to come to lift the body. When they came, the neighbors recognized them from their clothes, their language, the way they talked, and his caste was disclosed. He suffered. We say to such a man, "You see, you wanted to be a Brahmin or a Mahratta, why should we feel sympathy for you?"

Marriage remains the most formidable barrier in the path of anyone who wishes to escape his caste. Intercaste marriage was a generation ago, but such marriages involving [untouchables] are still extremely rare.

Animal skinners (untouchables) learning improved methods of hide processing.
(United Nations)

The point about marriage is that ex-untouchables who pass are unlikely to find mates for their children outside their caste, and if they do, they are unlikely to be able to keep their own caste background hidden. "It is possible, but not very likely," said one informant. "In India everybody knows everybody's caste one way or another, sooner or later. The educated people can separate, yet they can't separate, for community is part of this society. You can't be without a community. Without a community, it is awkward for a man in all his relationships. This is the culture of the country. *In India you have got to be connected.*"

The inescapable facts of caste life in India have led some ex-untouchables to devise an in-between style, a kind of semi-passing, as the solution to their problems. Put a bit roughly, it is a system for passing in public while not passing in private. In general it means that in all situations where self-advancement, comfort, and convenience dictate it, an ex-untouchable passes as a member of some higher caste. At the same time, in all circumstances that demand it—death, marriage, even voluntary work for the community—he leads a second or double life in the bosom of his community.

[Another way out is to convert to a different faith, such as Buddhism, Christianity, or Islam. But many do not regard this step as necessary. One young woman who had become a physician explained it the following way:]

> God has created us in this community and we are proud. I want to see our community come up to a higher level, to the standard of the others. It shall remain a caste, but will become like the others. . . . At present, marriage should stay within the caste. In the future if conditions change, it may not matter, but I would want my children to marry in the caste. We will tell our children that they are of our community. We will explain so that they will understand and know and help our community. . . .

This was essentially Gandhi's view of the way out: to

preserve the caste system but to reform it by doing away with untouchability, to give the untouchables access to the temples, access to the common utilities, such as wells, and assistance to raise their conditions of life to some more tolerable level, such as getting the night soil off their heads and into wheelbarrows. . . . What has been legally "abolished" is not caste but untouchability, and the problem is to transform this legal fact into social reality. Let the untouchable groups cross that line and rejoin the mass of lowly Shudras, let them remain as humble as they might be, let them retain all their divisions and subdivisions like everyone else, but let them be *touchable*
. . . .

Flickering here and there among these thoughts of the future was the gleam of an idea larger than untouchability and surviving caste. This was the notion that there was a larger common identity for all to share, an identity called Indian. . . .

> When anybody asks me, I say: "I belong to this nation, India. I'm an Indian." If they persist after that, I say: "Who are you, somebody from the census bureau?" And they keep quiet. I suppose they think: "He's an educated Mahar." And if they do, I am not ashamed. I am proud of this community, it is a fighting community, an honest community. But I do really feel like an Indian. This is the best answer. I consider myself one with my country.

As it does for so many Negro Americans, the question remained whether the rest of the people of his country were —or ever would be—one with him.

Affirmative Action, Indian-style

❧INTRODUCTION: Caste discrimination, like racial discrimination in the United States, is far from solved, despite much legislation, legal enforcements, and substantial social change in recent years. The Indian Constitution makes it illegal to discriminate against the ex-untouchables in employment, education, and housing. Moreover, the Constitution calls for an affirmative action program for the lower castes and tribals, officially referred to as "scheduled castes and tribes."

The affirmative action program adopted at the time of independence in 1947 reserved 22 percent of all government jobs for the so-called "backward classes." It also set aside places in state and national parliaments and in university admissions. Despite these efforts, lower castes often find it difficult to compete for jobs.

In such states as Rajasthan, Bihar, and Utter Pradesh, large landowners have increasingly exploited the ex-untouchables and have kept thousands in virtual bondage. The ex-untouchables, however, have not taken this unfair treatment quietly. During the past twenty years, thousands of bonded laborers in these areas have organized themselves into political action groups and have protested their treatment. They have elected representatives to both state assemblies and the national parliament.

The increasing political pressure from the lower caste in the past few years prompted the national government to establish the Mandal Commission to study and make recommendations on ways to correct the continuing problem of caste discrimination. After years of study, the commission issued its report in 1990. On August 7 of that same year, the then Prime Minister V. P. Singh, in one of his most controversial moves, announced that he had decided to implement the Mandal Commission Report.

The Report recommended an additional 27 percent of government jobs (about 100,000) be set aside for lower-caste Hindus, bringing to a total of 49 percent the number of all government jobs that would be reserved for the "backward classes." One of the most controversial aspects of the report was the call for the inclusion of a new group of lower-caste Hindus into an expanded affirmative action plan. The castes to be covered in the new policy were lower castes, but not ex-untouchables or tribals who were already covered in the Constitution. To identify these "Other Backward Classes" (OBC's), the Mandal Commission relied on the British census of 1931. A nearly sixty-year-old census, opponents of the report charged, could not possibly measure accurately the amount of lower-caste discrimination in the India of 1990.

The new quota policy set off an immediate wave of protest, especially in North India among university students who felt they already had a difficult time finding jobs. Although the new reform would actually set aside only 100,000 government jobs, millions of Indians felt angry at these quota systems and argued that special treatment for the scheduled castes discriminates against other caste groups and does not encourage the ex-untouchables to work hard and compete in an open system.

The protesters also insisted that in a democratic system everyone must be given a job and admitted to school on the basis of individual ability, talent, and effort. Finally, the protestors accused the prime minister of catering to the wishes to the lower castes simply to gain their votes in the future. These arguments are very similar to ones heard in the United States from those who protest affirmative action programs for women and racial and ethnic minorities who have suffered through a history of discrimination.

The following articles, taken from *India Today*, one of India's leading English-language news magazines, report on the agitations in the summer and fall of 1990, following the announcement that the Mandal Commission Report would be fully implemented. The first selection provides the reasoning of both sides in the affirmative action debate. The second and third ones document the student agitation that swept through North India in the fall of 1990.[21, 22, 23]

Does the Mandal Commission Help the Backwards?

For. Backward castes need better representation in the administrative machinery. Even though they constitute 52 percent of the country's population their representation in Central government jobs stands at an abysmal 4.69 percent. Reservations will also achieve social egalitarianism by break-

ing the psychological barriers of the backwards by bringing them into positions of power in the Government—
however minuscule the actual number of jobs involved.
Even though, as Prime Minister Vishwanath Pratap Singh
admits, only 1 percent of all jobs are created by the Centre
each year, the scheme is necessary because if gives the
backwards a sense of being part of governance—the system—and compensates for generations of discrimination.
Moreover, it also paves the ground for upward mobility.
Opposition to reservations is merely an attempt by upper
castes to preserve the monopoly that they have had over
the power structure for generations.

Against: Using percentiles of caste representation based on the
Mandal Commission report is an unmitigated fraud. The
very statistical foundations for the pro-Mandal argument are
unsustainable. Mandal's data [are] derived from the caste
enumeration of the 1931 census. He used this as his data
base to arrive at his conclusions taking into account population changes as reflected in the 1971 census which was not
broken down according to caste. In the 40 years that elapsed
between 1931 and 1971 there was no way of knowing which
castes had moved up or down the socio-economic ladder.
His conclusions, therefore, are hypothetical projections.

The Constitution advocates ameliorative measures for
deprived socio-economic classes. However, Mandal converted
class to caste without giving a precise definition of how he
arrived at his definition of "backward." In fact, Mandal himself admits that his methodology was faulty. Moreover, even
the three experts—B. K. Roy Burman, M. N. Srinivas and
Yogendra Singh—who were attached to his commission have
now come out and disowned the validity and accuracy of the
report.

Mandal also ignores the sweeping changes that have occurred throughout the country over the last 40 years—more
education, land reforms, industrialisation, proliferation of
skilled manpower—that have benefited the so-called backward castes, many of whom now are large land-holders. Reser-

vations are bound to help only a marginal elite of the backwards. Or why else is the Government resisting classifying the underprivileged according to economic criteria? The long-term cost in terms of caste-polarisation and flaring up of internecine hatreds will be far higher than any imaginary benefit.

Will It Promote Caste Equality?

For: What Gandhian ideology did for the Harijans (untouchables), Mandalism will do for the backwards. Because of reservations in jobs on the basis of caste, the backwards now have an identity which will help them unite and fight for equality. . . .

Against: This may lead to an Orwellian situation where some castes will be more equal than others. It will strengthen the caste-system because genetic heritage will become the basis for discrimination. Caste-based quotas will lay down that privileges should be extended to the groups and not to the individuals. It may unleash a more-backward-than-thou race among various castes for the limited spoils, lead to corruption in the certification of castes, and raise expectations. The already intense competition gets worsened when caste becomes the basis for selection. Thus it will lead to inter-caste rivalries. Since the new policy does not consider all castes equal, inequalities within the government departments will increase. . . .

Should the Government Do Social Engineering?

For: To achieve a just and equal society, the Government has the mandate to destroy social discrepancies by engineering a system of checks and balances. The Mandal Commission has identified caste-groups by several criteria, including the number of matriculates in the community, practice of child marriages, availability of potable water and the percentage living in thatched huts. This is a serious effort to improve the lot of the backwards who have only 4.69 percent rep-

resentation in class I jobs in the Central Government,
though they constitute 52 percent of the country.

Against: Reservations for the backwards in Central Government jobs do not improve the plight of their communities. Selection of an IAS [Indian Administrative
Service] officer from a backward village does not ensure
a high literacy rate, adequate potable water or better housing. Families that have benefited from job reservations
have not raised their real standards of living because they
have not practiced family planning. In a vicious circle,
they produce more children and ask for more reservations. Right now reservations reach only the individual,
who benefits from the collective backwardness of his caste.
Even if the argument of under-representation in Government was valid at some point, the reservation of Government jobs is a gratuitous exercise that ignores reality. The
real power in any society—political clout—has shifted in
favour of the backwards, almost wholesale in the south,
and in massive strides in Bihar and Uttar Pradesh where
they constitute nearly 40 percent of the legislative strength.
Reservations short circuit the responsibility of the state to
pave the way for overall progress. It is a political gimmick
aimed at grabbing the leadership of a vote bank.

Do Merit and Efficiency Suffer?

For: Merit is not determined by caste. There is a large chunk
of meritorious backwards who cannot rise because of their
socio-economic handicaps. The changing administrative
structures in Tamil Nadu and Karnataka have shown that
the governments can be run well despite more representation of the backwards. The upper castes dominate
the bureaucracy today, but the system is still plagued with
numerous evils. Apart from education capabilities, the
socio-political dominance of the upper castes is a powerful
factor influencing the selection process. Social responsibility demands that jobs should be shared with the backwards despite a little dilution of the meritocracy.

Against: This is a specious plea by the upper-class backwards to increase their clout in the power dispensation which is put before the nation by those in favor of Mandal. If the backwards need more efficient administration, they should seek to remove overall apathy and corruption in the bureaucracy. But they only want a bigger share in the present corrupt system to corner some spoils. The results of the lowering of standards do not reach the poorest of the poor. In effect its impact could be: same levels of corruption with added inefficiency. It cannot be denied that lowering test scores for entrance examinations to engineering and medical colleges and reserving promotion quotas in Government services according to caste will squeeze out the meritorious and demoralise these institutions. Says former director of Indian Institute of Advanced Studies, S.C. Dube: "In our concern for the less advantaged, let us not overlook the meritorious. Let us devise plans to nurture talent irrespective of its social origin."

Is It the Only Way to Right the Wrongs of History?

For: Giving backward castes advantages in return for centuries of oppression is a noble and just cause. Since the old Hindu order suppressed them on the basis of their genes, the present order has to make reparations. Competition is valid only among equals. Those treated as unequals in the past should be given a more-than-equal status to make them eligible for an equal competition. The wrongs of history have to be righted by turning their social handicap into economic privileges. Said V. P. Singh in Parliament: "Implementation of the Mandal Commission report is what little we can do to correct age-old imbalances."

Against: This is a dangerous tribal logic where an entire generation's blood feuds continue to the next. A modern democratic state recognises the necessity of preferential treatment to the disadvantaged. But if done on the basis of whole caste-groups, it will be holding responsible the present generation for the follies of its previous generation. Mandal revived this tribal mentality on a national level.

[Following Prime Minister Singh's announcement that he would implement the Mandal Commission recommendations, *India Today*, reported:]

. . . despite V. P. Singh's bravado, it was obvious that the virulence of the agitation, throwing together as it did some of his most ardent supporters—large sections of the urban middle class, students, professionals, lawyers and the press— had taken him by utter surprise. When the agitation began a month ago, it was in the form of scattered protests. Buses and trains were burnt. Traffic was blocked. There were police firings and *lathi* [police stick] charges. And the inevitable deaths. Still, political pundits insisted the agitation would die down. The agitationists belonged to the middle class and could never keep up the momentum, so the argument went.

And indeed, for a time the agitation did subside. Only to burst with renewed force into the consciousness of a horrified nation on September 19. That day, Rajeev Goswami, a Delhi University student, set himself on fire, sustaining 50 percent burns.

He was a faceless youth. But one act thrust him to national fame. As yellow tongues of fire licked his body, cameras clicked. The next morning, the picture of the youth attempting immolation was on the front page of all newspapers. Name: Rajeev Goswami. Age: 20.

Two days later, the crossing outside the Safdarjang Hospital—where he struggled for life—was renamed Qurbank Chowk (sacrifice square) and the road signs repainted Rajeev Goswami Marg. The anti-Mandal Commission student movement in the capital had finally found a rallying point.

What made this average third-year arts student attempt to immolate himself? Dr. B. K. Bhattacharya, the principal of Desh- bandhu College—where Rajeev studied—believes it was be- cause the press and the intelligentsia were decrying the Mandal report. His friends say the only option he had after V. P. Singh's decision to implement the Mandal report was suicide.

The only son of a middle class Punjabi Brahmin family, Rajeev has six sisters. His father, Madan Lal, is a clerk with the Postal Department. In college, Rajeev was on the Delhi University Students' Union (DUSU) Central Council, and had planned to stand for president or joint-secretary [of] DUSU. He had no concrete career plans as yet. His father wanted him to take up a government job. But he had told a friend he wanted to join politics—so it was logical for him to participate in the agitation against the Mandal Commission.

Tempers were running high after a nine-day hunger strike, which the students believed hadn't received adequate attention. Frustrated, Rajeev and his friends came up with the idea of self-immolation. Yet, Rajeev retained an element of sanity. The night before, he called his mother and reassured her: *"Hum sirf tamasha karne ja rahe hai"* (We are staging a drama).

But in an atmosphere charged with emotion, the initial plan of a mock self-immolation went awry. Having previously come with only his legs doused in kerosene, Rajeev then poured kerosene all over his body. And when he lit that match stick, he was at the back of the crowd and his friends, detailed to douse the fire, were not around.

* * *

If anti-Mandal agitation was looking for a novel form of protest, Goswami provided it. In quick succession, youths in a series of cities—Delhi, Hissar, Sirsa, Ambala, Lucknow, Gwalior, Kota, Ghaziabad—set themselves on fire.

Enraged by the reports of self-immolation attempts and police brutality, the anti-Mandal agitation flared up again, spreading to more cities, intensifying in violence.

In the capital, agitating students blocked one of the most important traffic intersections, naming it Qurbani Chowk and turning it into a mini-Tiananmen Square. For days, they disrupted traffic until in a pre-dawn swoop, a huge posse of policemen cleared the square and arrested about a thousand students.

Students stage a silent march in New Delhi, demanding that the prime minister hold a national debate on the controversial job reservation policy. At least thirty-eight people were killed by police or committed suicide in protests against the rally. (AP/Wide World Photos)

Next day, the students, in an attempt to recapture the square, engaged the police in pitched battles. When a lathi charge and tear gas failed to disperse the students, the police opened fire. Two were killed.

In Chandigarh, agitators burnt hundreds of government vehicles, buildings and offices. Finally the army had to be called out—the first time since Operation Bluestar in 1984. The army was also mobilised in about a dozen other towns, including Ambala and Sirsa, Kurukshetra and Rohtak. In unambiguous terms, the anti-reservationists had signalled to V. P. Singh and the National Front Government that they meant serious business. . . .

Almost overnight, campuses across the Hindi belt were politicised. Students for whom Hindi films were staple fare eloquently discussed why Laloo Prasad Yadav is for reservations while Chimanbhai Patal is against it. But while the politicisation may have been welcome, the agitation also sharply divided students along caste lines. Said Harinder Kumar, a political science research scholar: "We used to have Hindu College vs St. Stephens or Miranda House vs Lady Sriram College rivalries. Now they are forcing us to think on caste lines." Rajiv Sharma, an intern in King George Medical College, Lucknow, echoed that point: "Ever since the Mandal Commission report was announced and our agitation started, our Yadav and Gujjar friends have stopped talking to us."

But in most places, barring the occasional clash, the backward castes stayed off the streets leaving the field open for the anti-Mandal Commission agitators. At Delhi University, normally apolitical students braved police lathi charges to participate in protest rallies. When a speaker at a Delhi college seminar questioned the students' use of violence, a girl sprang up to scream: "This Government listens only to bullets. We are only breaking glasspanes."

Agitation proved a swift and effective political teacher. At many places, students have been quick to see through the efforts of political parties to exploit them. In Delhi, when BJP [Bharatiya Janata Party or Indian Peoples Party] President L. K. Advani and MP [Member of Parliment] Madan Lal Khurana visited Safdarjang Hospital to see the parents of Rajeev Goswami, students hooted them away. Advani was told to first denounce the Mandal Commission report, something he couldn't do since the party's election manifesto is committed to its implementation. Instead, he said he was opposing the police brutality. Said Devesh Kumar Singh, a second year law student: "They want to have their cake and eat it too. Only those publicly against the Mandal Commission can join us."

Kama in Classical India

࿘INTRODUCTION: The ancient texts instruct householders to seek not only *dharma*, which primarily concerns caste and family, but also *artha* and *kama*. *Kama*, the second goal of the householder, refers primarily to sensual, sexual pleasure but it includes physical pleasures of all kinds. *Kama* is anything that delights the senses. Good music, pleasing art, tasty food, scented perfumes, and love are among these sensual pleasures encouraged within the doctrine of *kama*.

According to Hindu values, people in the householder stage of life are to enjoy *kama*, not students or those who have renounced this life for the pursuit of religious goals. For a married man or woman, *kama* is quite appropriate. Without *kama* life would be very dull, and there would be no families or children to carry on the tradition. The following selection, taken from the ancient religious text the *Kama Sutra (Aphorisms on Love)* gives advice on seduction. The text was probably written about 2,000 years ago.[24]࿘

The young man in his effort to please the woman of his choice should try and give her everything she desires. Thus he should give her rare gifts and toys that her other companions do not possess. For example, he can give her a multicolored ball and other curiosities of this sort. He can give her dolls made of cloth, wood, buffalo horn, ivory, wax, plaster or clay, or utensils for cooking, suggestive wooden figures—such as a man and a woman, a pair of rams, goats or sheep. Also miniature temples made of clay, bamboo or wood consecrated to different goddesses, cages of parrots, cuckoos, starlings, quail, cocks and partridges, vases in a variety of elegant forms, water-drawing machines, [z]ithers and other musical instruments, wooden props for images, colored stools, lacquer, tilak, yellow mehendi, vermilion, and kajal or eye mascara, sandalwood, saffron and 'pan' made out of betel nuts and wrapped in betel leaves.

He should present these gifts on different occasions and they should also provide a good reason for meeting her often. Some of these presents should be made in public and some in private according to the circumstances. In other words, he should try and make her realize that he is ready to do anything she desires.

He should meet her in secret and tell her that he is afraid that her family and friends may not approve of him. He should also casually add that many of the gifts he gave her were very rare and much desired by others. When the young girl seems to like him better, he should tell her amusing stores—if she desires to be amused; or if she is impressed by conjurers he should show her some tricks; if she is curious to see the various arts he should not hesitate to show his proficiency in them— thus, if she loves song, he should sing for her, and on certain days when they go together to festivals or fairs, or when she comes home after a visit to some relatives, he should offer her bouquets of flowers, ornaments for her head and ears, and rings, for it is on such occasions that gifts should be given.

During his courtship the young man should take particular pains to dress well and be as courteous and charming as possible, for young girls like young men who are constantly with them to be handsome, pleasant, and well-dressed. Women, though they may love a man, make no effort to conquer the object of their affections, and it would be idle to wait for them to declare the true nature of their feelings.

Yet it is not impossible to discover the truth of a young girl's feelings; being as yet innocent and unschooled, they often betray themselves unconsciously. Here are some exterior signs which invariably betray the love of a young girl.

She never looks her loved one in the face, and blushes when he looks at her. Under some pretext or other she lets him get a glimpse of her ankles and arms. She looks at him secretly when his back is turned, and bows her head and

Lord Krishna and his beloved, Radha, seeking shelter from the rain. (National Museum, New Delhi)

answers indistinctly if he asks her a direct question. She likes to be in his company and speaks to her servants in a very special way to attract his attention if he is not looking at her. She never seems to want to leave his company, and tells him long stories very slowly as if she never wanted the conversation to end. She kisses and caresses a child in his presence, and draws ornamental symbols on the foreheads of her servants. She also takes care to be more quick and graceful than usual, especially if her servants speak to her jokingly in the presence of her lover. She confides in the friends of her lover and shows them respect and deference. She is good to her servants, speaks with them and orders them to do their work as if she were their mistress, and listens to them attentively when she hears them discuss her lover with someone else. She eagerly goes to the house of her nurse's daughter and arranges to see her lover there through the connivance of the former. She never lets her loved one see her when she is not carefully dressed, and she sends him her ring, earrings or her garland of flowers through a friend. She constantly wears some ornament that he has given her and is very sad when her parents speak of another suitor before her, and she avoids the friends and supporters of the latter.

A man who has noticed and correctly read the feelings of a young girl towards him, and who has accurately estimated her affection for him by a close observation of her movements and gestures should do everything possible to unite with this girl.

He should in general capture the affection of a very young girl by childish games, that of a slightly older girl by his proficiency in the arts, and that of a woman who loves him by having recourse to friends who are in her confidence.

Modern Indian Attitudes Toward *Kama*

❧INTRODUCTION: For millennia, Indians have valued celibacy before marriage and fidelity in marriage. Sexual pleasure is supposed to be enjoyed only within marriage. Young Indians today, however, are very much interested in romantic love, which they see portrayed daily in films, television programs, magazines, and rock videos, and they are changing their values about sex outside of marriage and their perceptions about relationships between the sexes. Young people in large cities, such as Bombay and Delhi, tend to be more outspoken about their attitudes toward dating and what is acceptable behavior between unmarried men and women. In 1989, one of India's leading English-language magazines conducted a public opinion poll to determine what Indians think about issues of love, marriage, and romance. The following charts are taken from that article and tell us something of contemporary Indian attitudes on these very personal questions.[25]❧

Premarital Sex is Out of Bounds
(Percent Agreeing)

	Married Women	Married Men
Bombay	88	65
Delhi	93	91
Madras	89	76
Calcutta	84	64

Will You Marry Someone with Sexual Experience?
(Percent)

	YES	NO
Female Students	34	66
Male Students	54	46

It's Wrong to Dismiss a Homosexual Employee
(Percent Agreeing)

	Female Students	Male Students	Married Women	Married Men
Bombay	63	51	43	35
Delhi	59	58	40	35
Madras	50	44	58	37
Calcutta	60	57	45	49

Women Have a Right to Sexual Equality
(Percent Agreeing)

	Female Students	Male Students	Married Men
Bombay	87	85	65
Delhi	69	81	59
Madras	51	71	58
Calcutta	64	62	47

Women's Lib Is Equivilant to Sexual Freedom
(Percent Agreeing)

	YES	NO
Married Women	86	14
Male Students	53	47
Female Students	66	34

Women's Liberation Is Not Equivalent
to Sexual Freedom
(Percent Agreeing)

	Female Students	Male Students	Married Men
Bombay	43	38	81
Delhi	71	44	93
Madras	77	46	78
Calcutta	83	76	89

Kissing and Necking Are Okay
(Percent Agreeing)

	If you like each other		If you love each other	
	Female Students	Male Students	Female Students	Male Students
Bombay	9	55	60	93
Delhi	10	77	54	81
Madras	13	40	54	86
Calcutta	7	30	60	86

It Is All Right to Make Love if in Love
(Percent)

	Female Students			Male Students		
	Agree	Disagree	Disagree Strongly	Agree	Disagree	Disagree Strongly
Bombay	14	47	38	47	35	18
Delhi	17	24	59	62	20	18
Madras	20	35	45	46	30	24
Calcutta	24	21	55	39	45	15

Do You Approve of Living Together?
(Percent)

	YES	NO
Married Men	27	73
Married Women	5	95
Male Students	51	49
Female Students	26	74

An Extramarital Affair Is Not Wrong
(Percent Agreeing)

	Female Students	Male Students	Married Women	Married Men
Bombay	9 (65)	25 (29)	2 (81)	25 (37)
Delhi	5 (77)	19 (30)	Nil (98)	6 (74)
Madras	5 (78)	30 (38)	1 (79)	21 (53)
Calcutta	5 (80)	18+(36)	3 (82)	10 (35)

(Note: Figures in brackets represent percent who disagree.)

How Do Women View an Unfaithful Wife?
(Percent)

	Bombay	Delhi	Madras	Calcutta
She is doing something wrong	38	57	38	44
She is immoral	17	20	17	31
Her husband must have been mistreating her	14	17	28	30
Husband and wife must have fallen out	29	9	19	17
She is a free woman and can do what she pleases	15	5	7	15

Artha: Survival and Success

🏵️INTRODUCTION: *Artha,* the pursuit of worldly wealth and power, is the third goal of the householder stage of life. Without *artha* how could a person support children and insure prosperity for the family? One must do well in this world, so Indian texts teach, otherwise one can never realize the nobler and higher goals of life. The following reading is adapted from a major text on *artha,* the *Arthasastra* by Kautilya, the chief minister to one of India's early kings. His advice on politics was written down sometime in the fourth century B.C. and may have influenced Machiavelli's *The Prince.*[26]🏵️

As the early Indian states were developing about 2,500 years ago, *artha* was seen as a method which would enable the warring states to survive and prosper. The goal of diplomacy in *artha* was to try to avoid war and to remain secure or even to win more power by superior diplomacy.

The game of amassing power in the *Arthasastra* is amoral. To win, a politician must be willing to do almost anything to outwit and prevail over his opponent. *Artha* is an attitude toward people that we might have toward doors. We simply twist the doorknob to open the door. We have no special feeling for the door. If we apply that attitude toward other people, we understand *artha.*

In the *Arthasastra,* Kautilya advises his king that the world is divided into circles of states. Put yourself in the middle of these rings and as you look out at the states that border your own, you must view these neighbors as enemies. The states that border your neighbors in the next circle are your friends because, "an enemy of my enemy is my friend." The people in the third circle of states are your enemies because they "are the friends of the enemies of my friends." This continues in circle after circle. All states are either friends or enemies and a king must form alliances with whichever states can most benefit his own interests. Being friends in this game has nothing to do with our likes and dislikes of the people who live in these states. Alliances are based purely on interests. In the amoral world of power politics, a leader will say or do anything and make friends with any state (temporarily, of course) which can help his country prosper. A new crisis will cause him to rearrange his alliances, but always with his own interest uppermost in mind.

Kautilya further advised his king how to approach his neighbors. He offered seven strategies to use in order to survive, get ahead and keep an advantage over his neighbors.

Seven Ways to Greet a Neighboring Power

1) *Sāman*: Appeasement, sweet talk, soothing words, conciliatory conduct, such things as non-aggression pacts.

2) *Danda*: Power, military might, punishment, violence, being well-armed, aggression of whatever kind.

3) *Dana*: A bribe or gift, a donation, an agreement to share the spoils of war.

4) *Bheda*: Divide the opposition so as to defeat them, splitting, cause a breach in the opposition, sow dissension in the enemy's party, use treachery, treason.

5) *Maya*: Deceit, illusion, fraud, or a diplomatic feat, such as a mission to the other power offering to negotiate as your military forces are readying for an attack.

6) *Upeksa*: Over-looking, taking no notice, ignoring the enemy until you have decided on the proper course of action.

7) *Indrajala*: A military *maya*, creating an appearance of power when you have none.[27]

♨POSTSCRIPT: The world of power politics is like the ocean where big fish eat little fish. To survive, little fish must live by their wits. Another text on *artha*, a series of animal fables called the *Panchatantra*, instructs poor and powerless people how to survive in a hostile world, just as the *Arthasasta* teaches the powerful how to compete against powerful heard, teach the common people that if they use their wits, cleverness, and learning (as well as their opponent's arrogance and egotism), they can survive and even prosper, despite their weakness. Thus, *artha* is a concept that applies to all strata of society. It is an inherent part of social life.✚

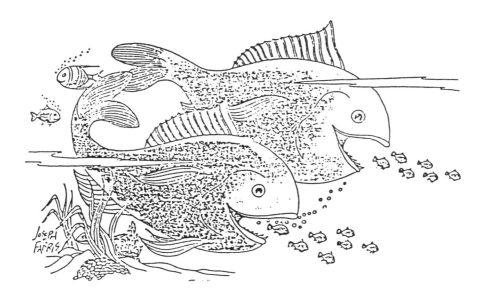

"'Big fish eat little fish.' I like that."
Drawing by Joseph Farris;
© 1979 The New Yorker Magazine, Inc.

The Hindu World View

❧INTRODUCTION: According to the Hindu world view, there are two stages in the first half of life: the student and the householder. It is here that a person's life is guided by the three goals of *dharma, kama,* and *artha.* Hindus pursue success through *artha,* fall in love and reproduce through *kama,* and carry out their student, family, and work responsibility through *dharma.*

The everyday world of pain and joy, work and success, birth and death is called *samsara* in Hinduism. No doubt *samsara* is important; it is life as we know it. And the goals of *dharma* and *kama* and *artha* are important for success in this world. But Hindus do not live for this world alone; they recognize a fourth and final goal of life—*moksha.* *Moksha* means reunion with the divine and it is the only goal of the second half of life. (The diagram below shows the goals and stages of life in the Hindu world view.)

GOALS

Dharma	Kama	Artha	Moksha

STAGES OF LIFE

Student	Householder	"Going to the Forest"	"Wandering Holy Man"

BIRTH   **DEATH**

In pursuit of *moksha*, Hindus pass through two more stages of life (beyond the student and householder stages). In the third stage, called "going to the forest," Hindus concentrate on trying to break loose from *karma*, their fate that locks them into endless rounds of birth and rebirth which keep them mired in the tediousness of *samsara*. Different people use different paths or *yogas* in their striving for *moksha*.

A person who experiences *moksha* enters the final state of life: the wandering holy man. Very few Hindus ever reach this stage, but it is respected by all believing Hindus as the culmination of life.

The following readings, compiled by the authors, weave together important sources of Hindu beliefs that guide individuals through birth and death and finally offer a way out of *samsara* to *moksha*. The chapter continues with the Hindu concept of God, Brahman, and *yoga*, written by the authors and drawing on traditional and other sources.ᵗᵉ

Samsara: The Cycle of Lives

"Two days ago the marriage feast was mine,
And only yesterday I bought milch kine [milk cows]
Wherewith to start my modest home. My field
Is bright with corn, with gold my coffers yield,
I cannot die." While yet thou speakest, fool,
Dread Yama's [God of Death] step comes near. Fare-
     well, vile soul.

    Chorus: How near is death? Mercy he cannot bring.
    Then, oh my heart, cease from the world, and cling
    With all thy power to tender Lakshmi's King [Vish-
    nu, the God of Preservation].

"My house is newly built. E'en now they say
The Mantras [holy verses] that have power to drive away
All evils from my home. My wife is great
With child. The day that weds my son we wait.
Life is so good, I cannot, will not die."
Vain fool! Death's hand now shades thy glazing eye.

    Chorus: How near is death? . . . [28]

Death can come at any time, as this Canarese folk song

suggests. But to the Hindu, death is but one point on the great span of endless time. An individual dies, but in India that is not the end of this story. All Hindus know:

> To him that is born, death is sure
> And for him who has died, birth is certain.
> This cannot be changed.

Another Hindu scripture explains:

> As the body of mortals undergoes the changes of infancy, youth and old age, even so will it be transformed, into another body hereafter; a sensible man is not mistaken about that. As a man puts on new clothes in this world, throwing aside those which he formerly wore, even so the self of man puts on new bodies which are in accordance with his acts in a former life.[30]

Although an individual may die, his life force or soul (called *atman*) never dies; it takes on a new form with each birth. *Samsara* ("rebirth") is more than a belief to the Hindu or Buddhist. It is the certainty on which all life is based.

KARMA: AS YOU SOW, SO SHALL YOU REAP

In what form will one be reborn? How is that determined? Snoopy asks the same question in the accompanying cartoon.

The factor that determines the form in which you will be born in your next existence is your *karma.* If you have lived a good life, you build up good *karma* and will be born into a higher station, or to a happier life. If you perform bad deeds, you build up bad *karma* and are certain to suffer in succeeding lives. Good and bad *karma* are built up over generations, the balance being passed on to future lives.

In the New Testament, Saint Matthew states, "As a man soweth, so also shall he reap." The difference between this statement and *karma* is that to Saint Matthew, a man's deeds are balanced out in a single lifetime, whereas *karma* is the balancing of good and bad deeds over hundreds of lifetimes.

Snoopy has analyzed the doctrine of *karma* and gives us

© 1960 United Feature Syndicate, Inc.

his thoughts in the cartoons on this and the next page. The Hindu holy book, the *Upanishads,* describes this process:

> Those whose conduct here [on earth] has been good will quickly attain some good birth—birth as a Brahmin, birth as a Kshatriya, or birth as a Vaishya. But those whose conduct here has been evil will quickly attain some evil birth—birth as a dog, birth as a pig, or birth as a *chandala* ("untouchable").[31]

Karma also helps to explain the seeming unfairness of life. Why does a child get hit by a car? Why does a young father die of cancer? Why did that housewife win the lottery ticket? Many Indians answer these kinds of questions by the law of *karma.* When they see a good man suffer, Indians might say: "It's because of some bad deed done in a previous life. Who can escape his *karma?*" Likewise, good *karma* follows a man:

In dark forests, amidst his foes in war,
In flood or raging flame;
In ocean depths or on precarious peaks;
Slumbering or courting dread danger
With reckless abandon;
Merits earned in former lives
Afford a man protection.[32]

Living, for the Hindu, can be seen as an attempt to build up good *karma*. But one builds good *karma* not by "doing good" or helping old ladies across the street, but by doing one's duty, one's *dharma*. If you are a son, you obey your father even if it means banishment. If you are a tailor, you bring up your sons to be good tailors. Each person has a *dharma*, determined in part by his position in the family, his caste, and his age. A son obeys; a sweeper cleans the street; a wife bears children. All are human, but each must be faithful to his own *dharma.*

BRAHMAN: THE HINDU CONCEPT OF GOD

The final goal in life for the Hindu is not to be born into a higher station in his next life. The final goal is not to be born again at all. At some point in his experience, after several lifetimes, or several thousand lifetimes, the Hindu grows weary of living on earth, no matter how pleasant it may be. Swami Ramakrishna, the great Hindu teacher, described the process:

> The world is like a stage, where men perform many parts under various disguises. They do not like to take off the mask, unless they have played for some time. Let them play for a while, and then they will leave off the mask of their own accord.[33]

Most everyone is still "playing for a while," but if we are Hindus we know that the time will come when we will want to "leave off the mask." When that times does come, we are ready to seek reunion with God.

What is the Hindu concept of God? Is it similar to Allah of the Muslims or Yaweh of the Jews or God the Father of the Christians? In the following passage, Krishna describes the nature of God to Arjuna. (Krishna is an incarnation of God, so he speaks of himself.) How does this concept of God compare to your own?

> I am immortality and death
> What is and what is not, Arjuna.
>
> I am the source of all.
> All things come forth from me.
>
> I am the beginning and the end
> And the middle of all creations
> I am the knowledge of the soul.
> I am the discourse of those who speak.
>
> I am the gambling of the cheat
> The sharp edge of the brilliant.
> I am victory. I am effort.
> I am courage to the stout-hearted.

Understanding, knowledge, non-delusion
Patience, restraint, truth, serenity,
Courage and fear, joy and sorrow,
Rising up and passing away.

Harmlessness, equanimity, content,
Austerity, open-handedness
Fame, ill-fame, however various,
These states of being arise from me alone.

And whatever is the seed of all beings
That I am, Arjuna.
No creature that moves or does not move
Could exist without me.[34]

Note that Krishna says that he and he alone is the "source of all"—of creation, destruction, fame, ill-fame, love, and hate. The single source is that invisible and subtle essence that pervades all things, which we call God. This God is all that is, and all that is not, as well. It is the ONEness of all reality. To be the ONE, it must combine all opposites within itself.

In the Judeo-Christian tradition and also in Islam, God generally stands for only good qualities, such as love, justice, truth, and peace. Another figure, usually the Devil, is the source of evil: hate, injustice, falsehood, sin, etc. In these religions, one has a choice between God, representing good, and the Devil, representing evil. You either go God's way or the Devil's. Notice the word *or*. The choice is good *or* evil, God *or* the Devil.

In the Hindu concept, however, ultimate reality is both rather than *either*. The ONE is both good and evil, both God and the Devil. Destruction is as much a part of the ONE as is creation. Both exist; therefore, they exist in the ONE.

But you and I exist as well. What is our relationship to the ONE? Listen to the way in which a father explains this to his son, Svetaketu, in the *Upanishads:*

"Place this salt in water and come to me tomorrow morning."
Svetaketu did as he was commanded, and in the morn-

ing his father said to him: "Bring me the salt you put into the
water last night."

Svetaketu looked into the water, but could not find it, for it
had dissolved.

His father then said: "Taste the water from this side. How is
it?"

"It is salt."

"Taste it from the middle. How is it?"

"It is salt."

"Look for the salt again and come again to me."

The son did so, saying, "I cannot see the salt. I only see
water."

His father then said: "In the same way, O my son, you cannot
see the Spirit. But in truth he is here."

An invisible and subtle essence is the Spirit of the whole
universe. That is Reality. That is Truth. THOU ART THAT.[35]

Christianity and Islam believe that man stands in
relationship to God. He may pray to God, walk with God,
perhaps even see and hear God, but he can never *be* God.
In the Hindu conception of the ONE, all things *are* God,
and therefore man is God too. The ONE is you, it is me, it
is All.

Yet God is not you. That is why many Hindus when
describing God speak in negative terms. God is not this, not
that, not knowing, not unknowing. What we see and experience is not God, yet God is All.

In talking about God we are like the six blind men dis-
puting the correct description of an elephant that none of
us can see. We have mistaken what we can see, touch, smell,
hear, and taste for the true and complete reality. This perception that physical phenomena are real Hindus call *maya*.
Maya, from the same root as the word "magic," means illusion. It is as if the universal reality were playing tricks on
us, making us believe that our bodies, this page, the mountains, and the birds are real. In Hinduism, one must go past
these material forms to the one divine mystery that en-
velops and manifests itself as all the little realities. That is
the one true reality. *Maya* is simply the mistaken belief that
lesser thinks are real.

A young woman performs a puja (act of worship) to the goddess Lakshmi during the Festival of Lights (Diwali). (Information Service of India, New York, N.Y.)

Joseph Campbell, a famous scholar of world mythologies, told the story of a kitten before a mirror who sees what he thinks is another kitten. He stalks it, boxes with it, even rubs noses with it. Finally he peeks behind the mirror and then realizes that he has been reacting to an image. Like the kitten, you and I spend our days loving and fighting things that are ultimately illusionary, according to the theory of the *maya*. Even you and I in our separate forms are illusions, say the Hindus, for we are all part of the ONE we call God.

The interior of the Mangesh Temple in Goa. (Government of India Tourist Office, New York, N.Y.)

MOKSHA: SEEKING REUNION WITH BRAHMAN

Because we live in the world of *maya*, we do not know that we are part of the ONE, Brahman, or God. In our daily lives, we experience life as separate beings, living, dying, being born again, living, dying, and being born again and again. Even if life is good, in fact, especially if it is good, at some point we begin to yearn for something deeper, some other reality. *Artha* and *kama* no longer tempt us; they have lost their taste. We begin to ask whether there isn't something else. A seventh century South Indian poet put it this way:

> If wealth which yields all desire is won,
> > What then?
> If your foot stands on the head of your foes,
> > What then?
> If honored men are drawn to you by your riches' force,
> > What then?

> If man's mundane body endures for an aeon,
> What then?[36]

When we ask "What then?" we are ready to give up our roles as householder and seek Brahman, the Oneness of all things. The Laws of Manu give clear instruction for this action:

> When a householder sees his [skin] wrinkled and [his hair] white, and the sons of his sons, then he may resort to the forest. Abandoning all food raised by cultivation and all his belongings, he may depart into the forest, either committing his wife to his sons or accompanied by her.[37]

[Many examples from the history and mythology of India describe this idea of "going to the forest." The individual personality (the ego) disappears.]

Once upon a time, in those bright ages when India was young, there lived a great king, Bharata, and so famous was he that even now the people speak among themselves of their country as Bharata Varsha, Bharata's Land; it is only foreigners who talk of it as "India."

In the days of this ruler, it was considered the right thing for every man, when he had finished educating his family—when his daughters were all married, his business affairs in order, and his sons well-established in life—to say farewell to the world and retire to the forest, there to give the remainder of his life to prayer and the thought of God. This was considered to be the duty of all, whatever their station in life, priest and merchant, king and laborer, all alike.

And so in the course of events the great King Bharata, [typical of a true] Hindu sovereign, gave up his wealth and power and withdrew. His family and people woke up one morning, and he was gone. That was all. But everyone understood that . . . he had passed out of the city during the night in the garb of a beggar, and the news spread through the country that his son was king. Just as the water of a lake closes over a stone thrown into it and leaves no trace, so

society went on its usual course, and the loss of Bharata made
no mark.[38]

[Seeking Oneness with God is still an important dimen-
sion of Indian life. In the selection that follows, taken from a
modern English novel set in India, a father decides to leave
his family and attempt to become a *sannyasi* ("holy man").
Notice that this is after his youngest daughter, Shalini, is married.]

Two weeks after Shalini's ritual return to her parents'
home, and one week after her final departure to Mayapore
with her husband, her father announced his intention to
divest himself of all his worldly goods, to depart from his
family and his responsibilities, and wander the countryside:
become, eventually, *sannyasi.*
   "I have done my duty," he said. "It is necessary to recognise
that it is finished. It is necessary not to become a burden.
Now my duty is to God."
   His family were shocked. Duleep pleaded with him but his
resolve was unshaken. "When are you leaving us, then?"
Duleep asked.
   "I shall go in six months' time. It will take until then to
order my affairs. The inheritance will be divided equally
among the four of you. The house will belong to your elder
brother. Your mother must be allowed to live here for as long
as she wishes, but your elder brother and his wife will become
heads of the household. All will be done as it would be done
if I were dead."
   Duleep shouted, "You call this good? You call it holy? To
leave our mother. To bury yourself alive in *nothing?* To beg
your bread when you are rich enough to feed a hundred
starving beggars?"
   "Rich?" his father asked. "What is rich? Today I have riches.
With one stroke of a pen on a document I can rid myself of
what you call my riches. But what stroke of a pen on what
kind of document will ensure my release from the burden of

another lifespan after this? Such a release can only be hoped for, only earned by renouncing all earthly bonds."

Duleep said, "Ah well, yes! How fine! In what way could you be ashamed now to find your son a little burra sahib [gentleman]? What difference could it make to you now what I was or where I was? Is it for this that I gave in to you? Is it to see you shrug me off and walk away from me and my brothers and our mother that I obeyed you?"

"While there is duty there must be obedience. My duty to you is over. Your obedience to me is no longer necessary. You have different obligations now. And I have a duty of still another kind."

"It is monstrous!" Duleep shouted. "Monstrous and cruel and selfish! You have ruined my life. I have sacrificed myself for nothing."

As he had found earlier, it was easier to blame anyone than to blame himself, but he regretted the attack. He suffered greatly at the recollection of it. He tried to speak about it to his mother, but these days she went about her daily tasks dumbly and unapproachable. When the time drew near for his father to go he went to him and begged his forgiveness.

"You were always my favorite son," old Kumar admitted. "That was a sin, to feel more warmly toward one than to the others. Better you should have had no ambition. Better you should have been like your brothers. I could not help but exert authority more strongly over the only son who ever seemed ready to defy it. And I was ashamed of my preference. My exertion of authority perhaps went beyond the bounds of reason. A father does not ask his son to forgive him. It is only open to him to bless him and to commit to this son's care that good woman, your mother."

"No," Duleep said, weeping. "That duty is not for me. That is for your eldest son. Don't burden me with that."

"A burden will fall upon the heart most ready to accept it," old Kumar said, and then knelt and touched his youngest son's feet, to humble himself.

Even in the business of becoming sannyasi old Kumar

seemed determined upon the severest shock to his pride. He underwent no rituals. He did not put on the long gown. On the morning of his departure he appeared in the compound dressed only in a loincloth, carrying a staff and a begging-bowl. Into the bowl his stony-faced wife placed a handful of rice. And then he walked through the gateway and into the road, away from the village.

For a while they followed him, some distance behind. He did not look back. When Duleep and his brothers gave up following him their mother continued. They watched but said nothing to each other, waiting for their mother, who, after a while, sat down on the roadside and stayed there until Duleep joined her, urged her to her feet, and supported her back to the house.

"You must not give in to sorrow," she told him later, lying on her bed in a darkened room from which she had ordered the servants to remove every article of comfort and luxury. "It is the will of God."[39]

YOGA: PATHS TO THE ONE

How will the father in the last selection seek union with the ONE? He can choose from among many paths. Sincerity, dedication, and years of discipline are the only requirements. The father will seek reunion with God through a form of *yoga* or *marga*.

Yoga means "yoking to God" or "union with God." It includes a variety of means that Hindus employ to experience *moksha*, thereby becoming selfless and egoless. It involves total dedication. *Yoga* does not mean improving your personality, finding peace of mind, learning how to do better in business, or how to cure headaches. Some of these things may result from the practice of *yoga*, but to say that they are its objective would be like saying that the objective of taking Holy Communion is a physical nourishment.

Yoga is a long process, which involves an attitude about life rather than a technique. It generally takes years, perhaps lifetimes, to achieve *moksha*.

There are three major *yogas*. One system is *Raja-yoga*—
seeking God through meditation and proper knowledge.
Raja-yoga is the "intentional stopping of the spontaneous activities of the mind-stuff."

Our minds are constantly on the move. Contemplation
of one object or idea immediately sets off a chain of other
associations and remembrances. As you sit in your seat in
the classroom, for example, imagine that you observe
through the window a man mowing the grass outside. This
mental picture reminds you at once that after school you
are supposed to mow the lawn at home. But you had
promised to meet Bill at four o'clock to look at stereo units.
Thinking of the stereo reminds you of music, the music of
the rock festival last summer, and thoughts of the festival
set in motion other images of the summer—swimming,
playing baseball, the day you got three hits and the crowd
cheered. Suddenly someone is calling your name. It is the
teacher, and you have not heard. You have lost your concentration on history all because of a man cutting grass
outside. Krishna might well have been talking to you when
he said: "The mind is restless, Arjuna: it is indeed hard to
train. But by constant practice and by freedom from passions the mind in truth can be trained."

The Hindu scriptures liken the mind to a pet monkey. A
pet dog can be trained to come when you call him and to
leave you alone when you are busy. A monkey, however, comes
when *he* wants to. You are usually the monkey's pet. But the
mind is not an ordinary mischievous monkey; imagine that
this monkey was drunk, and think how difficult it would be
to control. Now imagine that this drunken monkey has been
bitten by a scorpion. To control the mind, Swami Satchinanda
says, is like trying to control a drunken monkey that has been
bitten by a scorpion.

Raja-yoga is training to control the mind, to stop its images
and associations so that a deeper level of reality may be experienced. The training for the *Raja-yoga* is divided into eight
stages:

1) Self-control *(yama)*, the practice of the five moral rules: non-violence, truthfulness, not stealing, chastity, and the avoidance of greed.

2) Observance *(niyama)*, the regular and complete observance of the above five rules.

3) Posture *(āsana)*, sitting in ceratin postures, difficult without practice, which are thought to be essential to meditation. The most famous of these is *padmāsana*, the "Lotus Position," in which the feet are placed on the opposite thighs, and in which gods and sages are commonly depicted.

4) Control of the Breath *(prānāyāma)*, whereby the breath is held and the respiration forced into unusual rhythms, which are believed to be of great physical and spiritual value.

5) Restraint *(pratyāhāra)*, whereby the sense organs are trained to take no note of their perceptions.

6) Steadying the Mind *(dhāranā)*, by concentration on a single object, such as the tip of the nose, the navel, an icon, or a sacred symbol.

7) Meditation *(dhyāna)*, when the object of concentration fills the whole mind.

8) Deep Meditation *(samādhi)*, when the whole personality is temporarily dissolved.[40]

Just the first stage of *Raja-yoga* is demanding enough. Notice that posture, what we know as exercises, is number three on the list. It comes only *after* the attainment of the five moral rules. Control of breathing comes after that. It is understandable that an Indian would be skeptical of Americans who practice *yoga* exercises one evening a week.

Karma-yoga is a second way to realize *moksha*. *Karma-yoga* is based on action. It requires one to act without regard for the fruits of one's actions.

Imagine a mighty warrior about to fight in a great battle. On the eve of the conflict, he looks out at the enemy forces and there sees some of his dearest friends, his beloved uncle, his cousins, and even his *guru*. "How can I fight those whom I honor and love? Better I should die. I will not fight." With these words, he throws down his arms and sits despondently near his chariot.

This is the situation in the *Bhagavad Gita*, perhaps the best-loved Hindu sacred text. Arjuna, the brave Pandava war-

rior, refuses to fight against his cousins, the Kauravas.
But Arjuna's charioteer is an incarnation of God, the
Lord Krishna. Hearing Arjuna's words, Krishna advises
the warrior:

> You grieve for those you should not
> And yet you talk about wisdom.
> The truly taught do not mourn
> For the dead or the living.
>
> For to him that is born, death is sure
> And for him who has died, birth is certain.
> This cannot be changed. Therefore,
> You should not sorrow.
>
> And if you think just of your own place
> You should not recoil.
> For a warrior there is no better thing
> Than to fight out of duty.
>
> Here chance is offering you
> A door open to heaven.
> O Partha, those warriors are lucky
> Who are granted such a fight.
>
> But if you turn away from this battle
> Which your own duty requires
> Then, giving up duty and glory,
> You will only get trouble.
>
> People will talk of your shame
> Now and in years to come.
> And for one who has been honored
> Disgrace is worse than death.
>
> Those in the great chariots will be sure
> That you hang back from the battle through fear
> And they who once thought well of you
> Will come to hold you lightly.
>
> Those who wish you ill will talk of you
> And say what had best not be said.
> They will revile all that you are.
> What could be worse than that?
>
> Either killed, you shall gain heaven
> Or conquering, you will enjoy the earth.
> Therefore, stand up, son of Kunti
> And set your mind upon battle.

Holding pleasure and pain as alike
Gain and loss, victory and defeat
Prepare yourself for the fight
Only thus will you not reap evil.

Better do your own task imperfectly
Than do another's well.
Better die in your own duty.
Another's task brings peril.[41]

Lord Krishna instructed Arjuna to do his duty without
regard for the consequences. To act with a "holy indifference," with no concern for results is the essence of *karma-
yoga.* Think for a minute why *you* act. Why do you study for a
test? Why do you tell the truth? Why did you come to school
this morning? Why do you obey your parents?

Now put your answers aside and consider these words
Krishna says to Arjuna:

You have a right to the work alone
But never to its fruits.
Let not the fruits be your motive . . .

Steadfast in the Way, without attachment,
Do your work, Victorious One.
The same in success and misfortune.
This evenness—that is discipline.[42]

Your business is with the deed, not with the result. Just do
your duty and let the results fall where they may. As Krishna states:

The wise, whose minds are controlled,
Leaving the rewards of action,
Are released from the bounds of rebirth.[43]

This path of *Karma-yoga* is quite different from the *yoga*
of meditation, and yet it is just as valid. Many great Indians
believe in *Karma-yoga.* Mahatma Gandhi was a believer in
Karma-yoga. His teachings on nonviolence and his methods of
fighting the British through civil disobedience come out of
the ancient *Karma-yoga* system.

In *Karma-yoga,* there is no withdrawing from life. Life and the world are the stage on which we live out the truth. The "Pure Act" is an important idea in *Karma-yoga*. For example, if you had ten dollars, you might choose to use it in one of four basic ways: (1) You could buy yourself some topics; that would be a selfish act, (2) You could give the ten dollars to a needy person and say, "I am helping you. Aren't you thankful to me for my charity?" That would be an egotistical act, (3) You could simply tear the ten-dollar bill into pieces; that would be an absurd act. Finally, (4) you could give the money anonymously to a needy person or worthwhile cause. That would be the pure act and would come close to *Karma-yoga*.

The third major form of *yoga*, perhaps the one most frequently practiced by Hindus, is *Bhakti-yoga*. Here the devotee surrenders completely to God. Of all the *yoga* systems, *Bhakti* is perhaps the easiest to follow. It does not demand years of meditation, like *Raja-yoga*, or the difficult discipline of *Karma-yoga*. All one has to do is love God with all his being. It is not dissimilar to many Christian practices of surrender to God.

In Hinduism, a devotee may choose any one of several manifestations of the ONE. The *Bhakti* path does not require great learning, mastering of the scriptures, or elaborate rituals. One does not even have to be "well born." Lord Krishna states:

> He who works for me, who loves me, whose End Supreme I am, free from attachment to all things, and with love for all creation, he in truth comes to me.

> For all those who come to me for shelter, however weak or humble or sinful they may be—women or Vaishyas or Shudras— they all reach the Path supreme.[44]

The deity most often associated with *Bhakti* is Lord Krishna, one of the incarnations of God, who lived for a time as a cowherder with the milkmaids of Brindavan. The milkmaids adored Krishna. Krishna had but to play his flute and the women, even those who were already married, would risk all they held dear—family, home, and honor—to go to his call. Through identification with the milkmaids (gopist), the *Bhakti* devotee can love God with all the intensity of the romantic

The late Prime Minister Indira Gandhi lays a garland at a picture of Tulsi Das, Hindu poet and translator of the Ramayana. (Information Service of India, New York, N. Y.)

lover. In the following poem about a milkmaid and Krishna, remember that the one addressed is God:

> Let the earth of my body be mixed with the
>   earth my beloved walks on.
> Let the fire of my body be the brightness
>   in the mirror that reflects his face.
> Let the water of my body join the waters
>   of the lotus pool he bathes in.
> Let the breath of my body be air
>   lapping his tired limbs.
> Let me be sky, and moving through me
>   that cloud-dark Shyama, my beloved.[45]

Lord Krishna is not the only deity a devotee can choose to worship. Vishnu, Shiva, and Rama are also objects of *Bhakti* worship. In addtion, the female deities Lakshmi, Durga, and Kali are common inspirations of *Bhakti* devotion.

Certain *Bhakti* cults have spread all over the world. There are Krishna cults in several American and European cities. Devotees dance and pass out literature on the streets. Every year hundreds of Americans and Europeans travel to India in search of their own special *guru*. The Beatles and the film actress, Mia Farrow, are among those who have made these pilgrimages. Rennie Davis, a former radical political activist and one of the founders of Students for a Democratic Society, has become a devotee of Maharaja-Ji, the young religious leader. Some Indian *gurus*, such as Maharishi Yogi and Maharaja-Ji, have visited the United States.

Bhakti-yoga is often associated with saints who, through their poetry, songs, and way of life, helped to bring people to the love of God. All through Indian history such saints roamed the land, inspiring devotion to God. Many of these saints are in India today. Some are regarded by Indians as crackpots who appeal to Western seekers but who are not genuine holy men. Some, like Sai Baba in South India, perform miracles and have large followings of Indians and Westerners. Only time and the people can ultimately say who are authentic and who are fakes.

Whether they seek a spiritual *guru* or not, whether they follow one *yoga* or another, for Hindus, release from the con-

stant round of birth and rebirth is the ultimate aim of life.
Mahatma Gandhi put it in these words:

> What I want to achieve—what I have been striving and pining
> to achieve these thirty years—is self-realization, to see God face
> to face, to attain *moksha*. I live and move and have my being in
> pursuit of this goal. All that I do by way of speaking and writing,
> and all my ventures in the political field, are directed to this
> same end.[46]

Nataraj

ɪ♠INTRODUCTION: Another major deity for *Bhakti* is Lord Shiva. Shiva is the Nataraj, or Lord of the Dance. The Nataraj image of Shiva as the Divine Dancer comes from South India, and the image symbolizes many of the beliefs of Hinduism. If we understand what the Nataraj represents, we come close to understanding some of the deepest meanings of Hinduism.[47]♠

Shiva's Cosmic Dance brings the universe into existence and destroys it as well. At the same time, his dance points to the Oneness which lies beyond the flux of *samsara*. The Nataraj image of Shiva as the divine dancer symbolizes the Hindu life cycle that ebbs and flows in ever-occurring creation-destruction until the final release into *moksha*. The image also suggests the fleeting aspect of life: each moment, whether joyous or sad, soon passes. The old gives way to the new; life continually renews itself.

Look closely at the Nataraj. In his upper right hand, Shiva holds an hourglass-shaped drum which beats out the rhythm of the universe. The drum and its beat symbolize creation and the pulse of life. The serpents wound around Shiva's body, like a sacred thread, symbolize the life force that makes the universe possible. In his upper left hand, Shiva holds a ball of flame which symbolizes the world's destruction. The ring of flame which surrounds Shiva's dance stands for *samsara*, life fluctuating between creation and destruction, between the drum and the flame.

But *samsara* is not all there is, and part of the image breaks out of the ring of fire. Shiva holds his lower right hand in the

The Nataraj, or Dancing Shiva, is a classic Hindu image noted for the way it simultaneously captures movement and stillness in perfect balance. Like images of Jesus in Christianity, the Nataraj has been created by countless artists throughout the ages. The bronze Nataraj above dates from about 1000 A.D. (Donald Johnson)

gesture *mudra*, which means "Be not afraid." With his fourth hand he points to his raised foot, symbolizing the reason one need not fear. Shiva's raised foot, which is in front of the circle of fire and not caught in *samsara*, points away from the cycle of life and death and toward *moksha*. As we contemplate the raised foot, we realize we may escape *samsara* and break the bonds of ignorance. The dwarf on whom Shiva dances represents the ignorance or forgetfulness that stands between each of us and a true understanding of our own nature and of the nature of Brahman. If we can crush the dwarf of forgetfulness, we remember "Thou art That" and we realize we are one with Brahman.

Death: "Lower the Body to the Ground"

✒INTRODUCTION: Death is never easy to cope with; yet we know that it is the ultimate reality. One goal of all religions is to help man deal with his mortality.

It has been said, "As a man lives, so shall he die." What does this mean? Does it mean that our attitude toward life will determine our attitude toward death? Perhaps. Or it might be put in another way: In a man's attitude toward death, we can gain insight into his attitude toward the meaning of life. It may be possible, then, to infer the philosophy of a society from its handling of death.

The following selection, taken from the autobiography of a Punjabi businessman, describes the burial of Savitri, a young Indian woman who has died in childbirth.[48]✒

When the doctor realized that further effort was no use, he whispered to my mother the dreaded Hindu formula, "I think the girl should now be lowered onto the floor." Helped by others, she lifted Savitri from the bed and put her on the floor, which had been hastily plastered with water and some cowdung. . . . A few drops of water from the sacred Mother Ganga [the Ganges River] were put into her mouth, and the aromatic leaf of the holy Tulsi plant, which is grown in a pot in every Hindu home, was placed between her lips. Slowly life was leaving Savitri's body, burning with the heat of the fever, her baby lying already lifeless near her. A small lamp made out of dough, with melted *ghee* [oil] and a cotton wick, was put near her. As life would stop flickering in one body it would symbolically rise in a tiny flame in another. The soul would soar up and perhaps somewhere enter another body, till, purified of all sin, it would rise and merge into Nirvan [*moksha*], to be reborn no more. Who knows, my mother thought, where Savitri's soul was first born, and whether she was its last home. Had it finished its eternal quest, or would it continue the search for peace? Whatever its past or future, whether it stopped here or continued, in its sojourn, through Savitri's body, innocent and sinless, it could only have gone upward to a higher existence. It could only have gained a step nearer to Nirvan. . . .

As Savitri had no sons, my elder brother was chosen to perform certain ceremonies. He was bathed, Raja shaved his head, and he was put into a new, unwashed raw silk *dhoti* [draped clothing] and had to sit by the oil lamp in a corner of the room. The lamp had to be kept filled with mustard oil to keep it burning for ten days until all the ceremonies were over. Food would be served to him first and brought to him to eat near the lamp. As a mere boy, my brother was somewhat frightened by the role he was called upon to play. He must have thought of the happier role he had played as uncle's *sarbhala* [young male companion, age twelve to thirteen, accompanying bridegroom] when he rode behind him on the horse on our way to Savitri's house for the wedding. . . .

As the news spread, members of our *biradari* [caste brotherhood] began to drop in. As they passed through the street our neighbors joined them. . . . Our elders stood at the door, and as visitors came with folded hands and said, "Very much grieved, how much we cannot say," they replied with their hands stretched out in a gesture of infinity, "God's will." The elderly callers touched Dwarka Prashad [Savitri's husband] on the shoulder and said, "Son, have patience, there is no alternative but to accept God's will with fortitude. Bear the loss like a man, it will give courage to everyone else, especially to her mother and father."

One member of the *biradari* always came forward on these occasions and offered to make all the arrangements for the funeral rites. . . .

These were the moments when the *biradari* came into its own. Everything would be taken off the hands of the bereaved family, and without fuss, very quietly, everything would be taken care of. It was a great feeling for the family, a feeling of importance, of belonging and affection, to be waited on in their grief. With smooth and experienced efficiency, the men and women divided up their tasks, and someone took over-all direction. One person ran to the post office to send letters and telegrams; another went to buy materials for the ceremonies—incense, *ghee, mouli* [sacred red thread] and rice; another went to buy new unstitched cloth for the shroud, and handwoven red, purple or magenta cotton or silk for covering; another to buy flowers; another to buy bamboo sticks, some faggots of sandlewood, a mat woven from date-palm frounds, some string, an earthenware pitcher and bowl. A large variety of materials was needed for the coffin and the cremation. In villages a handcart would go round, and the *biradari* members would each give an unsplit log of wood as their contribution for the funeral pyre. . . .

[Inside the women prepared Savitri's body. It was then taken downstairs and placed on a bamboo mat bier.] Men came forward and lifted the bier and moved on. While passing through our *mohalla* [cluster of houses around a common courtyard] they held it low so that the neighbors and others waiting in the street could take a last look. At the end of the street they covered her face, lifted the bier on their shoulders, and started at a brisk pace. Every few steps another mourner would join the carriers out of duty and piety. It was considered a blessing to carry it. To the monotonous chant of *"Ram Nam Sat hai,"* [God's name is truth), sprinkling water with a tuft of kusha grass, throwing coins in the air over the body for the poor to pick up, the procession moved on through the streets till it reached the cremation grounds. . . .

Some people had arrived earlier to arrange the funeral pyre. The big and heavy logs were placed at the bottom, then the smaller ones; the still smaller logs formed rests for head and feet. Three iron bars were stuck in the ground on each side to prevent the logs from rolling off the pyre. The body was placed on the logs and covered with a few pieces of sandalwood and then smaller logs with some big ones on top again. A bundle of dried twigs and reeds was made into a small pillow and pushed between the logs under her head. Incense and ghee were then poured all over the pyre.

When everything was ready, some elders led Dwarka Prashad to the final and the most painful act. Everyone fell back and left him and the *acharya* [a Brahmin associated with

A Hindu worker looks on as a dead body burns on its funeral pyre. (United Press International)

death ceremonies] sitting near the pyre. The *acharya* recited
some last *mantras* [prayers] and lit a torch of dried reeds,
which he handed over to Dwarka Prashad, and then walked
away.

Dwarka Prashad stood alone, staring vacantly at the pyre.
Between the logs he could see the still form of Savitri, which
he had learned to know so well. He saw the shape of her
head, the curve of her breasts and her thighs, and her feet
pointing up. In deep youthful sleep he had sometimes seen
her lying on her back under a bedsheet, as still as she was
now. As intimacy grew he had seen her whole body lying ex-
pectantly vibrant, but now she looked so relaxed. He felt the
growing heat of the torch but he stood still. His feet would
not move. As the torch burst into a fierce flame and he still
would not move, granduncle came forward and put his hand
under his elbow and led him close to the pyre. "Dwarka
Prashad," he whispered hoarsely, "this is something which
only you must do."

There was a little smoke from the pillow of dry grass, a
crackle, and then a small tongue of flame leapt and licked
the red silk shawl. It grew into a fire which spread to the dry
logs. Fed by incense and *ghee*, as it rushed through the pyre,
the fire raged and flames leaped high. The mourners fell back
as the intense flames consumed everything in their way. "Let
us now go," said granduncle.[48]

POSTSCRIPT: Will this soul escape the "endless" cycle of birth-death-
rebirth? Nobody knows. Some rare souls, who follow their *dharma*
perfectly and ultimately, renounce this world and experience the ONE,
are released from the bonds of *samsara*. But for most people, the cycle
of life continues, and in some household a joyous young mother sings
out:

> Husband, call the midwife quickly,
> Let the child be delivered.

PART TWO

THE HISTORIC
TRADITION

Introduction

Most modern nations are built on their sense of past greatness and a common core of values. The people of modern India can look back on an unbroken tradition of almost 5,000 years, one of the longest continuous histories of any contemporary nation. Over the millennia of Indian history many invading groups have journeyed into the sub-continent and these groups have represented different religions, ethnic identities, and racial types. The great cultural diversity of modern India is the product of attempts over thousands of years to integrate new groups into an ever-expanding cultural framework. Most of the past and present leaders, as well as philosophers and artists, have tried and continue to try to work out a system where each of the many diverse groups that make up the nation can be respected even as the larger nation embraces them all.

Mark Twain, who traveled to India in 1896, was impressed with the great size and pluralism of the land. He wrote:

> This is indeed India; the land of dreams and romance, of fabulous wealth and fabulous poverty, of splendor and rags, of palaces and hovels, of famine and pestilence, of genii and giants and Aladdin lamps, of tigers and elephants, the cobra and the jungle, the country of a hundred nations and a hundred tongues, of a thousand religions and two million gods, cradle of the human race, birthplace of human speech, mother of history, grandmother of legend, great-grandmother of tradition, whose yesterdays bear date with the moldering antiquities of the rest of the nations—the one sole country under

the sun that is endowed with an imperishable interest for alien
prince and alien peasant, for lettered and ignorant, wise and
fool, rich and poor, bond and free, the one land that all men
desire to see, and having seen once, by even a glimpse, would
not vie that glimpse for the shows of all the rest of the globe
combined.[1]

The India as "the mother of history" mentioned by Mark
Twain, began some 5,000 years ago with the Indus civilization
which flourished at the time when both Ancient Egypt and
Sumer were at their height. Neither Egypt or Sumer enjoyed
a continual history as that of India.

Indian history may be broken into several periods. First
the Indus civilization flowered from about 2600 B.C. until 1600
B.C. This was followed by the Aryan period which lasted until
about 500 B.C. when the great religious reformers like the
Buddha and Mahavira helped usher in a new basis for the
social order. From 326-184 B.C. much of North India was
brought under the first great imperial rule of the Mauryans.
Following a period of foreign invasions from 184 B.C. to about
300 A.D., India entered into a great Golden Age under the
Gupta Empire. After 600 A.D. India functioned, not as a single
uni-fied empire but as dozens of smaller states, each developing its own language, culture, and art form. Most of these
northern states, after 1200, came under the domination of a
new group of invaders from the northwest, the Turkish and
Afghan Muslims. Finally, in the eighteenth century the British
came by sea to dominate Indian political life until independence in 1947.

Although the Indus is one of the oldest and largest of the
world's first civilizations, lasting from 2600-1600 B.C., little was
known about it until sixty years ago when archaeologists ex-
cavated the buried cities of Mohenjo Daro and Harappa.

Historians and archaeologists have determined some facts
about life in the Indus cities, but because no one has yet
deciphered the language, much of the life of the Indus people
remains shrouded in mystery. We do know the Indus people
grew barley and cotton, traded with the Middle East, used

ox-drawn carts, and developed very sophisticated urban planning that included a drainage system for the large cities and flush toilets in individual homes. The Indus people were apparently peaceful, as no great weaponry or other evidence of a standing army has been discovered. The art is graceful, yet modest, and the Indus people apparently knew the practice of *yoga* and probably worshipped the mother goddess, a tradition that has remained in Indian religion until today.

Sometime around 1500 B.C. the Indus civilization, then in sharp decline from its former greatness, was overwhelmed by groups of Indo-European nomadic herders known as the Aryans. The Aryans were a fierce warrior people who has mastered the art of iron for weapons and drove horse-drawn chariots, the scourge of the ancient world. As the Aryans moved down the Gangetic river plain with their cattle, cutting down the forests and conquering the local tribes, they soon dominated life in North India. The great cities of the Indus civilization fell into ruin, and new urban centers would not be rebuilt for hundreds of years.

At the end of the Aryan period, after much intermixing between the invaders and the Indus and other people of India, new religions like Buddhism and Jainism grew up to challenge the war-like culture of the Aryans. These religions, together with major reforms made within the Indo-European Aryan community, soon evolved into some of the most sophisticated philosophies known to the world. The new religions inspired great art and literature, including the *Mahabharata*, the oldest epic poem in world literature, and the *Bhagavadgita*, one of the treasures of world religion.

Gradually the Aryan peoples settled into villages and cities and gave up their nomadic ways. As the Aryans moved toward the eastern tip of India and intermarried with the local people, adapting many of their ideas and values, a new great civilization began to flourish in North India in the present state of Bihar. This great state, called Magadh, soon emerged in the early fourth century B.C. as the most dominant power in India and launched a new empire under the Mauryan dynasty. This dynasty lasted until 184 B.C. and produced one of India's greatest kings—the Emperor Ashoka who ruled from 269-232 B.C.

After the decline of the Mauryans, North India broke into a number of states ruled by invaders from the north and west. In the northwest of India, the state of Bactria, ruled by heirs of Alexander, took over the Punjab and created a new mix of Grecco-Indian culture. In the first century A.D., another foreign empire, built by the Kushans who came from China, also achieved great economic and artistic power in the North. During this time new kingdoms grew up in southern India, such as the Andhras, Kalingas, and several Tamil empires. These kingdoms were strongly influenced by Aryan culture from the north and many of their kings gave Aryan Brahmins large gifts for temple construction.

In 320 A.D., North India was once again united under the glorious Gupta dynasty. The Guptas, following the Mauryans, established the center of their power in Magadh. Under the Guptas, mathematics, chemistry, and the arts achieved world leadership. Iron pillars built during this time are still found today completely rust-free. The use of place numbers, including zero, were well known by this time and Buddhist and Hindu art, such as the Ajanta and Ellora caves, remain among the great artistic wonders of the world. Sanskrit drama also reached its height and the plays of Kalidassa circa 400 A.D., such as *Shakuntula*, are still performed today.

Following the decline of the Guptas, the sub-continent was divided into many prosperous states similar to the political divisions of Europe from 1500 onwards. During this time such states as the Pallavas and Cholas in South India, Rashtrakuta near the present city of Bombay, and Bundelkhand in Central India were examples of regional kingdoms that made up India.

Despite the great political divisions in India, cultural values embodied in Hinduism and Buddhism bound the people together. Sanskrit, the language of the educated elites, also formed a bridge across political boundaries, as did art

The Taj Mahal, one of the architectural wonders of the world, was built as a mausoleum (1631-1647) by the Muslim ruler Shah Jehan for his favorite wife, Mumtaz Mahal. The royal couple are now interred in the vault beneath the tomb chamber. (Maria Donoso Clark)

and literature. The caste system, too, seems to have been an important part of Indian life throughout her long history.

Beginning in the eighth century the new religion of Islam began its history in India. However, the early Arab traders and the small Muslim presence in northwest India were not very important. Only in the twelfth century did the invading Muslims from Afghanistan, who came to plunder the riches of North India, begin to make a significant impact in Indian history. The Muslims dominated northern India from approximately 1200 to 1700 and challenged Indian civilization in ways that had not been experienced since the Aryan invasions some 2,500 years earlier.

The impact of the West, beginning in the seventeenth century, was no less traumatic for the Indians. The Europeans were the first invaders to conquer the sub-continent from the sea and they soon dominated the politics of India. Bringing a new and dynamic culture with them, the Europeans, especially the British, intervened in nearly every aspect of traditional Indian culture.

This section of *Through Indian Eyes* focuses on a few aspects of the long Indian tradition as it deals with new groups and ways of life and attempts to integrate them into Indian civilization. After briefly introducing some of the more important eras in early Indian history, the focus shifts to the arrival of the Muslims in the sub-continent and the Hindu reaction to this phenomenon. Subsequent selections deal with British colonialism and the Indian nationalist movement.

Both Islam and Western civilization posed enormous threats to Indian civilization, and in many ways modern India is still responding to these two challenges. The Muslims confronted India with values that were alien to Hinduism. The Muslims championed an egalitarian social system based on revealed law. They also believed that the survival of prosperity of the Muslim community necessitated the frequent use of force. These ideas were largely alien to Hindu India. Similarly the British brought with them ideals of equality, private property, law, and individualism which were even more strange to traditional India. As the Indian nationalist movement developed, leaders such as Nehru and Gandhi sought to synthesize the best of the millennia-old Indian civilization with the best of the new ideas from the West. As India enters its sixth decade as an independent nation, this experiment at synthesis, itself a very old Hindu concept, continues.

Indian History: Time Line

The following chronology consists of a highly abbreviated list of major events in the 4,500-year history of India.

2600-1600 B.C.   Height of Indus Valley Civilization, largest civilization of the ancient world. Cities with urban planning. Language not yet deciphered. Worship of Siva and Mother Goddess. Practice of *yoga* developed.

1500 B.C.   Invasions into sub-continent by Indo-European Aryans. Major use of horse-drawn chariots. Worship of gods similar to Greeks and Romans.

1000 B.C.   Development of sacrifice as major form of religion. Rise of Brahmins as dominant group. Use of iron. Composition of *Four Vedas*, basis for Hindu religion.

700 B.C.   Writing of first *Upanishads*, a major source of Hinduism.

540 B.C.   Birth of Mahavira, founder of Jainism. The belief in *Ahimsa* or non-violence became a major influence in Indian life and led to the practice of vegetarianism.

527 B.C.   Buddha's first sermon at Benares. Founding of Buddhism as one of world's major religions.

326   B.C.   Alexander invades northwest India.

324-   Unification of North India under the Mauryan
184   B.C.   Dynasty.

269-   Reign of Ashoka, considered the greatest of early
232   B.C.   Indian kings.

100   A.D.   Worship of Krishna and Vishnu becomes common.
             The *Bhagavadgita* is composed.

200   A.D.   The *Ramayana* and *Mahabharata* are written down
             in Sanskrit.

320-   Rise of the Gupta Empire, a golden age of Indian
515   A.D.   civilization, producing the writings of Kalidasa and
             the Ajanta and Ellora cave temples and rock
             sculptures.

1206 A.D.   Beginning of Delhi Sultanate, first Muslim dynasty
             to rule North India.

1469 A.D.   Birth of Guru Nanak, founder of Sikh religion.

1498 A.D.   Vasco da Gamma sails around Africa to reach South
             India.

1526 A.D.   End of Delhi Sultanate; beginning of Moghul
             Empire under Babur.

1556-   Rule of Akbar, greatest of Moghul kings. India's
1605 A.D.   population reaches 100 million.

1532-   Life of Tulsi Das who wrote Hindi version of *Ra-*
1623 A.D.   *mayana.*

1600 A.D.   East India Company chartered by Queen Elizabeth.

1631 A.D.   Construction begins on Taj Mahal.

1707 A.D. Aurangzeb dies, last important Moghul king.

1757 A.D. Battle of Plassey, where Robert Clive defeated the Nawab of Bengal, paving the way for British control of North India.

1765 A.D. East Indian Company given right to collect taxes from provinces of Bengal, Bihar, and Orissa.

1770 A.D. Marathas occupy Agra and Mathura and present greatest competition to British rule in India, while under East India Company rule one-third of Bengali peasants die in famine.

1773 A.D. British Parliament passes regulating act to attempt to control actions of East India Company.

1785 A.D. Lord Cornwallis after defeat in America becomes Governor-General.

1793- A.D. Period of Liberal-Utilitarian reforms; introduction
1850   of British education in India.

1857 A.D. Revolt of Indians against British, called "Mutiny" by British and "First War of Indian Independence" by Indians.

1858 A.D. British monarch takes over direct rule of Indian empire.

1877 A.D. Victoria becomes Empress of India.

1885 A.D. Indian National Congress founded.

1911 A.D. New Delhi becomes capital of India.

1915 A.D. Gandhi returns to India from South Africa and introduces *Satyagraha* into nationalist movement.

1919 A.D.   Massacre of Indians by General Dyer at Amritsar.

1920 A.D.   Non-cooperation campaign.

1930 A.D.   Civil Disobedience Campaign: National Congress now a mass movement. Salt March. Gandhi begins work on his social program, especially to end untouchability.

1935 A.D.   India Act allows Indians some representatives in government.

1942 A.D.   Quit India Movement; Gandhi and Nehru in jail.

1947 A.D.   India and Pakistan gain independence from Britain. Nehru is first prime minister of India.

1948 A.D.   Struggle over Kashmir.

1963 A.D.   Nehru dies; Shastri is prime minister.

1965 A.D.   War with Pakistan. Shastri dies; Indira Gandhi becomes prime minister.

1971 A.D.   War with Pakistan and creation of Bangladesh.

1974 A.D.   India explodes nuclear device.

1977 A.D.   Moraji Desai is new prime minister under Janata government.

1980 A.D.   Ms. Gandhi again elected prime minister.

1981 A.D.   Agitation for Khalistan by Sikhs.

1984 A.D.   Ms. Gandhi assassinated; Rajiv Gandhi becomes new prime minister.

1989 A.D. Rajiv Gandhi and Congress lose elections. V. P. Singh and then Chandrasekar are interim minority prime ministers.

1991 A.D. Rajiv Gandhi assassinated. Congress, the largest single party in parliament but not a majority, selects P.V. Narasimha Rao as minority prime minister.

1991 A.D. India moves to a free market economy.

1992 A.D. The Vishwa Hindu Parishad (VHP) leads movement to reclaim Babri Masjid as temple to Ram's birthplace. Mosque is destroyed and Hindus attack Muslims throughout India.

1996 A.D. National government elections gives BJP (Bharatiya Janata Party) the largest number of votes but they are unable to form a coalition. In June, Deve Gowda is sworn in as prime minister of loosely knit coalition government, the first such low-caste leader in free India.

1997 A.D. National elections elevate the BJP to power with A.P. Vajpayee as new prime minister.

1998 A.D. India and Pakistan explode nuclear devices and the two countries exchange gunfire in Kashmir.

1999 A.D. Hostilities in Kashmir intensify. Sonia Gandhi elected president of Congress Party.

2000 A.D. Indian population reaches one billion mark.

The Discovery of India

ᶻ⁴INTRODUCTION: Jawaharlal Nehru (1889-1962) was India's first prime minister and one of modern India's greatest leaders. His daughter Indira Gandhi, also elected to the same office in 1967, was assassinated in 1984, and her son Rajiv, who succeeded his mother in 1984, was himself assassinated while campaigning in the election of 1991.

Born into a wealthy Brahmin family, Nehru received his high school and college education in England, where he was greatly influenced by Western ideas on science, democracy, and socialism. On his return to India in 1912, he, like his father, began to practice law, but soon turned his attention to India's struggle for independence from British rule. Often called a man of two worlds, Nehru attempted to reconcile Western ideas with the established values of the Indian tradition, always drawing on India's past for his inspiration.

In 1929 at age thirty-five, Nehru was elected president of the Indian National Congress, the political organization that fought for India's freedom. Between 1930-1936 he spent most of his time in jail for leading civil disobedience campaigns. During World War II he opposed giving aid to the British because of their refusal to give India independence, and was jailed once again.

In 1947, when India finally won its independence, Nehru became its first prime minister and held that post until his death in 1962. In an interview in 1954, Nehru said of himself:

> If any people choose to think of me then, I should like them to say: "This was a man who with all his mind and heart loved India and the Indian people. And they, in turn, were indulgent to him and gave their love most abundantly and extravagantly.[2]

The interaction between India's long past and her efforts to build a modern nation-state is a central theme of the last two sections of Nehru's book, *The Discovery of India.* Nehru wrote the book in 1944 while serving one of his many jail terms for agitating against British rule in India. In the following selection, Nehru raises important questions about India's past, her relationship to Europe, and the larger world history. In doing so, he also seeks to find his own roots in history to better enable him to lead an independent India.[3]❧

India was in my blood and there was much in her that instinctively thrilled me. And yet I approached her almost as an alien critic, full of dislike for the present as well as for many of the relics of the past that I saw. To some extent I came to her via the West, and looked at her as a friendly Westerner might have done. I was eager and anxious to change her outlook and appearance and give her the garb of modernity. And yet doubts arose within me. Did I know India?—I who presumed to scrap much of her past heritage? There was a great deal that had to be scrapped, that must be scrapped; but surely Indian could not have been what she undoubtedly was, and could not have continued a cultured existence for thousands of years, if she had not possessed something very vital and enduring, something that was worthwhile. What was this something?

I stood on a mound of Mohenjo-daro in the Indus Valley in the north-west of India, and all around me lay the houses and streets of this ancient city that is said to have existed over five thousand years ago; and even then it was an old and well-developed civilization. 'The Indus civilization,' writes Professor Childe, 'represents a very perfect adjustment of human life to a specific environment that can only have resulted from years of patient effort. And it has endured; it is already specifically Indian and forms the basis of modern Indian culture.' Astonishing thought: that any culture or civilization should have this continuity for five or six thousand years or more; and not in a static, unchanging sense, for India was changing and progressing all the time. She was coming into intimate contact with the Persians, the Egyptians, the Greeks,

Jawaharlal Nehru (1889-1963) was India's first prime minister, serving from 1947 until his death in 1963. Both his daughter, Indira Gandhi, and his grandson, Rajiv Gandhi, followed him as prime minister. (Indian Consulate, New York, N.Y.)

the Chinese, the Arabs, the Central Asians, and the peoples of the Mediterranean. But though she influenced them and was influenced by them, her cultural basis was strong enough to endure. What was the secret of this strength? Where did it come from?

I read her history and read also a part of her abundant ancient literature, and was powerfully impressed by the vigor of the thought, the clarity of the language, and the richness of the mind that lay behind it. I journeyed through India in the company of mighty travelers from China and Western and Central Asia who came here in the remote past and left records of their travels. I thought of what India had accomplished in Eastern Asia, in Angkor, Borobudur, and many other places. I wandered over the Himalayas, which are closely connected with old myth and legend, and which have influenced so much our thought and literature. My love of the mountains and my kinship with Kashmir especially drew me to them, and I saw there not only the life and vigor and beauty of the present, but also the memoried loveliness of ages past. The mighty rivers of India that flow from this great mountain barrier into the plains of India attracted me and reminded me of innumerable phases of our history. The Indus or *Sindhu*, from which our country came to be called India and Hindustan, and across which races and tribes and caravans and armies have come for thousands of years; the Brahmaputra, rather cut off from the main current of history but living in old story forcing its way into India through deep chasms cut in the heart of the northeastern mountains, and then flowing calmly in a gracious sweeping between mountain and wooded plain; the Jumna, round which cluster so many legends of dance and fun and play; and the Ganges, above all the river of India, which has held India's heart captive and drawn uncounted millions to her banks since the dawn of history. The story of the Ganges, from her source to the sea, from old times to new, is the story of India's civilization and culture, of the rise and fall of empires, of great and proud cities, of the adventure of man and the quest of the mind which has so occupied India's thinkers, of the richness and fulfillment of life as well as its denial and renunciation, of ups and downs, of growth and decay, of life and death.

I visited old mountains and ruins and ancient sculptures and frescoes—Ajanta, Ellora, the Elephanta Caves, and other places—and I also saw lovely buildings of a later age in Agra and Delhi, where every stone told its story of India's past.

In my own city of Allahabad or in Hardwar I would go to the great bathing festivals, the *Kumbh Mela*, and see hundreds of thousands of people come, as their forebears had come for thousands of years from all over India, to bathe in the Ganges. I would remember descriptions of these festivals written thirteen hundred years ago by Chinese pilgrims and others, and even then these *melas* were ancient and lost in an unknown antiquity. What was the tremendous faith, I wondered, that had drawn our people for untold generations to this famous river of India?

These journeys and visits of mine, with the background of my reading, gave me an insight into the past. To a somewhat bare intellectual understanding was added an emotional appreciation, and gradually a sense of reality began to creep into my mental picture of India, and the land of my forefathers became peopled with living beings, who laughed and wept, loved and suffered; and among them were men who seemed to know life and understand it, and out of their wisdom they had built a structure which gave India a cultural stability which lasted for thousands of years. Hundreds of vivid pictures of this past filled my mind, and they would stand out as soon as I visited a particular place associated with them. At Sarnath, near Benares, I would almost see the Buddha preaching his first sermon, and some of his recorded words would come like a distant echo to me through two thousand five hundred years. Ashoka's pillars of stone with their inscriptions would speak to me in their magnificent language and tell me of a man who, though an emperor, was greater than any king or emperor. At Fatehpur-Sikri, Akbar, forgetful of his empire, was seated holding converse and debate with the learned of all faiths, curious to learn something new and seeking an answer to the eternal problem of man.

Thus slowly the long panorama of India's history unfolded itself before me, with its ups and downs, its triumphs and defeats. There seemed to me something unique about the continuity of a cultural tradition through five thousand years of history, of invasion and upheaval, a tradition which was widespread among the masses and powerfully influenced them. Only China has had such a continuity of tradition and cultural life. And this panorama of the past gradually merged into the unhappy present, when India, for all her past greatness and stability, was a slave country, an appendage of Britain, and all over the world terrible and devastating war was raging and brutalizing humanity. But that vision of five thousand years gave me a new perspective, and the burden of the present seemed to grow lighter.

The hundred and eighty years of British rule in India were just one of the unhappy interludes in her long story; she would find herself again; already the last page of this chapter was being written. The world also will survive the horror of today and build itself anew on fresh foundations.

Letters from Prison

ॐINTRODUCTION: When the first British settlers arrived at Jamestown in 1607, India had lived through more than 4,000 years of history. English explorers traveled to India and to Jamestown about the same time. However, when they landed in western India they were not arriving in a continent like America with open spaces inhabited by a few hundred thousand people living mostly in small groups. The India the European traders saw was a highly complex urban civilization with a population of several hundred million and a much longer history than Europe's.

As India tried to free itself from European colonial rule in the twentieth century, her leaders often called upon the people to remember the rich Indian past and to once again rally themselves to greatness. The Indian tradition, as reinterpreted by nationalist leaders, was a major inspiration for the successful independence movement.

Jawaharlal Nehru, perhaps the most historically minded of the nationalist leaders, had a deep interest in both Western and Indian history. While serving one of his periodic jail sentences in the early 1930s, Nehru began writing a series of letters to his daughter Indira. These letters were no mere exchange of family and personal news. Nehru decided that his thirteen-year-old daughter needed some history lessons that would counteract the message of her predominantly British education. These letters became a book, *Glimpses of World History*, which includes Indian and Chinese history as well as Middle Eastern, Greek, and European history.

In the selection that follows, Nehru tries to convey to his young daughter the greatness of the Indian past and the role their civilization played in the drama of world history.[4]ॐ

January 8, 1931

The history we learn in school or college is usually not up to much. I do not know very much about others, but about myself I know that I learnt very little in school. I learnt a little—very little—of the history of India, and a little of the history of England. And even the history of India that I learnt was largely wrong or distorted and written by people who looked down upon our country. Of the history of other countries I had the vaguest knowledge. It was only after I left college that I read some real history. Fortunately, my visits to prison have given me a chance of improving my knowledge.

I have written to you in some of my earlier letters about the ancient civilization of India, about the Dravidians and the coming of the Aryans. I have not written much about the days before the Aryans, because I do not know much about them. But it will interest you to know that within the last few years the remains of a very ancient civilization have been discovered in India. These are in the north-west of India round about a place called Mohen-jo Daro. People have dug out these remains of perhaps 5000 years ago and have even discovered mummies, similar to those of old Egypt. Imagine! all this was thousands of years ago, long before the Aryans came. Europe must then have been a wilderness.

Today Europe is strong and powerful, and its people consider themselves the most civilized and cultured in the world. They look down upon Asia and her peoples, and come and grab everything they can get from the countries of Asia. How times have changed! Let us have a good look at Europe and Asia. Open an atlas and see little Europe sticking on to the great Asiatic Continent. It seems to be just a little extension of it. When you read history you will find that for long periods and stretches of time Asia had been dominant. Her people went in wave after wave and conquered Europe. They ravaged Europe and they civilized Europe. Aryans, Scythians, Huns, Arabs, Mongols, Turks—they all came from somewhere in Asia and spread out over Asia and Europe. Asia seemed to produce them in great numbers like locusts. Indeed, Europe was for long like a colony of Asia and many people of modern Europe are descended from the invaders from Asia.

Asia sprawls right across the map like a big, lumbering giant, Europe is small. But, of course, this does not mean that Asia is great because of her size or that Europe is not worthy of much attention. Size is the poorest test of a man's or a country's greatness. We know well that Europe, though the smallest of continents, is today great. We know also that many of her countries have had brilliant periods of history. They have produced great men of science who have, by their discoveries and inventions, advanced human civilization tremendously and made life easier for millions of men and women. They have had great writers and thinkers, and artists and musicians and men of action. It would be foolish not to recognize the greatness of Europe.

And in many other ways I could show you how great and vital was this old continent of ours in the days gone by.

How times have changed! But they are changing again even before our eyes. History usually works slowly through the centuries, though sometimes there are periods of rush and burst-ups. Today, however, it is moving fast in Asia, and the old continent is waking up after her long slumber. The eyes of the world are upon her, for everyone knows that Asia is going to play a great part in the future.

[Nehru's letter the next day, January 9, 1931, went on]:

Heigh-ho! I write on of foolish things although I sat down to write to you about past history. Let us try to forget the present for a while and go back 2000 or 3000 years.

Of Egypt and of ancient Knossos in Crete, I wrote to you a little in some of my previous letters. And I told you that the ancient civilizations took root in these two countries as well as in what is now called Iraq or Mesopotamia, and in China and India and Greece. Greece, perhaps, came a little later than the others. So that the civilization of India takes rank in age with its sister-civilizations of Egypt and China and Iraq. And even ancient Greece is a younger sister of these. What

This sculpture of the "Teaching Buddha" dates from the Gupta Age. (Donald Johnson)

happened to these ancient civilizations? Knossos is no more. Indeed, for nearly 3000 years it has been no more. The people of the younger civilization of Greece came and destroyed it. The old civilization of Egypt, after a splendid history lasting for thousands of years, vanished and left no trace behind it, except the great Pyramids and the Sphinx, and the ruins of great temples and mummies and the like. Of course Egypt, the country, is still there and the river Nile flows through it as of old, and men and women live in it as in other countries. But there is no connecting link between these modern people and the old civilization of their country.

Iraq and Persia—how many empires have flourished there and followed each other into oblivion! Babylonia and Assyria and Chaldea, to mention the oldest only. And the great cities of Babylon and Nineveh. The Old Testament in the Bible is full of the record of these people. Later, in this land of ancient history, other empires flourished, and then ceased to flourish. Here was Baghdad, the magic city of *Arabian Nights*. But empires come and empires go, and the biggest and proudest of kings and emperors strut on the world's stage for a brief while only. But civilizations went utterly, even as the old civilization of Egypt.

Greece in her ancient days was great indeed, and people read even now of her glory with wonder. We stand awed and wonder-struck before the beauty of her marble statuary, and read the fragments of her old literature that have come down to us with reverence and amazement. It is said, and rightly, that modern Europe is in some ways the child of ancient Greece, so much has Europe been influenced by Greek thought and Greek ways. But the glory that was Greece, where is it now? For ages past, the old civilization has been no more, and other ways have taken its place, and Greece today is but a pretty country in the south-east of Europe.

Egypt, Knossos, Iraq, and Greece—they have all gone. Their old civilizations, even as Babylon and Nineveh, have ceased to exist. What, then, of the two other ancients in this company of old civilizations? What of China and India? As in other countries, they too have had empire after empire. There have been invasions and destructions and loot on a vast scale. Dynasties of kings have ruled for hundreds of years and then been replaced by others. All this has happened in India and China, as elsewhere. But nowhere else, apart from India and China, has there been a real continuity of civilization. In spite of all the changes and battles and invasions, the thread of the ancient civilizations has continued to run on in both these countries. It is true that both of them have fallen greatly from their old estate, and that the ancient cultures are covered up with a heap of dust, and sometimes filth, which the long ages have accumulated. But still they endure and the old Indian civilization is the basis of Indian life even today.

Ashoka

&INTRODUCTION: From the many centuries of Indian history that Nehru wrote about to his daughter Indira, perhaps one leader rises above all others in the estimation of modern Indians. That leader was Ashoka, who came to power in 267 B.C. as the third ruler of the Mauryan Empire (324-184 B.C.).

Not much was known about Ashoka until a series of about fifty rock inscriptions were deciphered in 1837. Carved in both natural rock formations and on polished sandstone pillars, these inscriptions, usually referred to as the edicts of Ashoka, were discovered all over India, indicating the wide reach of Ashoka's empire. To date, eighteen rock edicts and thirty pillars have been found and translated. The following reading offers a picture of Ashoka's rule and his philosophy of government that emerges from the inscriptions.[5]&

Many of Ashoka's rock edicts deal with the concept of *dhamma*. By *dhamma*, Ashoka meant a combination of Hindu *dharma* and Buddhist ethics which stressed a compassion for both humans and animals. Ashoka's *dhamma* included compassion for those in need, respect for elders, performance of one's social duties, and tolerance for the beliefs of others. If, Ashoka reasoned, people could live by *dhamma*, and develop a society based on *dhamma*, all humans would be treated fairly and justly and the government would have no need to keep them under control with a large army. As both Indians and Westerners have come to know about Ashoka's unusual reign, many historians are struck by his devotion to non-violence as a way of life and as the basis for his political philosophy as well. Selections from Ashoka's rock edicts reveal Ashoka's philosophy of right rule and insights into his own transformation as a political leader.

Ashoka dictated one of his first rock edicts shortly after he had successfully conquered Kalinga, a country in eastern India. In the aftermath of this bloody victory, Ashoka, who had been a fierce warrior, began to doubt the way of war. Soon after his victory at Kalinga, he wrote:

> The Kalingas were conquered by His Sacred and Gracious Majesty when he had been consecrated eight years. 150,000 persons were carried away captive, 100,000 were slain and many times that number died.
>
> On conquering Kalinga the Beloved of the Gods [Ashoka] felt remorse, for, when an independent country is conquered the slaughter, death and deportation of the people is extremely grievous to the Beloved of the Gods and weighs heavily on his mind . . . those who dwell there whether [B]rahmins . . . or householders who show obedience to their superiors, obedience to mother and father, obedience to their teachers and behave well . . . all suffer violence, murder and separation from loved ones. Even those who are fortunate enough to have escaped . . . suffer from the misfortunes of their friends, acquaintances, colleagues and relatives. . . .
>
> Today, if a hundredth of a thousandth part of those who suffered in Kalinga were to be killed, to die or be taken captive, it would be very grievous to His Sacred Majesty [Ashoka]. If anyone does him wrong, it will be forgiven so far as it can be forgiven. . . .

He ended the edict on Kalinga by saying rulers who came after him:

> . . . should not think new conquests worth achieving. If they do conquer, let them take pleasure in moderation and mild punishments. Let them consider moral conquest the only true conquest.
>
> Not only was Ashoka influenced by Buddhist ethics, he was also deeply indebted to Jainism as well. His belief in non-injury (*Ahimsa*) was translated into policies forbidding animal sacrifices and a radical change in the daily diet prepared in the royal kitchens.
>
> Formerly in the kitchens [of the kings] many hundreds of

One of Ashoka's pillars, made of polished sandstone, dates from the third century B.C. during the peak of the Mauryan Empire. (Donald Johnson)

thousands of living animals were killed daily for meat. But now, at the time of writing this inscription on Dhamma, only three animals are killed, two peacocks and a deer, and the deer not invariably. Even these animals will not be killed in the future.

As a way of uniting his diverse empire, Ashoka encouraged people to travel on pilgrimages to the holy sites of India. To facilitate travel, the king supervised the construction of an elaborate network of highways. He also provided for medical care along the way:

Everywhere in the empire . . . the two medical services of [the king] have been provided. These consist of the medical care of man and the care of animals. Medicinal herbs, whether useful to man or to beast, have been brought and planted wherever they did not grow. Along the roads wells have been dug and trees planted for the use of men and beasts.

To make certain that the new concept of government through *Dhamma* was understood by all and that it would inform all government actions, Ashoka appointed cabinet ministers responsible for *dhamma*. A rock edict explains the principles that these ministers were to follow:

In the past there were no Officers of Dhamma. [Officers of Righteousness]. It was I who first appointed them, when I had been consecrated for thirteen years. They are busy in all sects, establishing Dhamma. . . . Among servants and nobles, Brahmins and wealthy householders, among the poor and the aged, they [Officers of *Dhamma*] are working for the welfare and happiness of those devoted to Dhamma and for the removal of their troubles. They are busy in promoting the welfare of prisoners should they have behaved irresponsibly, or releasing those that have children, are afflicted, or are aged. . . .

Everywhere throughout my empire the Officers of Dhamma are busy in everything relating to Dhamma, in the establishment of Dhamma and in the administration of charities among those devoted to Dhamma.

Although Ashoka converted to Buddhism and certainly infused his rule with Buddhist principles, ane even sent Bud-

dhist missionaries to other nations, he did not force his subjects to accept his own personal religious beliefs. He accepted
and encouraged many beliefs and urged all his subjects to be
tolerant of others' ways of life.

> The progress of the essential doctrine [*Dhamma*] takes
> many forms but its basis is the control of one's speech,
> so as not to extol [praise] one's own sect [belief] or
> disparage [criticize] another's. . . . All sects deserve
> reverence for one reason or another. By thus acting a
> man exalts his own sect and at the same time does ser-
> vice to the sects of other people.

Ashoka has become one of modern India's great heroes.
In the 1960s when India bought her first 747 passenger plane,
it was appropriately named Ashoka. Ashoka's symbol, a lotus
capital, was also chosen as the symbol of free India and appears on all Indian currency. A modern British writer and
historian has written of Ashoka:

> Amidst the tens of thousands of names of monarchs that
> crowd the columns of history, their majesties and gracious-
> ness and serenities and royal highnesses and the like, the
> name of Ashoka shines, and shines almost alone, a star.
> From the Volga to Japan his name is still honored. China,
> Tibet, and even India, though it has left his doctrine,
> preserve the tradition of his greatness. More living men
> cherish his memory today than have ever heard the
> names of Constantine or Charlemagne.[6]

Visitors Agree

ᐖ INTRODUCTION: Since Ancient India did not produce historians to tell us about life in those times, modern historians must rely on either archaeological evidence or reports from travelers to India to learn about various stages of Indian history. The Mauryan Empire that Nehru discussed in his letter to his daughter, and which Ashoka ruled so successfully, and the later Gupta Empire made deep impressions on several visitors from other countries.

Two of these visitors to India, Megasthenes, a diplomat from the Greek Empire who was stationed at the capital of the Mauryan Empire during Chandragupta's reign (324-301 B.C.), and Fa Hsien, a Buddhist pilgrim from China who came to India to study Buddhism from 405-414 B.C. during the height of the Gupta Empire, offer insightful observations about India during two of its great eras. Fa Hsien traveled to many parts of North India during the Gupta period and kept a record his impressions of the city of Mathura, a center of Krishna worship in Gupta India, in his journal.[7] ᐖ

The Indians all live frugally, especially when in camp. They dislike a great undisciplined multitude, and consequently they observe good order. Theft is of very rare occurrence. Megasthenes says that those who were in the camp of Sandrakottos, wherein lay 400,000 men, found that the thefts reported on any one day did not exceed the value of two hundred drachmae, and this among a people who have no written laws, but are ignorant of writing, and must therefore in all the business of life trust to memory. They live, nevertheless, happily enough, being simple in their manners and frugal. They never drink wine except at sacrifices. Their beverage is a liquor composed from rice instead of barley, and their food is principally a rice-pottage. The simplicity of their laws and their contracts is proved by the fact that they seldom go to law. They have no suits about pledges or deposits, nor do they require either seals or witnesses, but make their deposits and confide in each other. Their houses and property they generally leave unguarded. These things indicate that they possess good, sober sense; but other things they do which one cannot approve: for instance, that they eat always alone, and that they have no fixed hours when meals are to be taken by all in common, but each one eats when he feels inclined. The contrary custom would be better for the ends of social and civil life. (3rd century B.C.)

MEGASTHENES

* * *

[This country] has a temperate climate, without frost or snow; and the people are prosperous and happy, without registration or official restrictions. Only those who till the king's land have to pay so much on the profit they make. Those who want to go away, may go; those who want to stop, may stop. The king in his administration uses no corporal punishment; criminals are merely fined according to the gravity of their offenses. Even for a second attempt at rebellion the punishment is only the loss of the right hand. The men of the king's bodyguard have all fixed salaries. Throughout the country, no one kills any living thing, nor drinks wine, nor eats onions or garlic; but chandalas are segregated. Chandala is their name for foul men [lepers]. These live away from other people; and when they approach a city or market, they beat a piece of wood, in order to distinguish themselves. Then people know who they are and avoid coming into contact with them.

In this country they do not keep pigs or fowls, there are no dealings in cattle, no butchers' shops or distilleries in their market places. As a medium of exchange they use cowries. . . .

The elders and gentry of these countries have in their

capitals free hospitals, and hither come all poor or helpless patients, orphans, widowers and cripples. They are well taken care of, a doctor attends them, food and medicine being supplied according to their needs. They are all made quite comfortable and when they are cured they go away. . . .

There is no lack of suitable things for household use. Although they have saucepans and stewpans, yet they do not know the steamer used for cooking rice. They have many vessels made of dry clay; they seldom use red copper vessels; they eat from one vessel, [mixing] all sorts of condiments together, which they take up with their fingers. They have no spoons or cups, and in short no sort of chopsticks. When sick, however, they use copper drinking cups.

. . . The taxes on the people are light, and the personal services required of them is moderate. Each one keeps his own worldly goods in peace, and all till the ground for their subsistence. Those who cultivate the royal estates pay a sixth part of their produce as tribute. The merchants who engage in commerce come and go in carrying out their transactions . . . .

FA-HSEIN

The Muslims in India

➤INTRODUCTION: Hinduism, says one scholar, is "like a sponge." It is able to absorb many different cultures and still remain Indian. Indian civilization was able to integrate new groups into its system for more than 2,000 years. The Aryan invaders who entered the Indian sub-continent around 1500 B.C. gradually merged with the indigenous people, and over the millennia so did the Kushans, Huns, and many other groups who came into India. Each group brought new ideas and technology which influenced Indian life; each group adapted to its new environment and ultimately merged with the existing civilization.

Beginning in the eleventh century, the Indian sub-continent experienced invaders who were less willing to merge with the way of life they found in the sub-continent. Indians contended first with the Turkish Muslim conquerors and then with European colonialists. For nearly eight hundred years, from the twelfth century until 1947, outsiders ruled over the sub-continent. Muslim and Western influences challenged the older Hindu system and in many ways contemporary Indians are still trying to create a synthesis with these influences.

Muslim contact with the Indian sub-continent started peacefully in the middle of the seventh century. For several centuries, Muslim traders bought and sold goods with Indians and sometimes settled down in India. In the 1100s, contact was less peaceful. Muslim armies invaded India looking for riches which they could carry back to their home bases in Afghanistan and Iran. The Muslim invaders had superior military technology and organization, and their calvary easily defeated larger Indian forces composed of infantry and elephants. The Muslims also used gunpowder, which they had learned to make from the Chinese.

At first these Turkish Muslims only plundered and left, but gradually some of them were attracted to the rich civilization of North

170

India. They stayed on and in 1206 established the Sultanate of Delhi. Various groups of Turks and Afghans continued to control this Sultanate and much of North India until about 1500.

By 1526, the Moghuls, a group of invaders from the Asian steppes, had gained control over North India, and they established the Moghul Empire in India. Lasting from 1526 to the coming of the Europeans in the eighteenth century, the Moghul Empire stands as one of the most illustrious eras in Indian history, noted especially for its art and architecture.

Perhaps the greatest of the Moghul emperors and patrons of the arts was Akbar, who ruled from 1556 to 1605. Emperor Akbar had a keen interest in architecture. He encouraged the creation of a new style harmoniously merging traditional Hindu and Islamic elements. His style is exemplified by Fatehpur-Sikri, near Agra, built during Akbar's reign. Another Moghul emperor, Shah Jahan, built the Taj Mahal, "the miracle of miracles, the final wonder of the world," in memory of his wife. Completed in 1647, this white marble mausoleum, a brilliant combination of Hindu and Muslim styles, rests so gently on the ground that it seems likely at any moment to soar into the sky.

Akbar was continually searching for ways to merge Hindu and Muslim traditions in philosophy as well as in art and architecture. To learn about Akbar, we turn to another excerpt written by Jawaharlal Nehru to his daughter.[8]

For nearly fifty years Akbar ruled India, from early 1556 to the end of 1605. This was the period of the revolt of the Netherlands in Europe and of Shakespeare in England. Akbar's name stands out in Indian history, and sometimes and in some ways, he reminds one of Ashoka. It is a strange thing that a Buddhist Emperor of India of the third century before Christ and a Muslim Emperor of India of the sixteenth century after Christ should speak in the same manner and almost in the same voice. One wonders if this is not perhaps the voice of India herself speaking through two of her great sons. . . .

Physically, Akbar was extraordinarily strong and active, and he loved nothing better than hunting wild and dangerous animals. As a soldier he was brave to the point of recklessness. His amazing energy can be judged from a famous march of his from Agra to Ahmedabad in nine days. A revolt had broken out in Gujrat, and Akbar rushed with a little army across the desert of Rajputana, a distance of 450 miles. It was an extraordinary feat. There were no railways or motor cars then, I need hardly remind you.

But great men have something besides all these qualities: they have, it is said, a magnetism which draws people to them. Akbar had this personal magnetism and charm in abundant measure; his compelling eyes were, in the wonderful description of the Jesuits, "vibrant like the sea in sunshine." Is it any wonder that this man should fascinate us still and that his most royal and manly figure should tower high above the crowds of men who have been but kings? . . .

Akbar's capital was at Agra to begin with, and he built the fort there. Then he built a new city at Fatehpur-Sikri, about fifteen miles from Agra. He chose this site because a saintly person, Shaikh Salim Chishti, lived there. Here he built a splendid city, "much greater than London," according to an English traveler of the day, and for over fifteen years this was the capital of his Empire. Later he made Lahore his capital. "His Majesty," said Abul-Fazl, the friend and minister of Akbar, "plans splendid edifices and dresses the work of his mind and heart in the garment of stone and clay." . . .

It must have been a busy life of conquest and consolidation of a vast empire. But right through it one can see another of Akbar's remarkable traits. This was his boundless curiosity and his search for truth. Whoever could throw light on any subject was sent for and questioned. The men of different religions gathered round him . . . , each hoping to convert this mighty monarch. They often quarrelled with each other, and Akbar sat by, listening to their arguments and putting many questions to them. He seems to have been convinced that truth was no monopoly of any religion or sect, and he proclaimed that his avowed principle was one of universal toleration in religion.

A historian of his reign, Badauni, who must have participated in many of these gatherings himself, gives an interesting account of Akbar, which I shall quote. Badauni himself

The Red Fort in Old Delhi, built during the reign of Shah Jahan, shows the Islamic influences in Indian architecture. (Indian Consulate, New York, N.Y.)

was an orthodox Muslim, and he thoroughly disapproved of these activities of Akbar.

> His Majesty collected the opinions of everyone, especially of such as were not Muslims, retaining whatever he approved of, and rejecting everything which was against his disposition and ran counter to his wishes. From his earliest childhood to his manhood, and from his manhood to old age, his Majesty has passed through the most various phases, and through all sorts of religious practices and sectarian beliefs, and has collected everything which people can find in books, with a talent of selection peculiar to him and a spirit of enquiry opposed to every Islamic principle. Thus a faith based on some elementary principles traced itself on the mirror of his heart, and as a result of all the influences brought to bear on his Majesty, there grew, gradually as the outline on a stone, the conviction in his heart and there were sensible men in all religions, and abstemious thinkers, and men endowed with miraculous powers, among all nations. If some true knowledge was thus everywhere to be found, why should truth be confined to one religion?

Akbar died in October 1605 in his sixty-fourth year, after a reign of nearly fifty years. He lies buried in a beautiful mausoleum at Sikandra, near Agra.

❧POSTSCRIPT: Unfortunately, the last great Moghul ruler, Aurangzeb, opposed religious toleration. A devout Muslim and a Puritan in his habits, Aurangzeb dismissed the court musicians, artists, and historians. He discouraged poets, who "dealt in falsehood"; banned history, which "gave rise to feelings of undue pride"; and suppressed drinking and gambling. His military campaigns drained his resources. He also dismissed the Hindu clerks in his service and reimposed a poll tax on all "unbelievers." These oppressive measures against the Hindus were perhaps the most destructive acts of his reign, for memories of Aurangzeb's oppressive rule lingered in the minds of Hindu Indians for generations. By his death in 1707, the Moghul Empire was on the edge of ruin. The British came to fill the power vacuum.❧

The British Settle in India

ﾞ￠INTRODUCTION: At first the Moghul rulers hardly noticed the European traders who came, like so many groups before them, in search of the riches of India. The Portuguese, Dutch, French, and lastly the English all arrived at the Moghul courts asking permission to set up factories along the Indian sea coast. These factories were simply ports where European traders could purchase Indian goods, such as spices, cloth, and luxury items. The Moghuls thought the Europeans were guests of the far greater civilization of India. Although the Europeans had little that the Indian people needed or wanted, sometimes the Moghuls gave them permission to set up trading posts in a few cities. Goods went mostly one way, from India back to Europe; the Indians accepted gold and silver from the Europeans.

After Aurangzeb, who died in 1707, the Moghuls could offer little resistance to the Europeans and the factory trading posts gradually became enclaves controlled by the European powers. The East India Company, the trading company set up by private English investors, grew so powerful that it enlisted the support of the British government and defeated the Portuguese, Dutch, and the French enclaves, and by 1757 it was the most significant power in the Indian sub-continent.

For two centuries from 1757 until 1947—first as the East India Company, and after 1857 under the British Crown—the British dominated the Indian sub-continent. After 1757, the East Indian Company began to gobble up huge chunks of India which they exploited.

During that first century of control, even the British government could not stop John Company, as the East India Company was called, from annexing about half of the entire sub-continent. Some of it they governed directly; some remained under Indian control. By the early nineteenth century, Great Britain began to call the sub-continent the "Jewel in the Crown." After the events of 1857, India was the most important part of the entire British Empire, which covered nearly a

175

fourth of the world. The British controlled, governed, and increasingly introduced their way of life into India until after World War II.

As the British traders and entrepreneurs settled down in the new
trading cities in India, especially Calcutta, they enjoyed the good life
with all the trappings of both British high society and Moghul
opulence. A typical day for a middle-class East India Company worker
in Calcutta is described by a British visitor to Calcutta in the late
eighteenth century.[9]

At about the hour of 7 in the morning, his doorkeeper
opens the gate and the porch is free to his manager, servants,
messengers and spies, law enforcers, stewards and butlers,
clerks and solicitors.

The head porter and servant enter the hall and his
bedroom at 8 o'clock. A lady leaves his side and is conducted
by a private staircase, either to her own apartment, or out of
the yard.

The moment the master throws his legs out of bed, the
whole force is waiting to rush into his room, each making
three salaams [Muslim greeting], by bending the body and
head very low, and touching the forehead with the inside of
the fingers and the floor with the back part. He condescends,
perhaps, to nod or cast an eye towards the solicitors of his
favour and protection.

In about half an hour after undoing and taking off his
long trousers, a clean shirt, breeches, stockings, and slippers
are put upon his body, thighs, legs, and feet, without any
greater exertion on his own part than if he was a statue. The
barber enters, shaves him, cuts his nails, and cleans his ears.
The pitcher and basin are brought by a servant whose duty it
is, who pours water upon his hands and face, and presents a
towel.

The superior then walks in state to his breakfasting parlor
in his waistcoat; is seated; the butler makes and pours out tea,
and presents him with a plate of bread or toast. The hair-
dresser comes behind, and begins his operation, while another
servant softly slips the upper end of the tube of the hucca
[water pipe] into his hand; while the hair-dresser is doing his

duty, the gentleman is eating, sipping, and smoking by turns. By and by his moneyman presents himself with humble salaams and advances somewhat more forward than the other attendants. If any of the solicitors are of eminence, they are honoured with chairs.

These ceremonies are continued perhaps till 10 o'clock; when attended by his cavalcade, he is conducted to his sedan chair, and preceded by eight to twelve retainers, with the insignia of their professions and their livery distinguished by the colour of their turbans and sashes, they move off at a quick amble; the set of porters, consisting of eight generally, relieve each other with alertness and without bothering their master.

A "brown Englishman" with his entourage. (Industrial Media Services)

If he has visits to make, his footmen lead and direct the porters; and if business renders only his presence necessary, he shows himself, and pursues his other engagements until 2 o'clock when he and his company sit down perfectly at ease in point of dress and address, to a good dinner, each attended by his own servant. And the moment the glasses are introduced regardless of the company of ladies, the stewards enter, each with a water pipe, and presents the tube to his master, watching behind and blowing the fire the whole time.

As it is expected that they shall return to supper, at 4 o'clock they begin to withdraw without ceremony, and step into their sedan chairs; so that in a few minutes, the man is left to go into his bedroom, where he is instantly undressed to his shirt, and his long drawers put on; and he lies down in his bed, where he sleeps til about 7 or 9 o'clock, then the former ceremony is repeated and clean linen of every kind as in the morning is administered; his butler presents the pipe to his hand, he is placed at the tea table, and his hair-dresser performs his duty as before.

After tea he puts on a handsome coat, and pays visits of ceremony to the ladies; returns a little before 10 o'clock; supper being served at 10. The company keep together till between 12 and 1 in the morning, preserving great sobriety and decency; and when they depart our hero is conducted to his bedroom, where he finds a female companion to amuse him until the hour of 7 or 8 the next morning.

With no greater exertions than these do the Company's [East India Company] servants amass the most splendid fortunes.

The life of a young East India company worker is illustrated by the diary of Charles Metcalf on his arrival in Calcutta in 1801.

Tues. 6 Jan. Went with Plowden to see Miss Baillie at Barlow's. Received an answer from Crommelin. Dined at home.

7 Jan. Went with Plowden to Brook's. Saw Golding. Dined at Thornhill's. Got a Dhobee [washerman].

9 Jan. With Plowden in the morning. Was introduced to Sir Alured Clarke and General Baynard. Dined with the Governor-General who talked much about Eton. Went to Lady Anstruther's ball.

10 Jan. Shopping in the morning. Got a cocked hat (20 rupees). Dined and passed the evening at Dr. Dick's.

Sunday, Jan 11. Called on Mr. Bazett. Dined with them.

12 Jan. Strolling about in the morning. Went to the levee. Dined at home and passed the evening at Colvin's.

13 Jan. Dined at College. Went to the Governor's ball.

14 Jan. dined at Sir Alured Clark's. At Dick's in the evening.

15 Jan. Dined at Mr. Graham's. Went to Brooke's ball. Sat up till sunrise at a second supper.

16 Jan. Dined at Tucker's. Went to bed very much fatigued, not having slept the previous night.

17 Jan. Dined at College. Sat at Higginson's. Had a Moonshee [servant].

Sunday 18 Jan. Dined at home. Had a Moonshee.

19 Jan. Dismissed my Moonshee, finding him of no use. Determined to teach myself. Went on board the 'Skeleton Castle', the 'Malartique', and the 'London', taken from the French; and the 'Countess of Sutherland', a very large ship, in the company with the Plowden, Impey, Hamilton and Chester. Dined at home. Went to Lady Anstruther's.

20 Jan. Dined at Dick's.

21 Jan. Breakfasted at Bristow's. Wrote journal. Dined at Bristow's.

22 Jan. Tiffed [snacked] at Hamilton's. Dined at Plowden's.

23 Jan. Answered my Uncle Monson's letter. Ditto Richardson. Dined at home. Went to the Governor's ball.

Monday, 26 Jan. Dined at Bazett's.

28 Jan. Dined at College. Spent the evening at Hamilton's.

29 Jan. Dined at Brook's.

30 Jan. Dined at Butler's. Ball at Brooke's.

31 Jan. Tiffed at Law's.

Mrs. Fay gives an equally interesting account from the lady's point of view.

The dinner hour as I mentioned before is two and it is customary to sit a long while at table; particularly during the cold season; for people here are mighty fond of grills and stews, which they season themselves and generally make very hot. The Burdwan stew takes a deal of time; it is composed of everything at table, fish, flesh and fowl; somewhat like the Spanish Olla Podrida. Many suppose that unless prepared in a silver saucepan it cannot be good; on this point I must not presume to an opinion, being satisfied with plain food; and never eating any of those incentives to luxurious indulgence.

During dinner a good deal of wine is drunk, but a very little after the cloth is removed; except in Bachelors' parties, as they are called; for the custom of reposing, if not of sleeping after dinner, is so general that the streets of Calcutta are from four to five in the afternoon almost as empty of Europeans as if it were midnight. Next come the evening airings to the Course, everyone goes though sure of being half suffocated with dust. On returning from thence, tea is served, and universally drunk here, even during the extreme heat. After tea, either cards or music fill up the space, till ten, when supper is announced. Five card loo is the usual game and they play a rupee a fish limited to ten. This will strike you as being enormously high but it is thought nothing of here.

Tredille and Whist [card games] are most in fashion but ladies seldom join the latter; for though the stakes are moderate, bets frequently run high among the gentlemen which renders those anxious who sit down for amusement, lest others should lose by their blunders.

Formal visits are paid in the evening; they are generally very short, as perhaps each lady has a dozen to make and a party waiting for her at home besides. Gentlemen also call to offer their respects and, if asked to put down their hat, it is considered as an invitation to supper. Many a hat have I seen vainly dangling in its owner's hand for half an hour, who at last has been compelled to withdraw without anyone's offering to relieve him from the burden.

A British couple, Mr. and Mrs. J. P. Wildeblood, are surrounded here by their Indian servants in 1882. (Center of South Asian Studies, University of Cambridge)

Macaulay's "Minute on Education"

ঌINTRODUCTION: During the 250-year period of British influence in India from 1707 until independence in 1947, the leadership of the East India Company, parliament, and many intellectuals almost constantly debated the goals and philosophy of government best suited for the millions of people they controlled in the sub-continent. Many Englishmen thought that Hinduism and other aspects of Indian culture should be eliminated as soon as possible and replaced with British values and institutions. Others believed that Indian civilization should be respected by the new rulers and that British policy should simply provide law and order so that classical Indian culture could continue without interference from the East India Company or parliament.

The Englishmen who strongly advocated reshaping Indians in the mold of British culture were called the Liberal Utilitarians. They believed it would be relatively easy to help India develop into a modern nation if British governors worked to replace Indian customs with British law, government, economy, and values. Liberal Utilitarians like James Mill and his son John Stuart Mill argued that if a strong British government in India would pass laws which would actively transplant Anglo-Saxon democratic institutions to the unfortunate Indians, then the "tradition-bound" society would one day resemble their own modern, Western way of life. High on the liberal agenda for India were such goals as the introduction of Western law, the implementation of private property which would soon eliminate poverty, and the teaching of rationalism and the idea of progress.

The Orientalists, on the other hand, wanted to go slower in reforming Indian society and they also argued for a greater respect for traditional Indian culture. Many of the Orientalists were young civil servants who had developed a first-hand knowledge of Indian history

182

and culture and thought it foolhardy for outsiders to attempt to undo thousands of years of tradition and try to reshape Indian culture in the image of England. As Thomas Munro, one of the most respected Orientalist civil servants, wrote at the time of this great debate, "I have no faith in the modern doctrine of the rapid improvement of the Hindoos [*sic*], or of any other people."[10]

The dispute between the Orientalists and Liberal Utilitarians raged most heatedly between 1780 and 1850. The controversy was not merely an exercise of words because British policy-makers were forced to decide how best to govern the sub-continent, most of which was under British control. Because the Liberal Utilitarians believed that people of any race, tradition, and condition could be shaped into new human beings, they turned to Western education as the best way to achieve their goals of reforming India. The Orientalists agreed that an educational system should be launched in India, but forcibly championed a system which would stress a continuity of Indian civilization and would use as the language of instruction Urdu, Arabic, Sanskrit, Bengali, and the other major Indian languages.

The debate over the type of education to introduce into India turned out to be one of the most fateful and long-lasting decisions of the early years of British rule. The British Parliament set up a committee under the chairmanship of Thomas Macaulay to study this issue and to make recommendations for an Indian educational system. The committee published its report, called a "Minute," in 1834. The following excerpt is taken from Macaulay's "Minute on Education" and explains both the issues that divided the committee and its final decision.[11]

We have a fund to be employed as government shall direct for the intellectual improvement of the people of this country. The simple question is, what is the most useful way of employing it?

All parties seem to be agreed on one point, that the dialects commonly spoken among the natives of this part of India contain neither literary or scientific information, and are moreover so poor and rude that, until they are enriched from some other quarter, it will not be easy to translate any valuable work into them. It seems to be admitted on all sides that the intellectual improvement of those classes of the people who have the means of pursuing higher studies can at present be effected only by means of some language not vernacular amongst them.

What, then, shall that language be? One half of the Committee maintain that it should be English. The other half strongly recommend the Arabic and Sanskrit. The whole question seems to me to be, which language is the best worth knowing?

I have no knowledge of either Sanskrit or Arabic. But I have done what I could to form a correct estimate of their value. I have read translations of the most celebrated Arabic and Sanskrit works. I have conversed both here and at home with the men distinguished by their proficiency in the Eastern tongues. I am quite ready to take the Oriental learning at the valuation of the Orientalists themselves. I have never found one among them who could deny that a single shelf of a good European library was worth the whole native literature of India and Arabia. The intrinsic superiority of the Western literature is, indeed, fully admitted by those members of the Committee who support the Oriental plan of education. . . .

It is said that the Sanskrit and Arabic are the languages in which the sacred books of a hundred millions of people are written, and that they are, on that account, entitled to peculiar encouragement. Assuredly it is the duty of the British government in India to be not only tolerant, but neutral on all religious questions. But to encourage the study of a literature admitted to be of small intrinsic value only because that literature inculcates the most serious errors on the most important subjects, is a course hardly reconcilable with reason, with morality, or even with that very neutrality which ought, as we all agree, to be sacredly preserved. It is confessed that a language is barren of useful knowledge. We are told to teach it because it is fruitful of monstrous superstitions. We are to teach false history, false astronomy, false medicine, because we find them in company with a false religion. We abstain, and I trust shall always abstain, from giving any public encouragement to those who are engaged in the work of converting natives to Christianity. And, while we act thus, can we reasonably and decently bribe men out of the revenues of the

State to waste their youth in learning how they are to purify themselves after touching an ass, or what text of the Vedas they are to repeat to expiate the crime of killing a goat? . . .

To sum up what I have said: I think it clear that we are free to employ our funds as we choose; that we ought to employ them in teaching what is best worth knowing; that English is better worth knowing than Sanskrit or Arabic; that the natives are desirous to be taught English, and are not desirous to be taught Sanskrit or Arabic; that neither as the languages of law, nor as the languages of religion, have the Sanskrit and Arabic any peculiar claim to our encouragement; that it is possible to make natives of this country thoroughly good English scholars, and that to this end our efforts ought to be directed.

In one point, I fully agree with the gentlemen to whose general views I am opposed. I feel, with them, that it is im-

These pupils of the Maharani's Girls' College of Mysore studied both Indian and Western musical instruments during the British colonial period. (India Office Library, London)

possible for us, with our limited means, to attempt to educate the body of the people. We must at present do our best to form a class who may be interpreters between us and the millions whom we govern; a class of persons, Indian in blood and colour, but English in taste, in opinions, in morals, and in intellect. To that class we may leave it to refine the vernacular dialects of the country, to enrich those dialects with terms of science borrowed from the Western nomenclature, and to render them by degrees fit vehicles for conveying knowledge to the great mass of the population.

English Education in Action

❧INTRODUCTION: The introduction of English language education, after the British government accepted Macaulay's "Minute" as official policy, proved to be one of the most influential decisions made by the British during their rule of India. Colleges would now teach in English, which meant that secondary schools would also teach English, which ultimately meant that learning the new language would be the means of upward mobility for young Indians.

The English language soon became a permanent legacy in India. However, not everyone had an easy time with the new language as the following excerpts from modern Indian writers demonstrate. The first excerpt was written by R. K. Narayan, one of India's most famous twentieth-century authors, taken from his novel *Swami and Friends,* and the second comes from an autobiographical work called *My Brother's Face* by Dhan Gopal Mukerji. These selections describe young boys who not only found the language instruction sometimes poor, but the message of Christianity that came with the new schooling, sometimes just as difficult.❧

The scripture period was the last in the morning. It was not such a dull hour after all. There were moments in it that brought stirring pictures before one: the Red Sea cleaving and making way for the Israelites; the physical feats of Samson; Jesus rising from the grave; and so on. The only trouble was that the Scripture master, Mr. Ebenezar, was a fanatic.

"Oh, wretched idiots!" the teacher said, clenching his fists, "Why do you worship dirty, lifeless, wooden idols and stone images? Can they talk? No. Can they see? No. Can they bless you? No. Can they take you to Heaven? No. Why? Because

187

they have no life. What did your Gods do when Mohammed of Gazni smashed them to pieces, trod upon them, and constructed out of them steps for his lavatory? If those idols and images had life, why did they not parry Mohammed's onslaughts?"

He then turned to Christianity. "Now see our Lord Jesus. He could cure the sick, relieve the poor, and take us to Heaven. He was a real God. Trust him and he will take you to Heaven; the kingdom of Heaven is within us." Tears rolled down Ebenezar's cheeks when he pictured Jesus before him. Next moment his face became purple with rage as he thought of Sri Krishna: "Did your Jesus go gadding about with dancing girls like your Krishna? Did our Jesus go about stealing butter like that archscoundrel Krishna? Did our Jesus practise dark tricks on those around him?"

He paused for breath. The teacher was intolerable today. Swaminathan's blood boiled. He got up and asked, "If he did not, why was he crucified?" The teacher told him that he might come to him at the end of the period and learn it in private. Emboldened by this mild reply, Swaminathan put to him another question, "If he was a God, why did he eat flesh and fish and drink wine?" As a [B]rahmin boy it was inconceivable to him that a God should be a non-vegetarian. In answer to this, Ebenezar left his seat, advanced slowly towards Swaminathan, and tried to wrench his left ear off.[12]

[The author of the second selection grew up in the era of British colonialism, and he recalls his experiences with English instruction in a missionary school.]

The Missionary school to which Father sent me was the same as thine. Dost thou remember the lame teacher that taught the First English Reader? How ill-paid education generally is can be gauged by that poor old man's salary and training. He received 30 rupees [ten dollars] a month. He was taught a little English by an Englishman who once employed him as a clerk, but, since his pay was low, the wretched man never had any money to purchase leisure or books with which to improve himself.

He had been teaching the same English First Reader from time immemorial. He knew that Reader as a mariner knows his compass. Unfortunately for him, and unluckily for me, the year we began English this Reader was replaced by a different primer. At home we all learned our lessons with our elders; the son of a pariah learnt his from his father as did the son of the warrior from his. . . .

At last the day arrived when the lesson began with the new primer. The first word in it spelled—P S A L M.

The teacher asked the first boy to pronounce it.

The boy said, "Pallum."

The teacher: "Who taught thee that?"

The boy: "My father."

The teacher: "Thy father! Why, he is an oil-vendor; he can't be right. Next."

The next boy answered, "Sallum. My father taught me, sir."

The teacher: "Thy father is a Darwan [doorkeeper] at a bank. He sees and hears English people. Yet his pronunciation of this word may not be right. Next!"

More boys went on saying, "Pallum" and "Sallum." Then came my turn. We all knew English, even my sisters, and I answered, "Salm."

At this he flew at me. "What, thou darest to drop two consonants at once, both P and L? Thy family knows English, yet thou canst mispronounce this simple word."

He hit me with his cane again and again. After several minutes, he thundered at the class, "You are dismissed. Go home. Come back after you have learned your lesson."

The next day, when he came into the class, he said to me, "I looked in the dictionary. Salm is right."

"Then why did you hit me?" I asked.

"Another word and I will hit thee again." he shouted, and

with these words he resumed the lesson of *Psalm.*

That tells the story of the horrors of education that I endured when I was sent to study the Christian religion by my
father.[13]

History: Fact or Fiction?

æ•INTRODUCTION: The British presence in India is still one of the most debated topics in modern Indian history. Was British colonial rule a force for the betterment of the Indian people? Did it really begin India's involvement with the modern world, or was the period, as many historians argue, an era of exploitation where Britain used Indian resources, people, and markets for the enrichment of the mother country?

Textbooks attempt to be objective and impartial. The two readings that follow are both taken from high school textbooks. The first is from a world history text widely used in American schools; the second describes the same period from an Indian perspective. Whatever the ultimate answer to the question of the advantages and disadvantages of British domination of India may be, there is little doubt that the British left important legacies in the modern nations of Pakistan, Sri Lanka, Bangladesh, as well as India.æ•

AN AMERICAN TEXT

Britain completely dominated the Indian Peninsula following the Indian Mutiny in 1857. The British remained the masters until 1947, when India and Pakistan became independent. During those ninety years between 1857 and 1947, British rule changed India in many ways. One of the most important results of British rule was the political unification of India. From the start this was the British aim. In 1865 one Englishman wrote home that they were "making a people in India where hitherto there have been hundreds of Tribes but no people." Unification was achieved in five ways.

Government—First, the English established a government that directly or indirectly ruled all of the peninsula. Britain controlled about three-fifths of India, known as British India, directly through the bureaucracy headed by the viceroy. The rest of the subcontinent was governed indirectly through the semi-independent princely states. There were 562 of these scattered throughout the peninsula, and between Bombay and Delhi, a distance of 845 miles, the traveller would have to cross 36 frontiers. These kingdoms ranged in size from Hyderabad, which was about the area of Idaho, down to petty principalities no larger than a few city blocks. Some of the rulers were fabulously rich; the Nizam of Hyderabad was reputed to be the wealthiest man in the world. The link between British India and the princely states was the viceroy, who not only headed the bureaucracy which governed Brit-ish India, but also represented the British crown in its relations with the princely states. These states were independent except in matters of defense and foreign policy. Thus all of India was united under a single power—that of the viceroy at Delhi.

The restoration of order—Another way in which the British created Indian unity was by restoring internal order. During the twilight years of the Moghul Empire in the eighteenth century, India experienced a period of anarchy. Every village, by necessity, had to protect itself by a high wall. Robber bands roamed the countryside looting and killing, and the successful robber chief might set himself up as a local ruler of a small principality. It was unsafe to travel from Delhi to Agra, a distance of 200 miles, without an armed escort, and only the rich and the powerful could find either justice or security. The British restored order, first by martial law enforced by the army, and then through the creation of a policy force. The most difficult problem to solve was how to overcome the old suspicion that the police were corrupt and that the shepherd was more terrible than the wolf. By the early years of the nineteenth century, however, political and internal security had been achieved.

One law for all—A third unifying force was the establishment of what is called the rule of law, which means that the British enforced a single law for all Indians. Thus, Moslem and Hindu, outcaste and Brahmin, rich and poor, all were subject to one law and could find justice under this law. Before the British arrived, Indian law had been a jumble of Moslem and Hindu customs. At first, the English simply tried to curb the worst examples of barbarism and injustice. They tried to prevent brutal punishments, such as cutting off the hand of a thief, impaling a convicted robber, or turning over murderers to the vengeance of the dead man's family. Likewise, they tried to correct the worst aspects of Hindu family law whereby a husband had the right to cut off the nose of an unfaithful wife and to marry off his daughters as child brides.

In 1859 the British decided to abolish this hodgepodge of ancient laws and establish a single and uniform law for all. The principle that this law should be the same for everybody and should be administered honestly, without pressure from the rich and powerful, was one of Britain's greatest contributions to modern India. How revolutionary this idea was can be seen in the reaction of a rich Indian who bitterly opposed the introduction of English law into India. His chief complaint was that poor men should receive the same treatment before the law as rich men like himself. In the old days, he said:

> If any man without a well-established reputation ventured to go into court and lodge a complaint against a respectable person like myself, if he did not make good his accusation, he knew very well that he would probably have both his ears cut off and be turned out of court.
>
> Hence, in those days no such men ever ventured to make such a complaint or show their faces in any place near a court; but now see how it is. Any low-caste man can not only go to the English court and lodge a complaint against me, but he can compel me to meet him in open court face to face and answer his questions as if I were a common man of no standing whatever. It is this that we complain of. There is no honor, no sense of right, no justice left. That which you call justice and impartiality is really wrong and oppression.[14]

Communications—The British also unified India by solving the problem of transportation. India has only three river systems that can be used for navigation. The rest dry up in the hot weather, since they are not fed by mountain snows but by the seasonal monsoon rains. Food and supplies which were shipped inland had to be moved by ox cart or human carrier. Consequently, until very recent times, terrible fa-mines occurred in India because food could not be trans-ported from regions of surplus to regions of scarcity. The British met this problem by (1) building a network of roads, such as the Grand Trunk to the northwestern frontier; (2) constructing an extensive canal system; and (3) building railroads which became India's substitute for rivers. In 1870 there were 4,000 miles of track; by 1939, the mileage had risen to 41,000.

Language and education—Finally, the English language and an English educational system contributed to the unification of India. In 1835 English was established as the official language of the country. Also a string of universities were established and modeled after those in England. English education became the badge of an educated man, and there was created, as an English official put it, "a class of persons, Indian in blood and colour, but English in taste, in opinions, in morals, and in intellect." Just as Latin had once been the language of cultured men in medieval Europe, so now English became the language of educated men in India. And just as Latin had given unity to medieval Europe, so English now helped to unite modern India.[15]

AN INDIAN TEXT

The British Rule was inimical to the interests of almost all sections of Indian society. The peasants were suffering under the new land-tenure systems introduced by the British. The Indian industrialists were not happy because of the economic policy of the British government. For example, all import duties on cotton textiles were removed in 1882, which harmed the nascent Indian textile industry. The educated people suffered because they were discriminated against. Almost all sections of Indian society realized that their interests were antagonistic to British rule. The people of India became aware of the fact that the development of their coun-try was not possible unless British rule was ended. All these factors forged the people of India into a nation, and this consciousness expressed itself in the struggle for national independence.

Several other factors help in the growth of a national consciousness among Indian people. The exploitation of India by the British rulers worsened the condition of the already impoverished masses. There was a series of famines, which took a toll of millions of human lives, due to the indifference of the autocratic British administration. The British government made use of Indian resources to pursue its imperialist aims in other parts of Asia. The Governor-General (now also the Viceroy) was the supreme authority in the country, responsible only to the British Parliament thousands of miles away. He was assisted by executive and legislative councils, which consisted of persons, mostly Englishmen, appointed by him. The Indian people had no say in the administration of the country. The Indian Civil Service, which ran the administration of the country, also consisted mostly of Englishmen. Though Indians could appear for competitive examinations, it was difficult for them to get selected. The examinations were held in England, and few could afford to appear for them. Indians were put to a further disadvantage when the minimum age for examination was reduced from 21 to 19 years.

Another factor was the practice of racial discrimination. Before the revolt of 1857, many Englishmen, officials and others, associated with Indians on the social level. After the revolt, the feeling of racial superiority grew, and everything Indian appeared inferior and barbaric to them. There were exclusive clubs and railway coaches for Europeans where the entry of Indians was prohibited. As Jawaharlal Nehru put it, "India as a nation and Indians as individuals were subjected to insult,

The uprising of 1857: was it a mutiny or a war of independence? Here Indian participants in the rebellion are about to be shot from cannons by their British captors. (Culver Pictures, Inc.)

humiliation, and contemptuous treatment." The feeling of racial superiority may be seen from the failure of the Ilbert Bill in 1883. The bill sought to bring Indians and Europeans on a par as far as the criminal jurisdiction of courts was concerned and to withdraw the privilege enjoyed by Europeans of being tried by a judge of their own race. The Europeans launched an agitation against the bill, and it was withdrawn.

The British government consistently followed a policy of repression after 1857. Many measures of the government provoked widespread agitation. Two of these were the Vernacular Press Act of 1878 and the Arms Act of 1879. The former act imposed severe restrictions on the freedom of the press and the latter forbade the possession of arms by Indians.

Thus, various factors contributed to the rise of the

nationalist movement. In the last quarter of the nineteenth century, the movement started assuming an all-India nature. Beginning with the demand for small concessions, the nationalist movement in a few years became a movement for the complete independence of India.[16]

᠅POSTSCRIPT: Differences in the English and the Indian perception of British rule in India are reflected in the following poems. The first, "The White Man's Burden," was written in 1899 by the famous English author, Rudyard Kipling, who grew up in India. The second is an Indian parody of Kipling's poem. While some British readers took Kipling seriously when he described what his fellow countrymen must do "for" India, others detected irony in his language.᠅

The White Man's Burden

Take up the White Man's burden—
    Send forth the best ye breed—
Go bind your sons to exile
    To serve your captives' need;
To wait in heavy harness,
    On fluttered folk and wild—
Your new-caught, sullen peoples,
    Half-devil and half-child.

Take up the White Man's burden—
    In patience to abide,
To veil the threat of terror
    And check the show of pride;
By open speech and simple,
    And hundred times made plain,
To seek another's profit,
    And work another's gain.

Take up the White Man's burden—
    The savage wars of peace—
Fill full the mouth of Famine
    And bid the sickness cease;
And when your goal is nearest
    The end for others sought,
Watch Sloth and heathen Folly
    Bring all your hope to nought.

Take up the White Man's burden—
  And reap his old reward:
The blame of those ye better,
  The hate of those ye guard— . . .
By all ye cry or whisper,
  By all ye leave or do,
The silent, sullen peoples
  Shall weigh your Gods and you.[17]

[While English children were reciting "The White Man's
Burden," Indians were chanting their own song:]

Gold and gems that none could weigh
The wizard race did spirit away;
How they stole could none descry,
Such a spell did blind our eye.

From Haughty Isle in legions vast
Locusts come, devouring fast
All the corn in all our land,
To the people leave but sand.

In subject Ind from day to day
Men grow thin and pine away,
Starved of food and worn by thought,
By toil and hunger overwrought.[18]

And Then Gandhi Came

 INTRODUCTION: The middle decades of the twentieth century saw country after country in Asia and Africa win their freedom from their colonial "masters." Kenya, Ghana, Nigeria, Indonesia, Vietnam, India, to name just a few, have all achieved independence in the last forty years. India led the way.

The Indian Congress, the organizational army of the Indian independence movement, was established in 1885. At first it was composed largely of these educated, upper-class Indians. In its early years, its primary objective was for India, "in the course of time," to form a government "similar to what exists in the self-governing Colonies of the British Empire." Leaders of the Congress felt that whatever advances India made "must be within the Empire itself" and that these advances must be made gradually, by "reasonably cautious steps."

This moderate approach, which urged cooperation with Britain, was led by Gopal Krishna Gokhale, a Brahmin and a former schoolteacher, who urged his countrymen to work constructively for their country rather than just to make political demands of the British. Soon another voice was heard: Bal Gangadhar Tilak, a militant nationalist. "*Swaraj* [self-government] is my birthright," he stated, "and I mean to have it." Tilak believed that it was useless to appeal to the British for reforms in India. He told his fellow Indians: "Your industries are ruined utterly, ruined by foreign rule; your wealth is going out of the country, and you are reduced to the lowest level, which no human being can occupy. . . . The remedy is not petitioning but boycott."

Tilak based his approach on the fact that there were relatively few Englishmen in India. The whole bureaucracy was in Indian hands. The Indians, therefore, did not need arms to cripple the British rule; the means lay in refusing to cooperate with it.

Either approach, however, had to have a wider base than the educated upper class. One of the early tasks of the nationalist movement was to incite the masses, to fill them with a sense of national pride and power. Larger and larger crowds began to turn out to hear speakers tell of India's greatness and protest British policy. A landmark of the movement was a meeting in 1919 at Amritsar, in North India, where citizens gathered to protest the passage of the Rowlatt Acts. These acts gave British judges and officials the power to arrest Indians suspected of agitation and to hold them without trial, to search houses without warrants, and to deny defendants the right of counsel. In many ways, these acts were the antithesis of the rule of law that the British claimed to be introducing in India.

Over 1,000 Indians gathered in a garden at Amritsar to protest the Rowlatt Acts. Indian soldiers under British command fired without warning on the crowd, killing several hundred.

When Indians learned of the massacre at Amritsar, they also learned that General Dyer, who led the British troops, had been praised for his actions by the House of Lords. Amritsar became a turning point in the struggle for freedom. A new spirit of determination was developing, and a new leader came into prominence: Mohandas Karamchand Gandhi.

Gandhi, born in Gujarat in 1869 of middle-class parents, studied law in England before going to South Africa, where he worked for twenty years to improve the living conditions of Indians there. In 1914, he returned to India and several years later began to apply the techniques of non-violent resistance to the cause of Indian independence. In the next reading, India's first prime minister, Jawaharlal Nehru, speaks about the difference Gandhi's leadership made to the Indian people. [19]✺

We seemed to be helpless in the grip of some all-powerful monster; our limbs were paralyzed, our minds deadened. The peasantry were servile and fear-ridden; the industrial workers were no better. The middle classes, the intelligent-sia, who might have been beacon lights in the enveloping darkness, were themselves submerged in this all-pervading gloom. . . .

What could we do? How could we pull India out of this quagmire of poverty and defeatism which sucked her in?

And then Gandhi came. He was like a powerful current of fresh air that made us stretch ourselves and take deep breaths like a beam of light that pierced the darkness and removed the scales from our eyes, like a whirlwind that upset

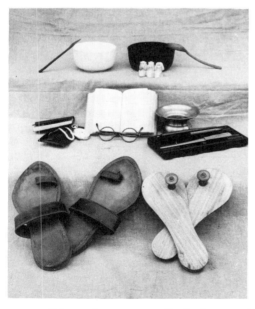

Gandhi's room at his ash-ram (above) and his total wordly possessions (left). (Information Service of India, New York, N.Y.)

many things but most of all the working of people's minds. He did not descend from the top; he seemed to emerge from the millions of India, speaking their language and incessantly drawing attention to them and their appalling condition.

Get off the backs of these peasants and workers, he told us, all you who live by their exploitation; get rid of the system that produces this poverty and misery.

Political freedom took new shape then and acquired a new content. Much that he said we only partially accepted or sometimes did not accept at all. But all this was secondary. The essence of his teaching was fearlessness and truth and action allied to these, always keeping the welfare of the masses in view. The greatest gift for an individual or a nation, so we had been told in our ancient books, was *abhaya*, fearlessness, not merely bodily courage but the absence of fear from the mind. Chanakya and Yagnavalka had said, at the dawn of our history, that it was the function of the leaders of a people to make them fearless. But the dominant impulse in India under British rule was that of fear, pervasive, oppressing, strangling fear; fear of the army, the police, the widespread secret service; fear of the official class; fear of laws meant to suppress, and of prison; fear of the landlord's agent; fear of the moneylender; fear of unemployment and starvation, which were always on the threshold. It was against this all-pervading fear that Gandhi's quiet and determined voice was raised: Be not afraid.

Satyagraha

୨⊷INTRODUCTION: As more and more Indians became aware of the possibility of independence, they also began to realize that Gandhi was calling for a very special method to obtain this freedom. Gandhi not only wanted his people to protest against unjust laws; he wanted them to break these laws, openly and publicly, and to be prepared to go to prison as a result. Moreover, he wanted them to act without hate or violence. "Nonviolence," Gandhi believed, "is the greatest force at the disposal of mankind."

This "greatest force" was at the disposal of womankind as well. Thousands upon thousands of women joined the cause, leaving the courtyard and walking beside the men in their saffron-colored saris. Their participation in protests greatly contributed to the emergence of women as full participants in the political life of India.

Gandhi based his social philosophy on the premise that what was moral for the individual was moral for the society at large. His own quest for truth in action was his philosophy of social reform in India.

In the following selection, a close associate of Gandhi speaks of the man on whom the Indian people conferred the title Mahatma (Great Soul), of the influences on Gandhi's philosophy, what Gandhi meant by *Satyagraha,* and whether Gandhi's approach has any relevance today.[20]୨⊷

Gandhi was truly a universal man. His ideas and philosophy were influenced by people and sources from all over the world. While studying in London, he read works of the Russian writer Leo Tolstoy and the American Henry David Thoreau. On the wall of his humble home hung the Sermon on the Mount from the New Testament. From his mother, Gandhi learned the *Ramayana* and other classical Indian stories and his beloved *Bhagavad Gita*. From the Indian villagers he loved, Gandhi learned a hard-headed practicality and resilience. His early experience in South Africa provided the setting for the development of his philosophy, which later was such an important factor in India's fight for independence.

Soon after he arrived in South Africa he was thrown out of his first-class accommodations on a train even though he had a first-class ticket. He was "colored." As he realized the inhumanity of the laws against blacks and colored, he decided he must refuse to obey the laws and be willing to take the consequences, to "go to jail, if need be, or die." Other Indians living in South Africa joined him in resisting, "not by inflicting suffering on their enemy, but by inviting suffering on themselves, as a price for their disobedience." Submit not to evil, and take the consequences, was the central theme. Gandhi, and a few others, knew that a new weapon was born.

Gandhi searched his brain to find a name for his new

Gandhi at his spinning wheel. (Information Service of India, New York, N.Y.)

weapon and to formulate its theory and practice. . . . His weapon had roots in Indian heritage. The ancient Vedas had a philosophy of suffering that brought divine as well as worldly results. Suffering, self-imposed and undergone in the spirit of grace, was an instrument of self-purification, and self-purification led to victory on a higher plane or even the highest. . . . To refuse to strike back and, at the same time, to refuse to submit is the height of dignity. To feel that the bully deprives one of one's dignity by physical abuse is to admit that one entrusts one's dignity to an outsider. Fundamental human dignity is part of one's character, and character cannot be changed by mere physical pressure. His weapon, therefore, was not for cowards and weaklings, claimed Gandhi. Were it a choice between cowardice and violence, he would prefer violence. More courageous than violence, argued Gandhi, was non-violence.

As the movement progressed in South Africa, Gandhi hit upon the idea of naming his new weapon of resistance *Satyagraha. Satya* means truth in Sanskrit and implies love; *Agraha* means firmness, which engenders force; they combine to say "The Force which is born of Truth and Love, or Non-Violence." He also described it as "soul force" for those who found it difficult to pronounce the Sanskrit compound.

Borrowing the phrase of Henry David Thoreau, the New England recluse who fought against slavery by refusing to pay taxes to a government which practiced slavery, Gandhi called the particular stratagem of *Satyagraha* which he was employing against the South African government "civil disobedience." Only those who are otherwise willing to obey the law, insisted Gandhi, could have a right to practice civil disobedience against unjust laws. It was quite different from the behavior of outlaws for it was to be practiced openly and after ample notice. It was not likely, therefore, to foster a habit of lawbreaking or to create an atmosphere of anarchy. And it was to be resorted to only when all other peaceful means, such as petitions and negotiations and arbitration, had failed to redress the wrong. . . .

Later on, in India, *Satyagraha* evolved into an intricate

strategy of non-violent direct action, which differs from war insofar as the latter is violent direct action. It includes such stratagems as agitation, demonstrations, negotiations, and the seeking of arbitration. Then come such economic measures as sanctions, strikes, picketing, the general strike, commercial boycott, and sitdown strikes to change the minds of his fellow Indians as well as that of the British government.

The Salt March

❧INTRODUCTION: The British establishment of the manufacture of salt as a government monopoly was one of the unjust laws Gandhi challenged. Gandhi understood the universal importance of salt and knew that a tax on it would burden even the poorest Indian. He decided to lead a march to the sea to obtain salt illegally as a symbol of India's desire to control her own destiny. He wrote to the British viceroy announcing his intention to break the law. For twenty-four days he and his followers walked through villages to the sea. There they broke the salt law and urged their countrymen to do likewise.

Villagers all along the coast started to make salt, and others followed Gandhi's example of marching to the sea. The British arrested and imprisoned Gandhi, but the protest continued. The following selection includes two news accounts of the salt marches by first-hand observers.❧

"I FOUND NO PEACE"

The sheds were literally swarming and buzzed like **a** beehive with some 2,500 Congress of Gandhi men dressed in the regulation uniform of rough homespun cotton *dhotis* and triangular Gandhi caps [ready to break the salt law]. . . .

Mme. Naidu called for prayer before the march started, and the entire assemblage knelt. She exhorted them: "Gandhi's body is in jail but his soul is with you. India's prestige is in your hands. You must not use any violence under any circumstances. You will be beaten but you must not resist; you must not even raise a hand to ward off blows." Wild, shrill cheers terminated her speech.

Slowly and in silence the throng commenced the half-mile march to the salt deposits. A few carried ropes for lassoing the barbed-wire stockade around the salt pans. About a score who were assigned to act as stretcher-bearers wore crude, hand-painted red crosses pinned to their breasts; their stretchers consisted of blankets. Manilal Gandhi, second son of Gandhi, walked among the foremost of the marchers. As the throng drew near the salt pans they commenced chanting the revolutionary slogan, *"Inquilab sindabad"* [Long live freedom], intoning the two words over and over. The salt deposits were surrounded by ditches filled with water and guarded by 400 native Surat police in khaki shorts and brown turbans. Half a dozen British officials commanded them. The police carried *lathis*—five foot clubs tipped with steel. Inside the stockade twenty-five native riflemen were drawn up.

In complete silence the Gandhi men drew up and halted a hundred yards from the stockade. A picked column advanced from the crowd, waded the ditches, and approached the barbed-wire stockade, which the Surat police surrounded, holding their clubs at the ready. Police officials ordered the marchers to disperse under a recently imposed regulation which prohibited gatherings of more than five persons in any one place. The column silently ignored the warning and slowly walked forward. . . .

Suddenly, at a word of command, scores of native police rushed upon the advancing marchers and rained blows on their heads with their steel-shod *lathis*. Not one of the marchers even raised an arm to fend off the blows. They went down like tenpins. From where I stood I heard the sickening whacks of the clubs on unprotected skulls. The waiting crowd of watchers groaned and sucked in their breaths in sympathetic pain at every blow.

Those struck down fell sprawling, unconscious or writhing in pain with fractured skulls or broken shoulders. In two or three minutes, the ground was quilted with bodies. Great patches of blood widened on their white clothes. The survivors without breaking ranks silently and doggedly marched

A mounted policeman scattering salt marchers. (Wide World Photos)

on until struck down. When everyone in the first column had been knocked down stretcher-bearers rushed up unmolested by the police and carried off the injured to a thatched hut which had been arranged as a temporary hospital.

Then another column formed while the leaders pleaded with them to retain their self-control. They marched slowly toward the police. Although everyone knew that within a few minutes he would be beaten down, perhaps killed, I could detect no signs of wavering or fear. They marched steadily with heads up, without the encouragement of music or cheering or any possibility that they might escape serious injury or death. The police rushed out and methodically and mechanically beat down the second column. There was no fight, no struggle; the marchers simply walked forward until struck down. There were no outcries, only groans after they fell. There were not enough stretcher-bearers to carry off the wounded; I saw eighteen injured being carried off simultaneously, while forty-two still lay bleeding on the ground awaiting stretcher-bearers. The blankets used as stretchers were sodden with blood. . . .

Finally the police became enraged by the nonresistance, sharing, I suppose, the helpless rage I had already felt at the demonstrators for not fighting back. They commenced savagely kicking the seated men in the abdomen and testicles. The injured men writhed and squealed in agony, which seemed to inflame the fury of the police, and the crowd again almost broke away from their leaders. The police then began dragging the sitting men by the arms or feet, sometimes for a hundred yards, and throwing them into ditches. One was dragged to the ditch where I stood; the splash of his body doused me with muddy water. Another policeman dragged a Gandhi man to the ditch, threw him in, then belabored him over the head with his *lathi*. Hour after hour stretcher-bearers carried back a stream of inert, bleeding bodies.[21]

"WE COVER THE WORLD"

One of the bravest things I have ever seen was the way those Hindus marched out on the field and grouped themselves in little knots. Hindus hate physical pain, but they knew what they were in for that day. Some of them quite confidently believed that they would soon be dead. In each group the Indian women, in their orange robes of sacrifice, made a thin ring around the men. They would have to be hit first. . . .

In a few seconds that field was a shambles of reeling, bleeding men; . . . . women shrieking and tearing at the policemen's clothes . . . throwing themselves before the swishing *lathis*. . . .

The Sikh leader was like that statue of the gladiator in Rome; a Herculean man, with his beard tied to his ears. He was being struck on the head. I stood about six feet from him and watched. He was hit until his turban came undone and his topknot was exposed. A few more blows and his hair came undone and fell down over his face. A few more and blood began to drip off his dangling black hair. He stood there with his hands at his sides. Then a particularly heavy blow and he fell forward on his face. . . .

I could hardly hold myself back. I wanted to grab that white sergeant's *lathi.* I stood next to him; he was so sweaty from his exertions. . . . I watched him with my heart in my mouth. He drew back his arm for a final swing, . . . and he dropped his hands down by his side.

"It's no use," he said, turning to me with half an apologetic grin. "You can't hit a bugger when he stands up to you like that."

He gave the Sikh a mock salute and walked off. [22]

Why Hindus and Muslims
Speak Hate

❧INTRODUCTION: Seventeen years after the Salt March, as a result of countless protests and prolonged negotiations, the Indian people won their independence from Britain. On January 30, 1948, less than six months after thousands of Indians celebrated their newly won freedom on August 14, 1947, Mahatma Gandhi was shot and killed by a Hindu extremist. In the weeks prior to his death, Gandhi had been fasting in an attempt to bring about peace between Hindus and Muslims. A small Hindu supremacy group, the Hindu Mahasabha, less interested in peace with the Muslims than in revenge, saw Gandhi as the enemy. Ironically, the leader of the most successful non-violent independence movement in history became the victim of one of the bloodiest post-independence political settlements in this century. How did this come about?

In 1940, the Muslim League, fearing the loss of political influence in a democratic India that was overwhelmingly Hindu, passed the Lahore Resolution, demanding the creation of separate, autonomous states for the areas in which Muslims were in the majority. The final terms of independence included the partitioning of the sub-continent. Thus, on August 14, 1947, not one nation but two gained independence, India and the newly created Muslim state of Pakistan.

As the boundary lines between India and Pakistan were being drawn, millions of Hindus living in what became Pakistan fled to India, and millions of Muslims in India sought refuge in Pakistan. This exchange of populations was one of the greatest uprootings of peoples in history. More than fifteen million people gave up their homes and possessions and sought new homes. Nearly three million refugees traveled by train. Millions of others traveled by bullock cart or walked with their few possessions in their hands. During this exchange of

Refugees from the partition riots compete for space in—and on—a train.
(Wide World Photos)

people, long-suppressed Hindu-Muslim hostilities came to the surface, and violence broke out on both sides.

Perhaps no one will ever know how many deaths resulted. Pakistan has estimated that more than 500,000 Muslims lost their lives during the three months that followed partition. It is probable that just as many Hindus were killed. Kidnapping, rape, and pillage were frequent in this bloody period. Throughout history, whenever religious symbols have become the focal point for cultural, political, or economic conflict, the resulting wars have been especially vicious. Think of the anguish of Protestants and Catholics in Northern Ireland, of Christians and Muslims in Turkey and Cyprus, and of Muslims and Jews in the Middle East.

The roots of Hindu-Muslim animosities can be traced in part to British policy. The British rulers, in an effort to maintain authority over the vast lands of India, encouraged Indians to direct discontent against other Indians rather than against the British rule. As the desire for independence grew, the British undermined the Muslims' trust in the Indian National Congress. Muslims feared the Congress spoke only for Hindu interests. Generally, the Muslim political party—the Muslim League—cooperated with the British in return for safeguards and concessions. When the British established elections for the central legislative council, they made the Muslims into a separate electoral group. "Divide and rule" was the British policy. It was in the British interest to foster Muslim separatism.

Dividing Hindus and Muslims was not difficult. Khushwant Singh, a prominent Sikh journalist formerly of the *Illustrated Weekly of India*, explains some of the differences between these two communities.[23]❧

India has been the home of many different religions—Hindus, Muslims [members of the Islamic faith], Christians, Sikhs, Buddhists, Jains, Zoroastrians, and Jews. But for practical purposes you can divide India's 500 millions into just two communities, Muslims and others. Hindus, who form 80 per cent of the population of the country, have been able to come to terms with all other religious communities except the Muslims. Muslims have always stayed outside the mainstream of Indianism. Very few joined the freedom movement against the British. Of the thousands of Indian terrorists who were hanged by the British, you cannot name more than half a dozen Muslims" [said Dr. R. M. Dandekar].

"Their bodies are in India, but their hearts are in Arabia," added Dr. T. R. V. Murti, professor of Hinduism at the Benares Hindu University. "It is hard to believe that nine out of ten Muslims on the subcontinent are converts from Hinduism and are Indians by race, language and way of living."

"I would not go so far as to accuse them of extraterritorial loyalty," protested Professor A. K. Saran of the Lucknow University. "Hindus and Muslims belong to two culture worlds. And the Muslims can never forget that for 700 years before the British occupied India, they ruled over the Hindus."

This is exactly what Mohammed Ali Jinnah, the found[er] of Pakistan, used to say—Hindus and Muslims are not one people with different religions, they are two separate and distinct nations.

Although Muslims belong to the same races and speak the same languages spoken by other Indians of the region in which they live, their customs and way of living differ in some respects. A Muslim child is given a distinctively Muslim name, such as Mohammed Ali. Sikhs and Hindus of northern India, particularly Jats, Rajputs, and Gurkhas, often have similar names; for example, my own surname, Singh. Even Christians in most parts of India retain their Hindu names; only conversion to Islam requires a change.

A Muslim boy is circumcised and learns verses of the Koran from a *mullah*. A Hindu boy has his head shaved, and, if he belongs to one of the three upper classes of Hinduism, he wears a sacred thread and is taught Sanskrit texts by a *pandit*.

The dietary laws of Hindus and Muslims are different. Hindus worship the cow. Muslims eat it. Hindus, if not vegetarian, eat pork. Muslims are seldom vegetarian and, like the Jews, consider the pig unclean. Muslims only eat the flesh of an animal slain by being bled to death. Hindus prefer to decapitate their goat; Sikhs go further and consider eating the meat of an animal slain in the Muslim fashion to be sinful. There are certain differences in the style of dress of the two peoples. Hindus wear Gandhi caps and *dhotis* [draped man's clothes]. Muslims prefer fezzes or caps made of lamb's

LET US FORGET 'I AM A HINDU YOU A MUSLIM' OR 'I AM A GUJARATI, YOU A MADRASI'. LET US SINK 'I' AND 'MINE' IN A COMMON INDIAN NATIONALITY

—MAHATMA GANDHI

WE ARE ALL ONE

(By M. Dutta Guptar, Directorate of Advertising and Visual Publicity, Ministry of Information and Broadcasting, Government of India, New Delhi)

skin and usually wear loose-fitting pajama trousers.

Hindu women wear saris and sport a little red dot on their foreheads. Muslim women prefer the Punjabi *salwarkameez* or the baggy *gharara*. Muslim women are often veiled. Hindu women never veil themselves.

Hindus worship a multiplicity of gods, read many sacred texts and venerate innumerable avatars. Muslims worship the one and only Allah, honor Mohammed as His one and only Prophet and read the Koran as the only true revelation of

God. Hindus go to many places of pilgrimage and wash off their sins in India's many sacred rivers. For the Muslim the only places of pilgrimage are Mecca and Medina or, if he is a Shia Muslim, Karbala in Iraq.

When a Hindu falls ill he consults a Hindu *vaid*, learned in the Ayur-Vedic system of medicine. When a Muslim falls ill he consults a Muslim *hakim*, learned in the *yunani*, or Greek, system of medicine. When a Hindu dies, he is cremated and his ashes are immersed in a river or the ocean. When a Muslim dies, he is buried with his face towards Mecca.

Muslims look upon Hindus as mean, cunning and cowardly, fit only to be *baboos* [clerks] or *banians* [shopkeepers]. They dismiss Hindu scholars as sanctimonious gasbags. "The only language a Hindu understands," say the Muslims, "is the language of the sword."

Hindus look upon Muslims as dirty, incapable of hard work, and grasping. "Give them Kashmir and they'll be asking for something else," say the Hindus. "Their mentality is that of the Arab Bedouin. They are not the sons of the desert but its father, because wherever they go they create a desert. Look what they did to Hindustan!"

In every Indian city there is a Muslim locality distinct from the Hindu. Even villages where the two live together are more often than not known by their religious character—Muslim village, Hindu village, Sikh village.

❧POSTSCRIPT ON BANGLADESH: The new Muslim nation of Pakistan was made up of two major parts: West Pakistan, composed mostly of Punjabis and Sindhis, and East Pakistan, a predominantly Bengali-speaking people. Even though these major linguistic groups were Muslims, their different languages and cultures soon led to arguments over power, jobs, and social status within the new nation. Not only was the new Muslim nation ethnically divided; the two major sections of West and East Pakistan were geographically separated by more than a thousand miles of Indian territory.

From its inception, Pakistani politics was controlled largely by the Punjabis of West Pakistan. The Bengalis of East Pakistan, although a majority, never were able to elect a prime minister. The Punjabis of West Pakistan also controlled the army. After 1954, Pakistan began to

accept large amounts of American military aid and soon undermined
the infant democracy of the new Muslim nation. For most of Pakistan's
forty-five year history, the army has dominated political affairs and has
been a major factor in determining the rise and fall of governments.

The Bengalis of East Pakistan shared a common culture with the
Hindu Bengalis of India. Both Indian and Pakistani Bengalis looked
to the Nobel prize-winning Rabindranath Tagore as their own poet.
They enjoyed the same food, music, and artistic traditions. Most importantly, they spoke a common Bengali language renowned for its
delicacy and poetry. Punjabis of East Pakistan shared much with their
Hindu Punjabi brothers. It is said that they are more practically
minded than Bengalis, being sharp traders and tending to be more
assertive then Bengalis. They are reknown for their tradition of warfare.

These cultural differences within a nation founded on Islamic principles gradually eroded the national spirit of a common nation. In 1971, the majority Bengali East finally elected a prime minister, but the Punjabi-controlled West refused to seat him. The tensions between the two wings of Pakistan broke into open warfare. Indira Gandhi, the Indian prime minister, actively supported the Bengali resistance.
Millions of East Pakistani refugees spilled over into India from East Pakistan as India stepped up its support for a civil war. Soon East Pakistan was calling itself Bangladesh (The State of Bengal) and demanding independence from West Pakistan.

Despite strong support from both China and the United States, Pakistan was unable to crush the independence movement in Bangladesh. Throughout 1971, the Pakistani army assassinated hundreds of Bengali intellectuals, raped thousands of Bengali women, and wiped out whole villages suspected of harboring independence sympathizers. These atrocities only strengthened the will of the new Bengali nation. Popular opinion all over the world supported Bangladesh. Entertainers such as George Harrison, diplomats like Chester Bowles, and religious leaders helped to raise money for the people of Bangladesh.

By the end of 1971, Bangladesh achieved its goal of becoming a new nation. With its Muslim population of one hundred forty million, Bangladesh is the second largest Muslim country in the world. Extremely poor, with a very small middle class and a highly overpopulated farming economy in a land devastated by ecological disasters, Bangladesh faces enormous social, political, and economic challenges.

The Struggle for Ayodhya: Temple or Mosque?

❧INTRODUCTION: The long-simmering animosity between Muslims and Hindus broke into the open once again during the election campaign of 1989. The symbol of the controversy this time was a four-hundred-year-old Muslim mosque in Ayodhya, which many Hindus believed should be a Hindu temple. An orthodox and militant Hindu political party, the Vishwa Hindu Parishad (VHP), pushed hard for the building of a Hindu temple on the site of the old Muslim mosque in Ayodhya. Ayodhya, according to Hindus, was the birthplace of one of their most important gods, Lord Ram, known to Hindus through the *Ramayana*, the epic story of Lord Ram. Ram Raj, (see page 34), or a rule like that of Lord Ram, was Gandhi's ideal all through the independence struggle.

When the first Moghul Emperor, Babar, invaded and subdued most of North India in 1526, he chose to build a mosque in Ayodhya even though this offended many Hindus. The mosque, known as the Babri Masjid, has been a source of conflict off and on between Muslims and Hindus ever since. As far back as 1949, Hindu militants broke into the mosque and placed several Hindu gods in various parts of the mosque. For the next several decades, Hindus tried to worship in the mosque and the building fell into general disuse by most Moslems.

The old issue was raised again in 1984 by supporters of then Prime Minister Indira Gandhi, when they proposed to "liberate" the Babri Masjid from the Muslims and make it a permanent Hindu shrine. Rajiv Gandhi, who succeeded his mother as prime minister, also supported the Hindu militants who wanted to tear down the mosque and build a temple dedicated to Ram. Meanwhile the Vishwa Hindu Parishad (or VHP) began plans to construct a new temple, called Ram Janmabhoomi Temple, on the very site of the Babri Mosque. The VHP repre-

220

sents the most organized political group of believing Hindus and they are the first group to achieve such a large political following among Hindus. The VHP encouraged Hindus all over India to make consecrated bricks called *Ramshilas* and carry them to Ayodhya to be used for the temple.

As the election campaign in 1989 continued, numerous clashes between Hindus and Muslims broke out. Often local police stood by and did nothing. By the end of 1990, the Babri-Janmabhomni controversy was still boiling. The December issue of *India Today,* one of the nation's largest English-language news magazines, summed up the violence around this issue.[24]❧

Compared with the October 30 kar sewa [holy march] that cut a bloody swathe of violence and destruction across Ayodhya, the December 6 "satyagraha" passed off relatively peacefully with the arrest of about 1,500 Ram sewaks [devotees] and about 800 on the next day. But even as the Babri Masjid-Ram Janmabhoomi tangle remained unresolved, the tension across the country and worsening of communal relations was palpable. Its most horrific manifestation was in Hyderabad and Aligarh where more than 100 people died in some of the worst communal rioting that the cities have ever experienced. As injuries from indiscriminate stabbings mounted to several hundred, life in Aligarh came to a standstill with the indefinite closure of all schools and colleges. . . .

But even while the mood in the cities and villages across the country remained ugly and militant—inflamed to a large extent because of the October 30 killings—there were voices of sanity, too. More, there was a surprisingly increasing awareness both among Hindus and Muslims that succumbing to fears and hatreds being fanned by politicians for electoral gains would simply pull the nation into ever deeper depths of religious and social despair.

But one thing was clear. The Hindus are in an uncharacteristically aggressive mood [with] Muslims insecure and searching and groping for ways to lower the temperature while trying to ensure that they will not be pushed into any abject religious surrender that would hurt their deepest sensibilities. . . . An additional trigger to Hindu rage, particularly

Some 2,000 Hindu fundamentalists transport the ashes of those killed in Ayodhya (under flowers between the two men) during a procession through New Delhi in support of the campaign to replace a mosque in the town of Ayodhya with a temple, shown here in the background. (AP/Wide World Photos)

in Uttar Pradesh, the crucible of the current strife, has been the *asthi kalash* [urns of ashes] of the kar sewaks killed in Ayodhya being taken around. At one level, albeit on a relatively small scale, these developments have led to preparations for an all-out communal conflict and the growing fear that the extremists may even resort to terrorism. . . .

In fact, except for big towns where they are in large numbers, the Muslims are running scared. More than the Babri Masjid—most of them refuse to talk about it—they are worried about their own lives. In Dediapada, a taluka [small government] town in Bharuch district, about 70 Muslim families are huddled together in a relief camp. The families fled their villages and hid in the jungles.

And for their plight these Muslims also blame their brethren in big cities who indulge in violence. Says Anwar Malik, 35, owner of a small *dhaba* [house] in Lunawada, near Godhra: "We are mortally terrified. Muslims in big towns don't realise that when they attack Hindus, it is we who have to face the music in the villages." . . .

But strangely, perhaps because they sense a coming victory, in a marked contrast to their vitriolic utterances in the past, Hindu leaders have shown considerable restraint this time. The Shiv Sena office, a fortress-like structure near Shaheen Talkies, is unusually shut, and there are no saffron banners or buntings. No Ram Janmabhoomi posters are plastered on the walls either.

But in private conversations Hindus are deeply struck by the call for Ram Janmabhoomi. Says Ajay Sakhalkar, a student at Bhiwandi's only college: "Muslims should realise that they are a minority and give the masjid for us to rebuild a big temple." And many ordinary Muslims seemed resigned to their fate. As one leading Muslim professional—unwilling to go on record—said: "We are willing to give up the masjid, because nobody prays in that . . . mosque anyway and there is even an idol there. We want to be left in peace. But we want this to be the end and not the beginning of such controversies. We do not want the VHP and the RSS [another Hindu party] opening the matter of 3,000 temples." . . .

What is most striking is the awareness of the temple dispute as an issue. It seems to have percolated down to the lowest rung of the society. Most people, on both sides, realise that the dispute is really political and it is being used by the politicians for their ends. But the knowledge doesn't prevent them from having an opinion which is mostly divided on communal lines.

And yet, because no one really wants to be the victim of communal rioting, good sense has been able to prevent imminent catastrophe. There have been numerous attempts to incite communal riots in half-a-dozen districts. In Lucknow beef was found in a temple last week and when the Hindus began to collect into a mob, somebody discovered a loaf of pork outside a mosque nearby. A potentially devastating riot was prevented when leaders on both sides promptly removed the meat from the religious places and pleaded for peace. . . .

Intones Gauri Pandit, 50, a potter . . . in Fatehja village, 20 km east of Patna: "We don't know about the past, we don't know if Ram was born in Ayodhya or not or if there was a temple before the masjid was built. We know only one thing: because of this controversy our livelihood is in jeopardy."

Even in communally sensitive places like Moradabad, the talk among Hindus, even though aggressively pro-temple and against "appeasement of minorities," is edging towards compromise. The fanatics, of course, are still there. But there is a sense of fatigue about the issue hanging fire for such a long time. People want to get over with it and get on with their lives. Everybody will be mighty relieved if the Ram Janmabhoomi issue is resolved through talks. But the bottom lines for both communities remain. For Hindus it is that the temple must come up and for Muslims it is that the Babri Masjid should remain.

Postscript on Kashmir

INTRODUCTION: One of the focal points of Hindu-Muslim antagonism has been the issue of Kashmir. At the time of independence from Britain there were about 563 so-called "Princely States" in the Indian sub-continent. These states were not officially a part of British India, but the British government conducted their foreign policy for them and otherwise intervened regularly in their affairs.

In Hindu princely states, the ruler was called Maharaja, meaning great (*maha*) king (*raja*). In the Muslim princely states, the leaders were called Nizams. At the time of independence, each of these states could (1) join the Indian union, (2) join with Pakistan, or (3) form a state of their own. Most of the states decided quickly to become part of either India or Pakistan. One princely state, Kashmir, became an immediate problem between India and Pakistan and this early conflict eventually led to three wars between the two neighbors.

India wanted to integrate Kashmir into the Indian Union, but since about 70 percent of the Kashmiris are Muslims, Pakistan has maintained that the state belonged in Pakistan. The issue was complicated by the fact that the Maharaja of Kashmir in 1947 was a Hindu. Soon after independence, Pakistani-backed guerrilla forces attempted to either "free" Kashmir (Pakistan's view) or to "conquer" Kashmir (India's view). The Maharaja of Kashmir, perhaps worried that he would soon be ousted from power, signed documents which made Kashmir a part of the Indian nation. India immediately sent armed forces to Kashmir and a war with Pakistan ensued.

Pakistan took the conflict to the United Nations and that body has continued to press for arbitration and negotiation on the matter. However, after 1972, both India and Pakistan accepted the existing boundaries of the area, which give Pakistan about one-third of the contested territory and India the remainder, including the lush and beautiful Vale of Kashmir, one of the major tourist attractions in South

Asia. In the years since independence, the people of Kashmir have
been agitating for greater power for the Muslim population, with
support from Pakistan and many other Muslim nations.

All through the decade of the 1990s, Pakistan and India have
fought an undeclared war in Kashmir. By 1999, the frequent artillery
exchanges had become almost a daily experience for Kashmiris. Pakistan has stepped up its active support of the Kashmir Liberation Front
and also increased its military presence in the area. Kashmir remains,
as it has since 1948, the most vexing challenge to India's national unity
and to her own commitment to democracy.

An American journalist traveled throughout Kashmir in 1999 and
interviewed several of the participants of the Liberation Front and
officers in the Indian Army. He also reports on the devastation that
the three-way struggle among India, Pakistan, and the independent
Kashmir movement has had in the region.[25]

. . . The story is that Kashmir has a long history of saints,
holy men, poets, and philosophers who were drawn to the
mountains and valleys for their beauty—snow in the winter
(but not too much and not too cold), green and fertile in the
summer, autumns like New England's, and spring floods from
the canyons of the central Himalayas. No less than the Buddha himself is said to have remarked that Kashmir is the best
land for meditation and leading a religious life.

But out on the street, just outside the tomb of the giant
Jesus, you can't walk a hundred yards in any direction without
passing a sandbag bunker manned by Indian security forces
pointing machine guns at passersby. . . . On the street, there
are burned buildings, empty buildings, and when the sun
goes down, the streets themselves are completely deserted except for roving packs of mongrel dogs. No one dares to ven-
ture ont, and yet people are not safe even inside, behind
locked doors, as it is not uncommon for six to twelve people
to be machine-gunned dead in their homes while they sleep.
In the past nine years, somewhere between twenty thousand
and fifty thousand Kashmiris have been killed. . . .

I have bought all fifty issues of *The Kashmir Monitor*, a new
Srinagar daily, four pages for one rupee. The headlines are
somewhere between breathtaking and unbelievable: "19 Muslims

Gunned Down in Cold Blood in Poonch Village"; "India and Pakistan Trade Artillery Fire, Charges—It Is All Out War Along LOC"; "Infiltration Bid Foiled, 16 More Lives Lost." The photos are of 155mm Bofors guns firing, dead bodies lined up, boys running on the street from soldiers with guns. . . .

On every bridge we cross, Majid [the journalist's driver] says, "This bridge bombed by the militants; the army rebuilds it." In every community we pass, he tells a tale of woe: "Here the militants put the bomb in the road. They do not tell the local people. The bomb explodes, killing a security-forces truck. The soldiers burn the houses and kill three men in the village, even though they did not know. And if they did know, if they tell the security forces, they are killed by the militants. It is the poor people who suffer; always it is the same." . . .

Majid takes me to the homes of some of the political-opposition leaders, all fundamentalist Muslims. Each of them tells me he is fighting for the right to self-determination, like America with the British two hundred years ago. Majid takes me to see Yasin Malik in jail. Yasin is one of four original insurgents who as teenagers went to Pakistan for training and weapons, then came back to Srinagar and convinced thousands of other youths to follow them. Then he was thrown in jail. He's now thirty-two and the chairman of the Jammu and Kashmir Liberation Front (one of many Muslim separatist organizations). Yasin, more than any other leader, seems to be respected, even trusted, among the Kashmiris.

I ask to go to Yasin's cell, but the police insist on bringing him to the jailkeeper's office to meet me. He slumps on a bench with his back against the wall as if he has no strength to sit up. He glares at me: What do I want? I tell him I'd heard that he had a bad heart, and I apologize for making him walk from his cell. He tells me that he's getting released in the afternoon and that I should come by and see him at his home.

We buy a chocolate cake for Yasin's family and find their home in the old part of the city. Yasin sits on the floor, leaning against the wall, and I ask him what happened to his heart. He says he got blood poisoning one of the first times he was

in jail and claims that later he had a heart transplant, also
while he was in jail. He seems weak. I ask him if he ever looks
back with regret on his decision to take up the struggle.
"There is no question of regret," he says. "We want to live with
respect, honor, and dignity. If there is no dignity, no respect,
no honor, then what for the life? It has no meaning. So this
movement will continue." . . .

[I then went to the local Indian Army officer in charge of
the district to get the official Indian side of the story.]

. . . "Why are you here?" asks Captain Vinot. I tell him I
want to know things like how many of them are actually Kashmiris. "They come through all over this area, and we shoot
them and take their weapons," he says. "Only 30 percent of
them are Kashmiris; the others are from Pakistan and Afghanistan, a few from Sudan. They come across, and we catch them
and shoot them. What else would you like to know?" . . .

We drive through town, and about 80 percent of the shops
are closed. Artillery guns go off on a plateau above the town.
Two minutes later, they fire again. Yesterday, Pakistan shelled
the town in three barrages—morning, noon, and night. We
wait for the Indians to return fire now, but nothing happens.
We head up the mountain to Goma, a hamlet of terraced
fields, of apricot and almond trees. On September 5, a young
mother was killed here, a piece of shrapnel piercing her heart
as she ran out to the fields to rescue her son. Some of the
men show us where she died. One man tells me that nearly
everyone in the village has left, moved to other places, and
that there will not be enough food this winter. He says their
homes are being hit, the roof of their school [bombed].

I ask [Masid] if he understands why India and Pakistan
are shelling each other, and he says no, he does not understand it. The other men say they do not understand it, either.
They don't know why the armies are shelling back and forth,
killing Kashmiris on both sides. One of the men asks me to
go home and tell people that the United States needs to stop
the shelling. And they all look at me, six or seven men, studying my face as if there might be some hope to be found there
. . . .

PART THREE

AN OLD CIVILIZATION
BUILDS A NEW NATION

Introduction

Nehru and the other leaders of the Nationalist movement soon found out after August 15, 1947, that winning independence from the British was one thing, but governing a new nation born in the midst of crisis was an even greater challenge. The new nation found itself immediately embroiled in war with Pakistan over Kashmir; and hundreds of thousands perished in the riots that came with the transfer of millions of Muslims to Pakistan and equal numbers of Hindus from Pakistan to India.

The Indian National Congress, the political organization which led the struggle for independence, formed the first post-independent government amidst this chaos. To make it even more difficult for the new Congress government, Mahatma Gandhi, father of the nation, openly suggested that Indians might not deserve freedom and it would be better to "dissolve" Congress than have it continue full of "decay and decline."

The political and economic difficulties for independent India were enormous from the outset. The balances that had to be struck in these areas called upon maximum use of the classical Hindu talent for synthesis and compromise. After nearly two centuries of colonial subjugation, India entered into the family of nations as an extremely poor country. With over 80 percent of the population engaged in farming, the new government under Nehru had to decide how to promote industrial growth with the grossly inadequate capital at its disposal, and at the same time meet the legitimate demands of all citizens for a decent standard of living. Even with a majority of its people in agriculture India had for centuries constantly flirted with the prospect of famine and now had to balance the basic need for food with the decision to industrialize on a massive level.

Politically, India is really a nation of nations. With some of its states the size and population of many European countries states and most with their own languages and cultures, the Congress government had to find some way to establish an equilibrium between a strong central government and pressures for a great deal of state autonomy. Too many regional demands could easily wreck the new nation. Too many compromises with the constant demands from linguistic, caste, and religious groups could lead to a paralysis of the central government.

Jawaharlal Nehru was the man unanimously chosen to lead the new government and address the almost intractable political and economic problems facing the new nation. He had very strong ideas about the direction his country should take, and would serve continually as prime minister until his death in 1963. Nehru almost certainly did not realize in his lifetime that his family would turn into something of a democratic dynasty and that his daughter Indira and grandson Rajiv would also be elected to the same office of prime minister.

From 1947 until 1989 the Nehru family held the post of prime minister for all but four years. In the election of 1991, Rajiv Gandhi would probably have returned as prime minister had he not been assassinated while campaigning for his party in South India. If Nehru could have predicted a family succession to India's highest office, he certainly could not have foreseen that both his daughter and grandson would tragically die at the hands of assassins. The parallel with a leading American political family also plagued with assassinations, the Kennedys, is striking.

The scorecard of successes and failures for India as a free nation over the past forty-five years has been mixed. Nehru's decision to launch a series of five-year plans, aimed at rapidly industrializing India, served to undercut immediate support for the agricultural sector, and during the late 1950s and throughout the 1960s, India's food problem was acute.

To meet her basic needs, India had to request large amounts of food grains from the United States, all the while enduring the pressures of the American government to move her political and economic policies toward a closer alignment with the United States. However, almost miraculously in the late 1960s, the so-called "Green Revolution" hit India with the force of a monsoon. By the early 1970s, her long-standing need for greatly increased and constant food production had been largely solved, although serious problems with equitable distribution remained and were to some extent aggravated by the Green Revolution.

In the much debated field of industrialization, India's growth has been constant but modest. Had it not been for the doubling of the population since independence, India's economic growth would have been far more spectacular. Nehru, with his strong belief in a planned economy, wanted the central government to own and operate such basic industries as steel, transportation, and mining while leaving most others to private enterprise. Despite pressures from the West, both Nehru and his daughter Indira clung to this hybrid mixed economy. Under Indira Gandhi the central government took on an even stronger role in the economy. When Rajiv Gandhi was elected to be prime minister in 1984, he began to turn to a freer market and also encouraged foreign investment far more than his mother had done. This orientation toward a more open market economy has been continued by the new Congress government, which assumed power in 1991. Perhaps as a consequence of this new philos-ophy, the 1980s saw India's most rapid economic growth in decades, but at awesome social and environmental cost and with a vast increase in the country's external debt.

Whatever the relative merits of a planned versus a more market oriented economy, India has, in a little over four decades since independence, made very good strides in economic development and now ranks among the top ten

This atomic power plant near Bombay stands as one of the symbols of modern India. (Donald Johnson)

industrial nations of the world. Moreover, India has the capacity to produce nearly every consumer product that its citizens might wish to buy, from automobiles, pharmaceuticals, and cosmetics to computers and television sets. The Indian scientific community ranks in the top four worldwide. Indian physicians, engineers, and mathematicians teach and work in many of the most prestigious universities and research centers in the world.

This, the last section of *Through Indian Eyes*, focuses on some of the approaches and strategies that independent India has chosen to follow while building a new state based on democratic principles. After consideration of the Indian political system, we move on to some of the major economic and political issues that India has dealt with since 1947, such as political separatism, economic development, and relations with the United States. India's independence from Britain, coming as it did soon after World War II, led the way for many other former colonial societies as they also moved to achieve freedom and to build their own nation-states. What sets India apart from almost all these other nations is that she has managed to maintain, except for one brief period, a democratically elected government. Trying to deal with the great number of serious problems facing such a vast country and attempting to do so democratically is an experiment that the whole world has been watching. Despite serious threats to the democratic process, particularly during the elections of 1991 with the assassination of Rajiv Gandhi, India remains one of the few genuine democracies among the world's nations.

Despite serious threats to the democratic process, particularly in the 1980s and 1990s, such as the assassinations of Indira and Rajiv Gandhi and the heightened tensions between Muslims and Hindus, India remains one of the few genuine democracies among the world's nations.

Indian Democracy:
The Constitution

&INTRODUCTION: India's leaders faced enormous challenges when they took control of their newly independent nation. Not only did they have to raise the living standard of the average citizen, but they had to bring together diverse language groups and regional political units to form a unified nation.

What kind of political system could best meet these challenges? India had a tradition of both dictatorial and democratic rule. The Moghul emperors and the Hindu *rajas* (kings) ruled with absolute power, but at the same time Indian villages for centuries had practiced a form of direct democracy called the Panchayat system, and the British had left behind elements of democracy in the form of laws, electoral processes, and political parties.

The Indian leaders, after fighting for decades against British colonial rule, formed a political structure that closely resembled the parliamentary democracy of Great Britain. In drafting a constitution, India not only drew upon the British political tradition, but it also examined constitutions from around the world to identify elements that would suit its circumstances. Many of the fundamental rights guaranteed Indian citizens are modeled after the U.S. Bill of Rights.

The following outline sets forth the "Fundamental Rights" of the Indian Constitution. It also presents the "Directive Principles of State Policy," which the framers of the Indian Constitution included to ensure economic as well as political justice.&

FUNDAMENTAL RIGHTS

Right to Equality:

i.   Equality before the law
ii. Equality of opportunity in matters of public employment
iii. Absence of any discrimination on grounds of religion, race, caste, sex, or place of birth
iv. Abolition of untouchability
v.   Abolition of titles (except for academic or military distinctions)

Right to Freedom:

i.   Freedom of speech and expression
ii. Freedom to assemble peacefully
iii. Freedom to move throughout India
iv. Freedom to reside in any part of India
v.   Freedom to form associations or unions

Right Against Exploitation:

i.   Prohibition of forced labor
ii. Prohibition of traffic in human beings
iii. Prohibition of employment of children below fourteen in risky occupations

Right to Freedom of Religion:

i.   Freedom to worship
ii. Freedom to practise and propagate religion and to manage religious affairs

Cultural and Educational Rights:

i.   Freedom to conserve the script, language or culture of any section of citizens

ii.   Freedom to establish educational institutions

Right to Property:

i.   Freedom to acquire property

ii.   Right to receive compensation for property acquired for public purposes; the amount of compensation to be determined by the law authorizing the acquisition of property

Right to Constitutional Remedies:

i.   Right to move courts for the enforcement of these rights

DIRECTIVE PRINCIPLES OF STATE POLICY

The Constitution also contains some principles which the state must follow both in law-making and in administration. According to these principles, the state should try to secure the social well-being of the people and establish social and economic democracy. The Constitution thus seeks to make India a Welfare State.

To achieve this aim, the state should strive:

India's first prime minister, Jawaharlal Nehru, signed the new Indian constitutution into law in 1949. (Embassy of India, Washington, D.C.)

i.   to see that all citizens have the right to an adequate means of livelihood

ii.   to provide equal pay for equal work for both men and women

iii. to organize village panchayats [councils]

iv.   to enact a uniform code for all citizens

v.   to provide free and compulsory education for children until they are fourteen

vi.   to raise the standard of living and to improve public health

vii. to organize agricultural and animal husbandry

viii. to protect the monuments and places and objects of national importance

ix.   to keep the functions of the executive and the judiciary separate

x.   to promote international peace and security.

Voting in the Villages

🎕INTRODUCTION: Every time India holds a general election, it enters the *Guiness Book of World Records* for sending the most voters to the polls. In 1991, more than 514 million Indians cast their ballots, more than four times the number of voters in the election of 1952. Indian elections are on such a scale that it takes several days to finish the balloting and to count the votes. To insure that all those eligible can vote, whether or not they can read, each party is assigned a symbol which voters recognize and mark as their choice on the ballot.

As the democratic system has taken root in India, it has adapted to Indian culture and remarkably has worked for most of India's history as an independent nation. The elections are generally free and fair and the candidates who receive the most votes form governments that stay in power at the peoples' pleasure.

In the following reading, taken from one of India's leading newspapers, we meet average Indian farmers who take their voting privileges seriously. Despite having to take time off from work, farmers do vote in great numbers. As the story suggests, many rural Indians also treat a general election as a great festival and fit the relatively new practice of voting into the longstanding tradition of holding public celebrations and rituals.[1]🎕

By five in the morning on June 15, Savitri Giri had finished her cooking and put her house in order. And by the time the rest of the family were stirring, she had bathed and donned a new sari, freshly starched. Nothing eye-catching by urban standards, but in Chalanti village of Balasore district, Orissa, it stood out, vivid and beautiful even among the bunting and flowers put up for the festival. When we reached her village about 10 km from the nearest town of Jaleshwar at 7 a.m.,

240

Giri was already setting up a small altar at the foot of the tree in her courtyard, decorating it with ritual patterns of flowers and vermillion.

Despite the importance of this local festival of the new moon, however, she was hurrying through her devotions, like thousands of other women in the neighbouring villages. For this year, a [religious] 'festival' threatens to overshadow the [secular] general elections. "Yes, it's festival day, but I have to somehow make time to go to the booth," says Giri. "How will a government be formed otherwise? Besides, this is one day when us [*sic*] small people get to play kingmakers. My vote will determine whether a hopeful gets to rule or not. Why should I lose out on all the importance? Why should I kill my rights?"

After four decades of democracy, sentiments like Savitri Giri's are not rare in rural India. Indeed, the Indian villager, if anything, appears to take elections more seriously than his urban brethren. To him (and her), exercising one's franchise has assumed the aura of a sacred duty. And he performs it with almost the same solemnity as the rituals of a religious ceremony. The act demands careful preparations, including, usually, a set of the new clothes so precious to villagers, which may have been originally set aside for a religious festival. And a bath of ritual purification, on par with the one you take before going to a temple, is absolutely mandatory. "People here think it's a sacred duty," affirms Thakkar Charan Giri, 72, a retired clerk from the Orissa Revenue Board, who has made it a point to get to the polling booth in his village of Olinda the moment it opens for business in every election right from Independence. "Of course, they don't exactly do a puja or anything like that, but the affair is not very different from a religious occasion."

But not all can go through the ritual purification. In his house about 1 km from the Olinda booth, 86-year-old Arjun Rana, who has also been voting right from our first general election, is feeling almost guilty because he can't take a bath. At his age and with the monsoons setting in, the cold water could well kill him. "A rubdown with oil will have to do," he says gloomily, but then perks up: "At least I'll be casting my vote. That's the real point, isn't it?" Having identified the point, he decides to exercise the prerogative of age and dispense with his new shirt: "What will an old man like me want with a shirt?" It is more fitting that he sees that his family of 12 makes it to the booth in time, for it is criminal to let a vote go to waste. His sons, who are party workers, have already gone. Now it remains for the womenfolk to eat and bathe before they are ready to vote, according to the dictates of their sons, of course.

Ten minutes' walk down the road, Nityananda Gharai, 28, who has to make do with weaving baskets and fishing from his little pond, cannot afford to go to the booth before the morning's work is done. I'll have to wait until 10 in the morning," he says. "Yes, this thing is a lot like a festival, but it's not all that special for us . . . we have to eat." Despite that, however, his family is quite motivated. "I even went to Bhubaneshwar to attend Bijubabu's (Biju Patnaik's) meeting two years ago," his mother-in-law Gelamoni Boru, 50, says proudly. And while Gharai protests that he will only change out of his work clothes—"I'm too poor to afford a new shirt"—the constraints of poverty obviously do not apply to his wife, [who] as he talks to us . . . sidles up to her husband in a sparkling new sari, ready to go voting. In fact, every member of the household will vote, down to the halt and the lame. Only the grandmother, whose age is "beyond reckoning," is exempt: she is blind.

In a paddy field in Chakara village, about 2 km down the dirt track from Olinda, Padmalochan Majhi, 22, his wife and his brother Madhu have been transplanting the new crop from before dawn, but it'll take another three hours before they are through. "We'll make it to the booth by noon," says Madhu, who is not yet of voting age but will go to the booth anyway. "There won't be time for a bath, but we'll be wearing new clothes." But this time, admits Padmalochan, the people's enthusiasm is not too high, though most of them hurried to vote as early as possible. "Elections are supposed to be held every five years, but this time, the problems at the Centre have disappointed us," he says. "Personally, I don't know whether this is good or bad, holding elections within one year, but the radio and TV tell us that it's very expensive."

But are elections necessary at all, especially if they are so expensive? In rural India today, some villagers are posing that question, impugning the very basis of democracy. "Of course, you need a leader to run a country", says Bhanucharan Majhi, 63, of Chakrara village. "But why so much fuss to choose a leader? In the old days, the kings and zamindars [landlords] ruled the country, and they ran it no worse than today's leaders. The king understood our problems; he cared. The zamindar would visit every village in his palanquin. Today's kings don't understand, they're only interested in making money at our expense. . . . There's not even a tubewell in our village. And the road (a dirt track which is the only link to the highway 5 km away) dates back to the times of the kings." Then why are they voting, if they're so disgusted with the system? "Mahatma Gandhi had said: 'Now that you are free men, you must vote.' It's a duty and a right." His sister Dukhi Mandal, 55, sees that we are not quite convinced and spells it out for us: "If you want to run a house, you have a leader. The old Rajas are gone, so now we have to elect a Raja."

But in a few isolated cases, innocence has already fallen victim to disappointment and the cynicism it breeds. At the Chalanti booth, while Ramachandra Patra insists that he must vote ("How will I call myself a citizen if I don't?"), his friends are not too sure. "Salt is now costing Rs 2.50 a kg and a couple of months on, rice will shoot up again to Rs 7," says one. "A lot of this price rise is caused by frequent elections," says another. "Sometimes, it's degenerating into a competition to see how many votes a single person can cast, one for the Congress, the next for the Janata Dal and maybe another for the BJP," says Santanu Paul, a long [time] transporter who brought in the ballot boxes. "No, these elections are coming too thick and fast for them to be taken seriously any longer."

Even the politicians are admitting a distinct fall in the voter turnout in this election. "We're expecting about 50-60% of the people to vote," says Aniruddha Kasta, BJP block president of Jaleshwar and vice-president of Balasore district. "But the villagers are pretty well-informed. We're still forming our organisation here, but in almost every village we entered, we found 20-30 BJP supporters already there." "We didn't even have to inform the voters," agrees Uriha Baske, a Congress I worker at the polling booth at Muhammadnagar, about 5 km from Jaleshwar. "Those who want to vote come anyway."

That's most of the people. At Olinda, there were 10 voters already in the queue when the booth opened at 7 a.m. Shyam Sundar Nayak, a carpenter, may have no idea when the last elections were held—"Maybe three years ago, maybe five, maybe more,"—but he has arrived in a sparkling new shirt. He always makes it a point to get to the booth with the first set of voters and brings his family along with him. He may not have attended any poll meetings, but he has carefully decided whom to vote for. A little behind him, Lakshmidhar Muklu is clearly displeased with the failure of the last government and is probably voicing his disappointment by turning up in seedy work clothes, but he definitely wants to be instrumental in forming the new government.

Further down the line, Thakkar Charan Giri of Taribatpur village comes out with a categorical indictment: "Politicians are playing with our blood. We are assured rice at Rs 2 a kg, but at what cost? And these elections are wrecking what little is left of the state machinery. Teachers drop in at the schools for an hour or so, then they're off to the BDO's [Block Development Officer's] office for a meeting. What are the children learning? It is we who understand the importance of elections, not the people in the capitals. There, five people can swing a majority now, and there's always a fat pension when you're voted out of power. That's all that matters to them." Agrees Padmanabha Jana, a prosperous farmer: "What's the advantage, whether we vote or not?"

But then, why have they bothered to turn up in the first batch of voters? The answer comes from Kausalya Behra, 52, at Rajpur village: "This is our adhikara [right]; this is our kartabya [duty]. This is our only link with the rulers." Is she

Indian villagers line up to cast their ballots in the general election. (United Press International)

enthusiastic about this election then? Not really. Every eligible member of Behra's family will turn out, "but we won't go dancing and rejoicing and beating drums. Some people understand what's going on, some don't. But we must carry out our kartabya."

Testing Democracy

ॐINTRODUCTION: The framers of the Indian Constitution were well aware of the problems that can arise when power is divided between the states and the central governments, such as found in the U.S. and in India. Conflicts over "who controls what" are almost inevitable. The Civil War in the United States was in part caused by such a conflict.

As one means to solve power disputes between states and the central government, the Indian Constitution provides for the dissolving of state governments and even the national parliament in certain cases. There are three types of situations where democratic rule can be dismissed and replaced by Emergency Rule, as stated in the Constitution: "(1) war, external aggression, or internal disturbances; (2) failure of state governments to maintain law and order; and (3) crises which threaten the financial credit or stability of the central government or any of the state governments."

Indian leaders have used the Indian Constitution several times to suspend state governments, but only once has any prime minister requested that the national parliament be suspended. In 1975, Prime Minister Indira Gandhi called for a "State of Emergency," and all democratic rights and processes throughout India were suspended for almost two years.

Why such drastic action? The answer is not simple, but at least part of it can be found in the actions of the Prime Minister herself. Born during the independence struggle as the only child of former Prime Minister Jawaharlal Nehru, Indira Gandhi (no relation to Mahatma Gandhi) grew up in the center of political action. She worked closely with her father and served as his official hostess in the later years of his leadership.

After her appointment as prime minister in 1965 following the untimely death of Lal Bahadur Shastri, Mrs. Gandhi in 1967 won the general election as the candidate of her late father's Congress Party

246

and became the first woman to be elected prime minister in Indian history. Many of the party leaders who supported Mrs. Gandhi expected her to be a weak leader, which would allow them to rule from behind the scenes. But she surprised them all and became a very strong prime minister and an astute politician.

In 1969, she backed her own nominee for president of India against the choice of the Congress Party, and her candidate won. Her victory split the Congress in two, and her wing became known as the Congress I (for Indira).

Early in 1970, Mrs. Gandhi nationalized the banks and popularized the phrase *garibi hatao* or "end poverty." The slogan became the rallying cry for her lower-class supporters, raising their expectations that at long last the government and Gandhi Devi (Goddess Gandhi) were really going to help the poor.

During the same period, however, there were signs of serious unrest in the nation. Various groups expressed their discontent in almost daily strikes and protests. Peasant movements, student demonstrations, and labor stoppages gained momentum. The rate of inflation increased, unemployment soared, and the black market flourished.

When the opposition mobilized sufficiently to threaten her possible re-election, and even brought a court case against her, Mrs. Gandhi invoked the Emergency provision of the Constitution and suspended certain constitutional rights, thereby granting extraordinary powers to herself as prime minister.

From June 1975 to March 1977, Mrs. Gandhi ruled with almost absolute power. She imprisoned opposition leaders, muzzled the press, and dictated parliament's actions. Her son, Sanjay, became increasingly powerful and led campaigns to clean up slums and accelerate birth control programs, especially sterilizations of both men and women.

In January 1977, Prime Minister Gandhi, hoping to gain voter support to legitimize her "Emergency Rule," surprised her opponents and almost everyone else, by calling for a national election. In one of India's most exciting political contests, she and Sanjay were both defeated in their bids for seats in parliament, and the Congress (I) was soundly defeated by the newly formed Janata Party. In the following selection, Ved Mehta, a well-known writer, gives his interpretation of who was responsible for Indira Gandhi's defeat less than two years after her declaration of Emergency Rule.[2]

Mrs. Gandhi and her party were turned out of office

primarily by the poor. . . .

The rumors—a blend of fact and fiction—about the dire effects of the Emergency on the poor had for some time been travelling rapidly through the villages by word of mouth. It was rumored, for instance, that the government was using the Emergency as an excuse to demolish the hutments of the poor, with the homeless poor being shipped out to prison labor camps in the desert—a rumor based on Sanjay's "beautification of the cities."

It was also rumored that the government was using the Emergency to drive rice, wheat, lentils, cooking oil, and soap off the market. In reality, such necessities had become scarce because their prices were held down during the Emergency.

It was said that the country was being run by "the boy"— people's derisive term for Sanjay—while venerated elders were in jail. In the years of the freedom struggle against the British raj, the poor had learned that the government could personify vice and that jail could personify virtue, and that a politician's most important credential could be his jail sentence, for there was hardly a major politician who had not once served some time in a British jail.

Above all, it was rumored that "the boy" was using the Emergency to castrate the poor much as village bulls were castrated to make bullocks—a rumor based on Sanjay's sterilization program. The villagers understood very little about the effects of vasectomies—hastily performed as they were by the government, with regard only for statistics. Superstitiously, people associated sterilization with sexual impotence, emasculation, and loss of life-giving energy and spiritual strength—an assault on their bodies, their families, and their religions. Relatively few of the poor had direct experience of vasectomies, but it seemed that a great many of them had heard of people who had undergone the operation and suffered disastrous consequences. . . .

At the polls, the lines of the poor were longer, and there were larger numbers of frightened-looking men and women in them than in any previous elections. Certainly a poor vil-

lager understood the meaning of the choice between dictator-
ship and democracy, between Emergency measures and
democratic procedures, if only, perhaps, from his daily experience with the local constable and other petty officials.
During the Emergency, these government functionaries, with
no legal checks on their power, had become increasingly
remote and arbitrary, exacerbating the villagers' customary
fear of authority.

ᏜᲮPOSTSCRIPT: India not only survived authoritarian rule, but the Indian
people voted it out in a democratic election. What is perhaps even
more amazing, in January 1980, Mrs. Gandhi was voted back into
power and became prime minister once again.

The Janata Party, unable to deliver on its election promises, was in
disarray by 1980. Critics were once again attacking the government
for its inability to end poverty and to stop the country's economic drift,
and for placing political interests above the interests of the people.

These factors plus Mrs. Gandhi's tireless campaigning produced
an overwhelming victory. She served until 1984, when she was assassinated and succeeded by her son, Rajiv Gandhi. (Her older son,
Sanjay, had been killed in a plane crash in 1980.)

Despite the two assassinations, the Gandhi dynasty still continues.
In the wake of several Congress defeats in the 1990s, the leaders of the
old party turned to Rajiv's Italian-born wife Sonia as their new hope.
In 1998, Sonia Gandhi was elected as president of the Congress Party
and in the new elections would be the party's candidate for prime
minister. ᏜᲮ

India's Diversity

INTRODUCTION: Since the beginnings of Indian civilization more than 4,000 years ago, people from many places and with a variety of cultural styles have entered the sub-continent. Today that diversity is reflected in the languages Indians speak, in the way Indians dress and the food they eat, the jokes they tell, and the values they hold. The challenge to India's democracy is to create unity out of so much diversity, to create a political process in which almost nine hundred million people can all participate equally.

In the following reading, Tara Zinkin, a long-time observer of India, identifies some of the elements of diversity that characterize India's population.[3]

One cannot stress enough India's diversity, a diversity which is found everywhere. Standing at a street corner one can watch the many varieties of people flash by and attempt to identify all the types of people. Everybody in India tries to underline the way in which he or she is special, by the use of clothes, make-up, color, hairstyle, headgear, footwear, jewelry. Women from Uttar Pradesh wear their wedding rings on the middle toe. Women from the South wear a wedding necklace which varies in shape from place to place. In Bengal women wear a wedding bangle. But except for those who go abroad, no Indian woman wears a wedding ring on her finger. In South India jewels have to be, or pretend to be, gold, in the North silver is the fashion. In some places women go barebreasted once they are too old to be attractive to men, in other places it is the other way round.

With experience one can place an Indian by his looks, just

This model displays a traditional Indian sari made of modern synthetic fabric.
(Embassy of India, Washington, D.C.)

as one can place an American by his accent. Bengali men sway about draped in long, white, pleated loin-cloths, called *dhotis*; South Indians wear a spotlessly white straight piece of cloth, usually folded back over the knee; while North Indians wear long trousers of varying shapes—which are Indian inventions such as pajamas (and Western men owe their trousers to India). There are as many types of headgear as there are stars in a midsummer's night. So long as women are not fashion-conscious they can be identified by their appearance. In the Punjab they wear one braid of hair down the back; in North Malabar they wear a heavy bun on one side of the head; in South Malabar they let their hair hang loose; in Western and Eastern India they wear a bun on the nape of the neck, but in Central India the bun is tucked under the hair much as a modern beehive hairdo in the West.

And their clothes vary in a hundred different ways. There is the plain white sari of Bengal with its floral border; the somber silk sari of Madras tucked between the legs and around the hips, [which in turn is] in contrast to the Christian sari of the North wound twice around the hips, in contrast to the Christian sari of the South that is pleated at the back instead of the front; the Coorgi sari worn over the opposite shoulder from anybody else; the Gujerati sari hung over one side; the Maharashtrian sari worn almost like trousers; the bouffant trousers of the Punjabi women; [and] the tent-like contraption with which Muslim women hide themselves from male eyes. By the color of the sari and its texture one can place the wearer, not only religion-wise but region-wise. The expert can tell a Catholic woman from Bombay city from a Catholic woman from Cochin by her earrings, just as he can tell a Patiala Sikh from a Punjabi Sikh by his beard. Patiala Sikhs roll their beards upwards over their chin; Punjabi Sikhs downwards under their chin.

Diversity is underlined by every human trick. But diversity does not stop at the way people look for dress; it is rooted in the very soil of India.

Wanted: A National Language

❧INTRODUCTION: Since independence Indians have fiercely debated what the official language of India should be—what language to use for election ballots, postal instructions, civil service exams, and all the other official communiques produced in a nation.

More than 40 percent of the Indian population—almost 400 million people—speak some form of Hindi, making it the fourth most spoken language in the world, but almost 500 million other Indians speak other languages. How could these 500 million, almost double the population of the U.S., compete for government jobs or pass national examinations if Hindi were the national language? Indeed, how could South Indians, who speak languages unrelated to Hindi, maintain their own rich literary traditions if Hindi became the official language and northerners dominated the central government and the national culture?

There are sixteen official Indian languages, one of which is English. Indian advertisements, newspapers, and education all reflect this vast linguistic diversity. India's sixteen languages do not even all use the same script. The rupee, India's official currency, is inscribed with all official languages.

Indians tend to identify strongly with their language group. This identity was enhanced when the Indian government, soon after independence, redrew state boundaries on the basis of language. For example, most people in the state of Andhra Pradesh speak Telegu; most in Gujarat speak Gujarati; most in Tamil Nadu speak Tamil, and so forth.

Does India need a single national language? Certainly it is difficult to create and sustain a sense of national unity in so large a country when the people have difficulty understanding one another. An article in the *Illustrated Weekly of India* addressed the possibility of establishing a link language, at least for a period of time, instead of one official language.

> The most difficult decision we have to make is with regard to a link language—maybe we shall not be deciding it for an indefinite period. There is a great deal of anger in the South over Hindi being "thrust" on its people. But the term "South" need not mean the entire area in which Dravidian languages are spoken. One feels there is not so much opposition to Hindi in Andhra, Mysore, and Kerala as in Tamil Nadu. There is also reason to hope that in the next fifty years Hindi will be accepted unofficially in the South. At any rate we cannot push Hindi as a common language—we must let it evolve as one.

> It is suggested that we have already a link language in English. Whatever unity there exists in India, it is claimed, is due to that language. If we rely on a foreign tongue for the preservation of our unity, then that unity is not worth having. In fact it is no unity at all, but a pathetic admission of the fears and suspicions prevailing between one part of India and another.[4]

Is English really a "foreign tongue" in India? It was the official language from 1835 to 1947. It is the language of Western science and technology. But fewer than 2 percent of the Indian people are literate in English. In the following selection, R. K. Narayan, a famous South Indian novelist who writes in English, comments on some of the ambiguities in Indians' attitudes toward English.[5]⬦

Language has become a profoundly embarrassing subject nowadays. The thought of it gives a peace-loving citizen a pain in the neck. I mean it with particular reference to the English language. An average citizen today is in the position of appreciating the language but not wanting it. We are not so far away from the time when people used to say as a matter of prestige, "He speaks perfect English," and a bride who could write her letters in English and who could claim to have read Scott and Dickens was considered fully accomplished. In the matter of employment, too, a young man who could draft an English letter with ease and confidence stood a better chance of being employed than the one who was proficient only in the regional language. And there were people who didn't know English and who said with a sigh, "If I had only learned English

I would have conquered the world—"

This may not be a very comfortable memory for anyone now, but it would be false to pretend that such values did not exist at one time. However, various causes, practical, political, etc., have demanded the abolition of English from our midst. It is almost a matter of national propriety and prestige now to declare one's aversion to this language and to cry for its abolition.

But the [English] language has a sirenlike charm and a lot of persistence, and (if we may personify it) comes up again and again and demands, "What have I done that you hate me so much?" The judge does not lift up his head for fear that he might weaken. He assumes the gruffest tone possible and says, "You are the language of our oppressors. It is through you that our nation was enslaved, and it is only through you that the people were divided, so that those who were masters of English could rule others who didn't know the language. Your insidious influence wrought a cleavage in our own midst—"

"You speak very good English."

"Well, well, I won't be flattered by it," says the judge. "All of us are masters of English, but that proves nothing. You are the language of those who were our political oppressors. We don't want you any more in our midst. Please, begone."

"Where shall I go?"

"To your own country—"

"I am afraid this *is* my country. I fear I will stay here, whatever may be the rank and status you may assign me—as the first language or the second language or the thousandth. You may banish me from the classrooms, but I can always find other places where I can stay. . . . I am more Indian than you can ever be. You are probably fifty, sixty, or seventy years of age, but I've actually been in this land for two hundred years."

"When we said, 'Quit India,' we meant it to apply to Englishmen as well as their language. And there doesn't seem to be much point in tolerating you in our midst. You are the language of the imperialist, the red-tapist, the diabolical legalist, the language which always means two things at the same time."

"I am sorry, but red tape, parliament, and courts have a practical purpose in having a language which can convert shades of meaning and not something outright. That reminds me: have you got the criminal and civil procedure codes in the language of the country now? . . . "

"You need not concern yourself with this problem. We want you to go. . . . The utmost we shall allow you will be another fifteen years. . . . "

"Fifteen years from what time?" asked the English language, at which the judge felt so confused that he ordered, "I will not allow any more discussion on this subject," and rose for the day.

⁂POSTSCRIPT: Something has to be done to resolve the language problem. One Indian remarks: "I can't stand speaking English. It makes us nervous and turns our voices falsetto, which never hap-pens when we speak any tongue native to India. . . . How dreary it all sounds when a man talks an alien language. . . . When we speak English even elephants could not drag a jeweled metaphor out of us."

But what language should be chosen instead? Everyone has a different solution. A businessman speaks of Punjabi as "a quaint language, slow, indelicate, and lusty . . . Punjabi excels in love and abuse. Its abuse is of the genealogical kind which can trace one's family history in the most revealing and incestuous terms." How different from Bengali, for example, as this passage from *My Brother's Face* by Dhan Gopal Mukerji suggests:

> The first Bengali sentence that Calcutta spoke to me on my return was, "Come, amuse thyself with kind words, the day is young, and we all know that life is brief as a sparrow's hop." The speech of men is the ring of gold in which may shine the precious stone of Thought, and there is no speech as attractive as Bengali. . . .
>
> Of course, we Bengalis are tremendous talkers, but what a picturesque speech we utter! The best poet of India as well as the best scientist is a Bengali, and Jagadish Bose is as much of a poet . . . as Tagore is a scientist. So when I am accused of being a talkative Bengali I am complimented and I say to myself, "If you had such a tongue as mine you would talk also."[6]

India has sixteen official languages, all of them represented on this one rupee note.

Kumrakadu Adigalar, a Tamil religious leader, claims that "Tamil, of all the languages of the world, is the most fit for the feeling of piety. Songs which melt the heart are only in Tamil." It is hard to imagine a man with these sentiments switching easily to Hindi or English as his language.

The language controversy has thus far defied solution. On a proposal currently being considered is the so-called three-language formula. Under the terms of this plan, education would be conducted primarily in the regional languages, with Hindi as a required second language. English would be an "associate national language" for an unspecified period of time.🙿

Primordial Politics: The Punjab

⌘INTRODUCTION: "Out of many, One," Indian leaders like to say in response to their nation's great diversity. However, keeping the larger nation together often means responding to the political demands of highly emotional ethnic, religious, linguistic, and cultural groups that make up the tapestry of Indian society.

Long before India became an independent nation in 1947, these cultural conflicts were a regular feature of Indian history, and the British often played one group off against another as a way to suppress a growing nationalism in the sub-continent. The struggle between Muslims and Hindus which led to the formation of Pakistan still goes on in Indian politics. Language riots, tribal movements, and religious separatism have all played a part in Indian politics.

Soon after independence, the Telegu-speaking citizens in southern-India began agitating for their own state based on their language. Over the years political parties in the various linguistic areas have continued to press their demands for greater power and autonomy within the Indian union and some have demanded their own independence. Kashmir, Tamil Nadu, Andhra Pradesh, the Punjab, and tribal groups in northeastern India have all agitated for regional autonomy. From time to time each of these areas bursts into violent protests calculated to obtain self-rule for their particular cultural or linguistic group.

Such group demands for more power and autonomy are not new to the world of politics and certainly not restricted to India. In recent years, ethnic groups—such as the Armenians and Ajerbaijainis in the Soviet Union, the Serbs and Croates in Yugoslavia, the Kurds and Shiite Muslims in Iraq, the Gio and Mano in Liberia, and scores of other groups around the world—have asserted their need for recognition and self-determination, sometimes leading to secessionist movements, bloodshed and civil war. In the United States, African-

Americans, Hispanics and Asians have likewise demanded greater acceptance of their unique contributions to American history.

Group movements based on language, religion, or ethnic identity are held together by what has been called "primordial loyalties." One of the seeming mysteries of primordial politics is that the most vociferous and violent activities often come from those groups that are the most prosperous, educated, and active in the larger society.

In recent years, one of the most intractable of these regional struggles has centered on the demands of the Sikh community to gain greater control of the government and economy of the Punjab State. Ironically, the Sikh community and the Punjab in general is the area of India with the highest per capita income in the nation. The average family in the Punjab enjoys an income of more than twice that of the average farm family elsewhere in India. More wheat per acre is grown there than in any other farming area in the world. There is little poverty, and village life in the Punjab now includes families with tractors, television sets, and other signs of prosperity. Soon after independence some Sikh leaders began calling for Khalistan, a "Promised Land" of their own. To understand why, it is important to understand the history of the Sikhs.

The Sikhs number about fifteen million, most of whom live in the northern Indian state of Punjab. Despite their small numbers, Sikhs are very visible in modern India since the men do not shave or cut their hair and usually cover their head with turbans. Sikhs also wear a bracelet and special undershorts, and carry a sword (usually a small symbolic one).

Sikhs make up 10 percent of the officers in the Indian army and are prominent in business, engineering, and technology.

The majority of Sikhs farm their rich lands in the Punjab where they have been leaders in the "Green Revolution" that has greatly increased food production.

The following reading by Khushwant Singh, a prominent Sikh writer and intellectual, explains the origins of Sikhism and provides a historical background to the Sikh call for a homeland—for Khalistan.[7]

The founder of Sikhism, Guru Nanak (1469-1539), was a Hindu Bedi (or Vedi, one who knows the *Vedas*) of the Kshatriva caste. He preached the one-ness of God who was *nirankar* (formless) and rejected the worship of idols. He denounced the caste system and insisted that all his followers (*shishyas* from which the word Sikh is derived) ate together in the *garu*

ka-langar (the Guru's kitchen). For his disciples he set up
separate places of worship, first called *Dharamsalas,* later *Gurud-
waras.* The process of separation from Hinduism was carried
further by the successor Gurus with the evolution of a new
script, Gurmukhi, in which the Guru's writings were compiled
and different ceremonials prescribed for births, marriages and
deaths. By the time of the fifth guru, Arjun Dev (d. 1606), the
Sikhs [had] their own sacred city, Amritsar, and their own sacred
scripture, the *Granth Sahib.* Hence Guru Arjun was able to state
categorically: "We are neither Hindus nor Mussulmans."

Guru Arjun's son, the sixth guru, Hargobind (1595-1644),
began arming his followers. He built a *Akal Takht* (throne of the
Timeless God) facing the Harimandir and made it the seat of
both spiritual and temporal authority from which edicts
(*hukumnamas*) could be issued to the community. Despite these
deviations, Sikhs regarded themselves as the militant wing of
Hinduism. The ninth guru, Tegh Behadur, appeared before the
Mughal Court in Delhi as a leader of the Hindus of northern
India. His execution in 1675 A.D. in Chandni Chowk was later
described by his son and successor, Guru Gobind Singh, as mar-
tyrdom in the Hindu cause: "to protect their right to wear their
caste-marks and sacred threads, did he in the dark age, perform
the supreme sacrifice."

Guru Gobind Singh, who brought about the final transformation of the Sikhs from a peaceful sect to a militant frater-
nity, sought inspiration from the deeds of martial Hindu
deities, like goddesses Chandi, Sri and Bhagwaiti. At the same
time by establishing (in April 1699) the *Khalsa* (from the Per-
sian word *Khalis* for pure) and enjoining on his followers to
be *keshadhari* (with unshorn hair and beard) with a community name, Singh, he gave his Sikhs an outward form distinct
from the Hindus. Nevertheless, the dividing line between Hindus and Sikhs remained extremely thin. For one, there were
people who did not grow their hair and beards who called
themselves *sahajdhari* (slow adopter) Sikhs; then there were
Hindus who preferred to read the *Granth Sahib* which they
could understand in preference to the *Vedas* or the

Upanishads which they could not, and who visited *Gurud-waras* rather than Hindu temples. To this category belonged most Sinahi Hindus, notably the Amils. Many Hindu families brought up one of their sons as a *keshadhari* Sikh and Hindus in urban areas continued to give their children in marriage to each other. . . .

The real seeds of Hindu-Sikh separatism were sown by the British by conferring minority privileges on only *keshadhari* Sikhs in the matter of recruitment to the services and later introducing separate electorates and reservation of seats in legislatures. Sikh leaders of the time realised that maintaining a distinct identity apart from the Hindus brought them economic benefits. . . .

What prevented the Hindu-Sikh divide [from] getting wider during the later years of British rule was the rising tide of Muslim communalism and its demand for a separate Muslim State. In every communal conflict in the Punjab, Hindus and Sikhs put up a united front against the Muslims. This was much in evidence in civil strife that preceded the partition of the province. No sooner were the boundary lines of India and Pakistan demarcated, Punjabi Hindus and Sikhs trekked out of Pakistan into India.

Freed of the fear of Muslim domination in independent India, Punjabi Hindus and Sikhs had to redefine their relationship. It should be born in mind that as a community the Sikhs were the worst losers in the partition. Hindus were largely an urban people and were able to salvage some of their properties and cash which enabled them to rehabilitate themselves in cities and large towns. The majority of Sikhs were farmers. They lost not only their homes but also their lands and cattle which were their only means of livelihood. They had been the richest landowners in undivided Punjab (13 percent of the population paying over 40 percent of the land revenue and water rates). They had to change places with the landless Muslim peasantry of East Punjab. With rustic logic they maintained that while Hindus got Hindustan and the Muslims got Pakistan, all they got was poverty.

With independence, Sikhs also lost privileges they had

This painting depicts Guru Nanak (1469-1539), the founder of Sikhism; the name guru *means teacher.* (Embassy of India, Washington, D.C.)

enjoyed under British rule. Their numbers in the Defense Services declined rapidly; their representations in the legislatures likewise dwindled. For the first time they realised that when it came to counting of heads, they were less than two for every hundred Indians. Even from amongst the less-than-two, those who had observed the Khalsa symbols of unshorn hair and beard only for the privileges that derived from them began to give them up because they were no longer economically advantageous. A minority complex began to build up. And with it a sense of grievance that they had been hoodwinked and wronged by the Hindu leaders of the Congress party.

In the new Punjab, Sikhs found themselves in majority only in a few districts contiguous to Pakistan. They had two alternative choices before them: as an expansive community to assert themselves in all parts of the country as farmers, transport operators, tradesmen and industrialists; or to work towards a state in which they would have absolute majority, a

Punjabi Suba which would in fact be a Sikh state. For the first decade-and-a-half after independence, the first point of view gained acceptance and Sikhs prospered in their home state and as farmers in Haryana, Ganganagar district of Rajasthan and the Terai region of Uttar Pradesh. They set up industries in different parts of India and gained virtual monopoly over the transport industry of the country. . . .

As long as the Green Revolution which brought unprecedented prosperity to Sikh farmers continued, little was heard of Sikh grievances. When the revolution reached its plateau and peasants realised that the land could not give them much more, grievances began to build up. As sizes of families increased with every generation, holdings of land became smaller. At the same time avenues of employment abroad closed up as one foreign country after another clamped down on [the] issue of work-permits and visas. There was hardly any major industry in the Punjab to absorb the ever-growing numbers of educated unemployed young men. There were not even enough flour, cotton and sugar mills to process its excess produce of wheat, rice, cotton and sugar cane. It was the educated unemployed Sikh youth who became pliable material in the hands of Marxists or Sikh fundamentalists. At times, both joined hands to put administration of the State in jeopardy.

Assault on the Golden Temple

&INTRODUCTION: Whatever concessions the central government had made to the Sikhs over the years were not enough to cool the rising passions and demands for more political power. The leading Sikh political party, the Akali Dal, had for years demanded that Chandigarh be handed over to the Punjab to serve as their capital city and for more autonomy in the Indian system.

Attempting to offset these demands, Prime Minister Indira Gandhi and her son, Sanjay, tried to set up their own Sikh leader whom they could control. They discovered and supported a then-unknown Sikh fundamentalist, Jarnail Singh Bhindranwale. However, once Bhindranwale became well known, Mrs. Gandhi could no longer dictate his actions. Bhindranwale became increasingly popular because he advocated violence to gain Khalistan, the very thing Mrs. Gandhi had hoped to avoid.

Obeying Bhindrawale's directives, young Sikhs, sometimes even from their bicycles, murdered opposition leaders and sprayed bullets into Hindu crowds, assassinating police chiefs and Congress government officials. Bhindranwale and his followers took control of the holiest of Sikh shrines, the Golden Temple at Amritsar, and in early 1984 they began stocking weapons in the temple. They vowed they would not leave the temple until Indira Gandhi's government gave complete autonomy to the Sikhs in the Punjab.

These actions threatened the unity of India. After months of vacillation, Mrs. Gandhi, in June 1984, imposed martial law in the Punjab and sent the Indian army into the Golden Temple. This move explains the events and calculations leading up to the attack on the temple.[8]&

The hard decision to dispatch the Army to the troubled State to flush the terrorists out of the gurdwaras—above all

The Golden Temple at Amritsar, the holiest of Sikh shrines, was invaded by the Indian army in 1984 to oust Sikh separatists. (Embassy of India, Washington, D.C.)

the Golden Temple, from there they had operated with impunity—seemed unavoidable. Even then hope was not given up completely—for some unpublicised informal contacts between the Centre and the Akali Dal leaders, including its president, Sant Harchand Singh Longowal, were still on. This was an extension of the exercise that began after the Government agreed to consider the Akali Dal's demand for amending Article 25 of the Constitution which, according to it, had the effect of diluting the separate identity of the Sikhs.

With this victory in the pocket, the Akalis—so reasoned New Delhi—would be in a mood to settle other issues, without any loss of face. It was not to be. The Centre saw no reason to revise the earlier tentative decision.

And with this ended the prolonged phase of negotiations, of hope alternating with despair, with numerous missed opportunities. At least on three occasions in the preceding two years, reconciliation was in sight but somehow the issue was not clinched. The Opposition blamed the Government for backing out of its semi-commitments on account of narrow or unreasonable considerations, while the Centre took the non-Congress (I) parties to task for their "double talk" and the Akalis for adding new demands to the old list.

The main impediment, of course, was the 39-year-old fundamentalist, Jarnail Singh Bhindranwale, a preacher who despite his protestations to the contrary moved to the world of politics, and virtually took command of the situation in the wake of the Akali agitation. The outlook and the methods adopted were obscurantist and semi-fascist. When the Akali leaders went to Delhi for talks, his men struck with deadly ferocity, claiming innocent men and women and even children as their victims, with the sole object of scuttling negotiations.

He, a "man," had nothing but contempt for a "woman," Mrs. Gandhi, so he told a correspondent in terms that reflected his social outlook. Why, he would go to Delhi only to hoist the Khalsa flag on the ramparts of the Red Fort, he bragged. It was his writ—not that of the Akali Dal which controlled the Shiromani Gurudwara Prabhandak Committee—that was the law within the Golden Temple complex. Longowal & Co. were a pretty nearly helpless lot.

Bhindranwale believed in the gun, not in the conference table. Arms, it was clear, were not a problem for him and those extremists who grouped round him. In flowed medium machine guns, rifles, pistols, grenades of various makes and origins—including country-made hardware. Ironically, he chose the Akal Takht, the highest seat of the Sikh religion, as his headquarters.

This became the nerve centre, the central point of the elaborate defense structure, planned with the help of a dismissed Major General, Shuhbeg Singh, on military lines. The bunkers, the interconnected manholes, the improvised gun positions on terraces, the arched apertures, the doors and windows spoke of the extensive fortification of the place of worship.

Once the decision was made, Army units swiftly moved to their positions in Amritsar and other cities in the first days of June. By the time Mrs. Gandhi announced in a nationwide broadcast on June 2 that the Government would not surrender to violence and terrorism, the deployment was nearly complete.

The job was not easy in the absence of intelligence or detailed information, and speed was of the essence. Some quick steps were taken to coordinate the action with para-military forces, already positioned in the State, as Lt. Gen. Ranjit Singh Dayal was named the Governor's Security Adviser.

"Inadequate"—the word used by the GOC [General Officer Commanding], Western Command, Lt. Gen. K. Sunder-ji—intelligence was not the only handicap of the troops. They were required, and rightly so, to show reverence to all the holy places and especially to guard against damage to Harmandar Sahib, the sanctum sanctorum of the Golden Temple. The use of high trajectory weapons and incendiary ammunition was barred. Troops were not to take any leather items to the temple area.

A 36-hour curfew was clamped all over Punjab from 9 p.m. on June 3 which, of course, was extended more than once. It covered all the cities and towns, big and small, although villages and clusters of huts had to be left out. "Mind you. It is the Army curfew. It is not porous," said the Union Home Secretary, Mr. M. M. K. Wali, briefing correspondents in New Delhi.

The curfew was enforced particularly rigidly in the walled city of Amritsar, and in the areas around the Golden Temple, which were put in as tight a cordon as was possible in a densely populated locality.

What followed is well known. Exhortations beamed to the armed extremists inside the temple complex to come out and surrender were of no avail.

Troops began moving into the temple complex on June 5, at 10:30 p.m., with darkness affording them some cover. Yet they drew a heavy fire from the terrorists in the narrow streets around, at close range. Despite the casualties, the troops closed in on the temple after overcoming the initial resistance.

A Sikh preacher addresses a group at the Golden Temple. (United Nations)

❧POSTSCRIPT: After two days of fighting on June 5 and 6, thousands of Sikh militants lay dead, including their charismatic leader, Bhindranwale. More than a hundred Indian soldiers also lost their lives in the assault. Other losses included hundreds of rare sacred manuscripts and the sanctity of Sikhism's most holy temple.❧

Killing the Prime Minister

‰INTRODUCTION: What Mrs. Gandhi had in mind when she ordered the assault on the Golden Temple, we will probably never know. Certainly one clear message she intended to send was that the growing and often violent minority opposition to the central government would no longer be tolerated. Soon after Operation Bluestar, the prime minister removed the popular Muslim Chief Minister Farooq Abdullah from Kashmir and a well-liked chief minister from Andhra Pradesh. With the approaching general elections, Mrs. Gandhi perhaps believed that her Congress Party could not win if the growing regional political movements, like the agitation for Khalistan, continued to paralyze the central government.

Whatever Mrs. Gandhi's intentions were, the results became painfully and tragically clear five months after the assault on the Golden Temple. The following selection, written by the editors but drawing heavily on Indian press reports, describes what happened.‰

The armed removal of the Sikh occupation of the Golden Temple did not solve the Sikh problem. With the death of Bhindranwale and the other militants inside the temple, Khalistan had its new martyrs. Mrs. Gandhi's decision to use armed force against the Khalistan movement by sending the army to Sikhism's equivalent of Mecca or the Vatican further solidified Sikh armed resistance and determination to fight on. One direct result of Operation Bluestar was to place Mrs. Gandhi's own life in grave danger.

Indeed, on October 31, 1984, while preparing to meet with British writer and director Peter Ustinov, who was working on a documentary of her life, Mrs. Gandhi was gunned down by two of her own bodyguards, both Sikhs. One of India's leading English language news magazines described the assassination this way:

> It was a path that she knew well, a daily walk of 10 to 15 seconds at her brisk, no-nonsense pace from her home at 1 Safdarjung Road to neighboring 1 Akbar Road for a daily darshan with the public, or an early morning meeting with a visiting dignitary or an interview with a newsman. On that morning of October 31, the darshan had been cancelled and Mrs. Gandhi's appointment was with well-known actor writer Peter Ustinov. His crew was to record an interview for Irish TV.
>
> But it was one appointment that Mrs. Gandhi didn't keep. Her life ended abruptly that morning in a hail of assassins' bullets just as she was about to cross from the Safdarjung Road house to the Akbar Road bungalow. She died [because of] the one contingency that her legion of security officials had been unable to guard against: traitors from within her own security guards. Confessed a shaken intelligence officer: "We thought that we'd taken care of every contingency, but who could have foreseen that the enemy could have come from within the house."[9]

In the aftermath of Mrs. Gandhi's assassination, India faced one of its darkest hours as Hindus began taking vengeance on any and all Sikhs. In the capital of Delhi especially, the Sikhs suffered greatly at the hands of marauding bands of young people who indiscriminately killed innocent Sikhs and looted their shops and homes. Unfortunately, the police did little to stop the carnage and the new Prime Minister Rajiv Gandhi did not call out the army for several days, even though the violence continued.

According to one news report, "the most shameful incident of mob violence" took place at Morena, about twenty miles from Gwalior, south of Delhi.

> Angered by a rumour—which turned out to be unfounded—that a wealthy Sikh set upon by a mob had killed 18 of them, a crowd 10,000-strong collected near the outer signal of the

Prime Minister Indira Gandhi with her sons, Sanjay (left) who died in a plane crash, and Rajiv (right) who was assassinated in 1991 while serving as prime minister. (Embassy of India, Washington, D.C.)

railway station at noon. They first stopped the Utkal Express going towards Delhi, but found no Sikh passengers in it. Almost immediately, the Chhatisgarh Express from Delhi steamed in and was brought to a halt by the mob. They dragged out two dozen Sikhs and slaughtered 12, including a ticket examiner.[10]

Violence leading to retaliation and then leading to counter-retaliation had seemed to become part of the Indian political scene. Where it would stop, nobody knew.

Which Road to Development?

๛INTRODUCTION: As the former colonial possessions of Europe gained independence in the decades following World War II, each new nation was faced with the question of how best to achieve economic development. The new nations looked to the two "superpowers," the United States and the Soviet Union, as examples of two very different paths to development. The U.S. represented the idea of a market economy where most economic decisions are made by individuals operating freely in response to the laws of supply and demand. The Soviet Union, on the other hand, represented the idea of centralized planning with the government controlling almost all aspects of the economy.

India, perhaps because of its long history of synthesis, chose to create a "mixed economy," combining major features from both the Soviet and Western economic systems.

Even before independence, leaders of the nationalist movement had debated the proper mix between central planning and the free market and whether to invest India's limited resources in heavy industry or in village development. The two major protagonists in the development debate were Jawaharlal Nehru and Mahatma Gandhi.

While Nehru favored rapid industrialization brought about by a series of five-year plans, Gandhi distrusted industrialization which he believed to be an important source of Western materialism and lack of community. He preferred instead a policy which would improve the lives in India's villages where more than 80 percent of the population lived.

In the following two readings by Nehru and Gandhi, the two great leaders offer their views of India's future and what they considered the best economic program for achieving their respective visions. These two views of development have been argued throughout the years of Indian independence, and both views have shaped India's political economy.𝕚

THE NEHRU WAY

We are, all of us, working together to make a new India—
not abstractly from a nation but for the 360 million people
who are wanting to progress as individuals and as groups.

In fact, we are trying to catch up, as far as we can, with the
Industrial Revolution that occurred long ago in Western
countries and brought about great changes in the course of a
century or more. That Revolution ultimately branched off in
two directions which are, at present, represented by the high
degree of technological development in the United States of
America on the one hand and by the Soviet Union on the other.

These two types of development, even though they might
be in conflict, are branches of the same tree. The Industrial
Revolution has a long history from which we can learn many
lessons. We are apt to think in terms of European history
when we consider India. I do not understand why we should
repeat the errors of the past. We must make an effort to learn
from the past.

It is obvious that India must be industrialized as rapidly as
possible. And industrialization includes, of course, all kinds
of industry—major, middling, small, village and cottage. However rapid our industrialization may be, it cannot possibly absorb more than a small part of the population of this country
in the next ten, twenty or even thirty years. Hundreds of millions will remain who have to be employed chiefly in agriculture. These people must, in addition, be given employment
in smaller industries like cottage industries and so on. Hence,
the importance of village and cottage industries.

I think the argument one often hears about big industry
versus cottage and village industry is misconceived. I have no
doubt that we cannot raise the people's level of existence
without the development of major industries in this country;
in fact, I will go further and say that we cannot even remain
a free country without them. Certain things, like adequate
defense, are essential to freedom, and these cannot be had

unless we develop industry in a major way.

But we must always remember that the development of heavy industry does not by itself solve the problem of the millions in this country. We have to develop the village and cottage industry in a big way, at the same time making sure that in trying to develop industry, big and small, we do not forget the human factor. We are not merely out to get more money and more production. We ultimately want better human beings. We want our people to have greater opportunities, not only from an economic or material point of view but at other levels also.

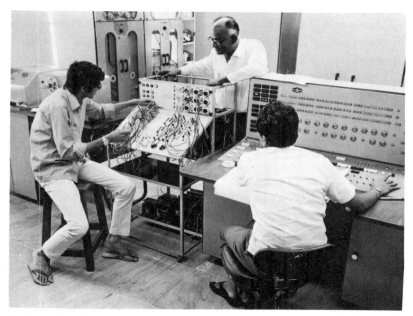

India's scientific community is one of the largest in the world, including the advanced industrialized countries. (United Nations)

We have seen in other countries that economic growth by itself does not necessarily mean human growth or even national growth. We have to keep this in mind and also remember that the growth of a nation has little to do with the shouting to be heard in the market places and the stock exchanges of the country. So, an integrated plan for the economic growth of the country, for the growth of the individual, for greater opportunities for every individual and for the greater freedom of the country, has to be drawn up and drawn up within the framework of political democracy.

Political democracy will only justify itself if it ultimately succeeds in producing these results. If it does not, it will have to yield to some other kind of economic or social structure which we may or may not like. Ultimately, it is the results that decide the structure a country will adopt. When we talk of political democracy, we must remember that it no longer has the particular significance it had in the 19th century, for instance. If it is to have any meaning, political democracy must gradually or, if you like, rapidly lead to economic democracy. If there is economic inequality in the country, all the political democracy and all the adult suffrage in the world cannot bring about real democracy.

Therefore, our object must be to put an end to all differences between class and class, to bring about more equality and a more unitary society—in other words, to strive for economic democracy. We have to think in terms of ultimately developing into a classless society. That may still be a far-off ideal; I do not know. But we must, nevertheless, keep it in view.

We, in this country, must not think of approaching our objectives through conflict and force. We have achieved many things by peaceful means, and there is no reason why we should suddenly abandon that method and take to violence. There is a very special reason why we should not do so. I am quite convinced that if we try to attain our ideals and objectives, however high they may be, by violent methods, we shall delay matters greatly and help the growth of the very evils we are fighting. India is not only a big country but a country with a good deal of variety; and if anyone takes to the sword, he will inevitably be faced with the sword of someone else. This clash between swords will degenerate into fruitless violence and, in the process, the limited energies of the nation will be dissipated or, at any rate, greatly undermined.

Now, the method of peaceful progress is ultimately the

method of democratic progress. Keeping in mind the ultimate aim of democratic thought, it is not enough that we should simply give our votes and leave everything else to look after itself. The ultimate aim is economic democracy. The ultimate aim is to put an end to the differences between the rich and the poor, between the people who have opportunities and those who have very few or none. Every obstacle in the way of that aim must be removed, whether it is in a friendly and cooperative way or by State pressure or by law. Nothing should be allowed to come between you and the achievement of that social objective.[11]

THE GANDHIAN WAY

I have believed and repeated times without number that India is to be found not in its few cities but in its 700,000 villages. But we town-dwellers have believed that India is to be found in its towns, and the villages were created to minister to our needs; I have found that the town-dweller has generally exploited the villager. The village movement is as much an education of the city people as of the villagers. It is only when the cities realize the duty of making an adequate return to the villages for the strength and sustenance which they derive from them, instead of selfishly exploiting them, that a healthy and moral relationship between the two will spring up.

My idea of village *Swaraj* [self-rule] is that it is a complete republic, independent of its neighbors for its own vital wants and yet interdependent for many others in which dependence is necessary. An ideal Indian village will be so constructed as to lend itself to perfect sanitation. It will have cottages with sufficient light and ventilation, built of a material obtainable within a radius of five miles of it. The cottages will have court-yards enabling the householders to plant vegetables for domestic use and to house their cattle.

The village lanes and streets will be free of all avoidable dust. It will have wells according to its needs and accessible to all. It will have houses of worship for all; also a common meeting place, a village common for grazing its cattle, a co-

The economic challenge in India is how to meet the needs of almost 600 million villagers.

operative dairy, primary and secondary schools in which industrial education will be the central factor, and it will have village *Panchayats* for settling disputes. It will produce its own grains, vegetables and fruit, and its own *Khadi* [handwoven cotton cloth].

Khadi to me is the symbol of unity of Indian humanity, of its economic freedom and equality. . . . Moreover, *Khadi* mentality means decentralization of the production and distribution of the necessities of life. Therefore, the formula so far evolved is, every village to produce all its necessaries and a certain percentage in addition for the requirements of the cities. Production of *Khadi* includes cotton growing, picking, ginning, cleaning, carding, slivering, spinning, sizing, dyeing, preparing the warp and the woof, weaving and washing. These, with the exception of dyeing, are essential processes. Every one of them can be effectively handled in the villages. I feel convinced that the revival of hand-spinning and hand-weaving will make the largest contribution to the economic and the moral regeneration of

India. The millions must have a simple industry to supplement agriculture. Spinning was the cottage industry years ago, and if the millions are to be saved from starvation, they must be enabled to reintroduce spinning in their homes, and every village must repossess its own weaver.

Mechanization is good when the hands are too few for the work intended to be accomplished. It is an evil when there are more hands than required for the work, as is the case in India. The problem with us is not how to find leisure for the teeming millions inhabiting our villages. The problem is how to utilize their idle hours, which are equal to the working days of six months in the year.

The revival of village industries is but an extension of the *Khadi* effort. Handspun cloth, hand-made paper, hand-pounded rice, home-made bread and jam, are not uncommon in the West. Only there they do not have one-hundredth of the importance they have in India. For with us, their revival means life, their destruction means death. If the cloth manufactured in mills displaces village hands, rice and flour mills not only displace thousands of poor women workers but damage the health of the whole population in the bargain. Where people have no objection to taking flesh diet [eating meat] and can afford it, white flour and polished rice may do no harm, but in India, where millions can get no flesh diet even where they have no objection to eating it if they can get it, it is sinful to deprive them of nutritious and vital elements contained in whole wheat and unpolished rice.

If rice can be poured in the villages after the old fashion, the wages will fill the pockets of the rice-pounding sisters and the rice-eating millions will get some sustenance from the unpolished rice instead of pure starch which the polished rice provides. That branless wheat flour is as bad as polished rice. Whole wheat flour ground in one's own *chakki* [hand mill] is any day superior to, and cheaper than, the fine flour to be had in the bazaars. According to medical testimony, *gur* [raw sugar] is any day superior to refined sugar in food value.

My idea of society is that while we are born equal, meaning that we have a right to equal opportunity, all have not the same capacity. Every human being has a right to live, and therefore to find the wherewithal to feed himself and clothe and house himself. I want to bring about an equalization of status. Economic equality is the master key to non-violent independence. A non-violent system of government is clearly an impossibility so long as the wide gulf between the rich and the hungry millions persists.[12]

The Greening of Agriculture

➲INTRODUCTION: When India achieved political freedom, it was one of the poorest nations in the world, although in the sixteenth century, prior to major Western impact, Indian cities flourished under the Mogul Empire and contained perhaps 30 percent of the population. The number of people living in cities when the British departed had shrunk to around 15 percent.

Furthermore, because of British economic policies, the thousands of skilled craftsmen who had lived in the cities had been forced out of their crafts and back to their villages. These craftsmen, particularly in textiles, had helped in the years before the coming of the Europeans to give India a favorable balance of trade and a high degree of prosperity. Another legacy of the colonial era was the diversion of huge tracts of land, formally used for foodstuffs, to plantations which the British used to grow sugar, tea, coffee, cotton, and indigo as cash crops for export.

No one knows what the economic status of India would have been in 1947 without the long period of British rule, but for whatever reason, India in 1947 was an agricultural nation without major industries and with half the population living in abject poverty. The 360 million Indians at the time of independence could look forward to a life expectancy of hardly more than thirty years. The production of food grains was only about fifty million tons, far short of even a basic diet for a large minority of the people. Largely because of the British Permanent Settlement policy, the Zamindar class and other absentee landlords owned huge tracts of land on which bonded laborers worked for subsistence wages with little chance of paying off their debts in their own lifetimes. In any case, there is simply too little arable land in India to provide adequate acreage for the hundreds of millions of peasants who live by farming.

The lack of self-sufficiency in food plagued Indian economic efforts from independence until 1970. During that time, Indian leaders had to continually ask for foreign food aid, mostly from the United States. By the end of the 1960s, however, a near miracle had happened in Indian agriculture. In the 1950s, Indian farmers were using age-old seeds and tools to cultivate lands largely without irrigation. In the 1960s, thanks to the new genetic varieties of wheat and rice developed by Dr. Norman Boulag and other scientists, revolutionary new farming techniques were being introduced into India. The new high-yielding seeds needed extensive water and required much more fertilizer than the older seeds, but enough farmers voluntarily began to use the technique so that by 1970 the term "Green Revolution" was being used to describe the new system of farming.

In 1966, about 2 percent of Indian agriculture was utilizing the new wheat and rice seeds. By 1975, approximately 34.4 percent of the cultivated land was being planted with the new breed of seeds. During the same period, the total Indian food grain production had increased from 74.2 tons in 1966 to an astounding 100 million tons in 1975. From that time onward India has produced not only enough food for her own use, but even some for export.

The most dramatic example of the Green Revolution in India occurred in the Punjab, where by 1985 farmers were harvesting more wheat per acre than anywhere else in the world. Until the political unrest caused by the Sikh demands for Khalistan, the Punjab continued to lead the way in India's Green Revolution. In the following selection, journalists Ramindar Singh and Raj Chengappa interview several successful Punjabi farmers and explain how their lives have changed in the few short years of the Green Revolution.[13]

He is already a celebrity, a Midas among farmers, with an uncanny ability to coax enormous amounts of golden grain from the soil of his 80-acre farm on the outskirts of Ludhiana. He is a show-piece introduced to dignitaries and ambassadors when they visit Punjab. His district, Ludhiana, leads the world in wheat and rice yields but gentleman farmer Jagjit Singh Hara, 49, beats Ludhiana's best by a wide margin. He extracts a bounty of 4.4 tonnes of grain from every acre of his land every year, half of it wheat and half rice. A city slicker who became a legend in a state which has many, Hara has now won widespread acclaim—from the Philippines-based International Rice Research Institute which recently adjudged him one of the 14 outstanding farmers from 10 countries, from the Agriculture Ministry which anointed him a *Dhan Pandit* and from the nearby Punjab Agricultural University which has made him a visiting professor. The centre-piece in a display of trophies, plaques and citations that crowd the walls of his drawing room is Hara's picture with Norman Borlaug, the Nobel laureate who helped India's green revolution.

Further north, on a picturesque 25-acre plot near Pathankot, overlooked by the snow-clad Dhauladhar range, lives Kuldip Singh Gill, who has made a fortune out of Hi-Sex. No, he is not in the pornography business. Hi-Sex is his favourite breed of hen and Kuldip Singh Gill is to eggs what Hara is to grain. One day last fortnight, Gill contemplated the day's production of 105,000 eggs, which raised the fragile hoard in his storeroom to an impressive 3.5 lakh [350,000]. The size of his poultry farm—with its 2.10 lakh hens—is no cackling matter; even the description sounds odd considering that it is registered with the Director-General of Technical Development as a medium scale industry. In fact, egg manufacturer would be a more appropriate description for Gill, 40, and a pioneer who introduced modern mass production techniques to the industry in Punjab where a unit was considered big if it had 40,000 to 50,000 birds. He had no formal training in poultry. He says he learned by keeping his eyes and ears open and his mind receptive to new techniques of bird management. He was the first person in north India to introduce the practice of keeping the birds in wire cages—three to a cage. The birds stay clean and so do the eggs. And their reduced mobility saves a considerable amount of feed. Hard work has made him perhaps the largest commercial poultry farmer in the country—the King of Cluck.

They are both ordinary looking, the kind you would not notice on the street. Hara, tall and jovial, unlocks his heart and his bar to visitors. Gill, short and dapper, is more reserved. Both started out in somewhat identical fashion: Hara as a refugee from Pakistan and Gill as a farmer's son at a loose end. And both have achieved remarkable success in their respective fields.

Like them, there are others elsewhere in the country—

Farmers irrigating their land in Tamil Nadu state. (United Nations)

the potato growers of Farrukhabad and Meerut in Uttar Pradesh and Biharsharif in Bihar, the cotton planters of Surat and Maharashtra, the dairymen of Gujarat and the paddy growers of Andhra Pradesh's West Godavari district and Tamil Nadu's Thanjavur—who symbolise equally well the growing community of farmers whose easy receptivity to modern and mechanised techniques has helped the country cross the hump in the quest for self-sufficiency in food and other commodities. In this quest, the crucial ten-year period from 1975 to 1985 has been a turning point. In a microcosm, their story is also the story of Indian agriculture for this period. In 1974-75 India produced 99.83 million tonnes of foodgrains and 6.23 million tonnes of potatoes, around 65 lakh [6.5 million] bales of cotton. Catalysed by the efforts of innovators like Hara, foodgrains production increased to 151.54 million tonnes in 1983-84, a not unimpressive increase of 51.82 per cent. Few other countries have achieved similar breakthroughs. In other areas too, the achievement was equally impressive: potato production more than doubled from 6.23 million tonnes in 1975 to 13 million tonnes. "Potato has produced as big a revolution as wheat," says Deputy Director-General M.V. Rao of the Indian Council of Agriculture Research (ICAR). "Previously potatoes were a luxury. Now a glut has caused prices to crash." Cotton output too swelled from about 65 lakh bales in 1975 to 93 lakh bales in 1985. Ten years ago long staple cotton worth Rs 70 crore [Rs 700 million] was being imported, now it's surplus. Thanks to the Gills of the business, egg production jumped from 8,204 million to 13,500 million and broilers literally took wing, from 10 million to 50 million.

Success stories all, spurred mainly by the availability of improved seeds from agricultural universities and seeds corporations (70,000 tonnes were distributed in 1984-85 compared to only 25,000 tonnes five years ago), progressive mechanisation (annual production of tractors has gone up from 33,146 in 1976-77 to around 90,000 this year), easier bank credit (Rs 5.810 crore [Rs 58.1 billion] disbursed in 1984-85 as against Rs 3,387 crore [Rs 33.87 billion] in 1980-

Farmers in North India harvest high-yielding wheat, a staple of the "Green Revolution." (Donald Johnson)

81), increased fertiliser usage (84 lakh tonnes in 1984-85 compared to 55.16 lakh tonnes in 1980-81) and increase in irrigated area and grassroots application of research breakthroughs in university laboratories. These achievements often get lost in the welter of publicity about droughts, shortages and price rises, but they have infused the farming community and the nation with a new confidence. This is echoed in the words of ICAR Director-General Dr. N. S. Randhawa: "The strength of our agriculture lies in its improved ability to withstand droughts." In the 1970s a drought spelled disaster; the one in 1979-80 caused a shortfall of 22 million tonnes and wiped out a buffer stock accumulated over ten years. But some success in drought-proofing made a foodgrains production of 151 million tonnes possible in 1983-84, a drought year. Two areas of worry remain—oilseeds, whose shortage forces the country to import edible oil worth more than Rs 1,000 crore every year, and pulses, whose per capita availability over the years has fallen from 72 grams to only 34 grams.

That apart, Punjab remains the brightest lighthouse on the agricultural landscape, says Randhawa. There are others too, but their number will have to increase if the country is to produce the 235 million tonnes of foodgrains required by the year 2000 to feed an estimated population of one billion people. Expectations of an increase of that order are based on the hope that the coming decade and a half will multiply the tribe of agricultural entrepreneurs like Hara and Gill and transform the operations of others like Karnataka coffee planter Ajjicutira Ponnappa who rejoices in his new-found prosperity after years of marginal earnings. Ponnappa's lean face lit up in anticipation as he admired the coffee berries ripening in the winter sun on his 20-acre estate near Mercara. It promised to be a good crop and Ponnappa was satisfied: "God has set me free from worries."

Life was not always a bed of berries for the aging Ponnappa, 60. With insignificant yields from five acres of paddy fields left him by his father, his youth was one of despair as he slogged it out as a clerk in the state Industries Department. With a wife and three children to support, he was terribly insecure. "I spent sleepless nights worrying about our future," he remembers now. In 1972, with the coffee boom under way, Ponnappa decided to invest his life's savings of Rs 35,000 to convert ten acres of jungle land into a coffee estate. Taking all the help he could get—high yielding seeds from the coffee board and development loans from a bank—he tided over the five years it takes for the plants to bear fruit. "Growing a coffee plant is like taking care of a baby," he says. "In the first five years we spent money with no returns." When the returns came, they gladdened his ears. Because of steadily rising coffee prices he started grossing over Rs 1 lakh [Rs 100,000] a year. He bought another 10 acres near his estate and applied for more loans. Last year he spent Rs 1 lakh on a sprinkler system. The fact that he owes banks about Rs 2.5 lakh does not faze him. "No city job can give me the security that my estate does," he says. Security also means having the money to send his son to engineering college and the daughter to a college in Mangalore, and a Rs 5 lakh concrete house with attached bathrooms which is nearing completion on the estate. "It's a paradise," he gloats.

Others have traversed different paths to the paradise of prosperity. Gill was doing pre-engineering when his father died leaving him, the only son, with 40 acres of land. "I used to ask people what's a good industry to start," he says. And a relative sold him the idea of starting a poultry farm. So he started out with 1,500 birds in the early 1970s. It soon became clear that he had a way with chicks. By 1975 he had grown to 10,000 birds and to 50,000 three years ago. Then he really expanded with the help of a bank loan of Rs 30 lakhs and now has 210,000 hens. The farm even has its own feed mill to process the 20 tonnes of feed needed every day. Yet another expansion is under way. Gill attributes his success to the farm's location, with the huge market of Jammu and Kashmir, Himachal Pradesh and the army at his very doorstep, and availability of cheaper feed ingredients. With characteristic modesty he plays down his own role in husbanding his massive brood into a medium scale industry. Gill too has only one son who he hopes will join him in the business. Understandably, Gill is not overly fond of eggs; he eats only about two a week and chicken meat graces his table only once a fortnight.

Hara came to Kanganwal village adjoining Ludhiana's industrial estate in 1951 from Multan. His father was allotted 20 acres in exchange for the land they had left behind in Pakistan. Says Hara: "For three years we lived in a tin shed under the banyan tree. Little by little we saved and built a house." And bought more land. "Agriculture has to be run like a business," he says, "it's no use saying it's in the blood." Hara confesses that his businesses boomed 10 years ago when he adopted high-yield paddy [rice] as a summer crop. "Paddy has brought prosperity to Punjab as a summer crop," but the wheat-paddy rotation is taking a heavy toll of soil fertility. Hara displays a passionate concern for the health of the soil on his farm and is worried at the way farmers around him are neglecting their basic resource.

He has prepared a soil fertility map of his entire farm and gets soil samples tested every two years at the Punjab Agricultural University which provides this service free to neighbouring farmers. Any deficiency of nutrients is quickly remedied. He plants an intermediate crop of green manure (*jantar*) which is mashed and buried in the soil to replenish depleted nutrients. Not afraid of dirtying his hands, Hara still works on the farm. The care he lavishes on his land has paid dividends. He now lives in a bigger house surrounded by exotic trees and plants with a small swimming pool he likes to plunge into after he has finished entertaining his frequent guests. Such is his reputation that every grain he produces is purchased by the National Seeds Corporation to be sold as seed to other farmers.

Entrepreneurs like Hara who have assured means of irrigation represent a minority of 30 per cent of the farming community. The remaining 70 per cent of the cultivators still depend largely on nature since they cultivate the rain-fed areas. But however small their number, the Haras of this country produce 60 per cent of its food and the ripples of their achievements reach even those on the boundaries of the sphere. That is their importance.

The Little Match Girls

𝕰INTRODUCTION: The benign human results, which were supposed to have flowed from Nehru's concept of planned industrialization, have not always been evident in real practice. Indian industrialization, like industrial revolutions all over the world, has often meant the exploitation of labor by factory owners.

Among the millions of workers who make up India's labor force, many are young children who will never know the luxury of school or the leisure time for carefree play. They will likely spend most of their life working for mere survival. The following selection focuses on the practice of child labor in a match factory in South India. This factory was the subject of a government investigation, the results of which were to have been released in 1977. However, the report was withheld until *India Today* published the commission findings in 1983. Ironically, the owners of the factory, the Nadars, were once a lowly untouchable caste who raised themselves up the social scale. Now as factory owners, they too exploit others for profit.[14]𝕰

Down the long hall, lit patchily by sunlight coming in the rough open windows, sat row upon row of children, almost 250 of them, all of them around 10 years of age, all immersed in their work. In front of each one of them lay a small mountain of headless matchsticks, and the children's hands flew from those piles to frames they balanced on their laps, inserting each matchstick painstakingly into its slot in the frame. There was obviously pressure to fill each frame fast, for the children never looked up. Even at "lunchtime," as their right hands unconsciously pecked at the food they had brought from home, their left hands mechanically continued to insesert matchsticks in the frames. On every face was an expression of utter blankness, masks on an army of child robots.

This was "D" unit of the Standard Match Industries at the Madathupatti village crossing, not very far from Sivakasi, a small municipal town in Tamil Nadu's Ramanathapuram district, only one of the hundreds in the region, a cog in the wheel of the huge handmade match industry. Sivakasi is also famous for the fireworks it produces, and in the cracker factories, too, most of the workers are children, some above 14 years of age, but a lot below. Standard Fireworks, for instance, has 12 units spread in the taluk [district subdivision], each employing between 100 and 300 people; at the Tayyalpatti village unit, the foreman says: "We prefer child labour. Children work faster, work longer hours and are more dependable."

The world's largest concentration of child labour works in the Sivakasi units. Out of a total population of 100,000 workers in the match and fireworks industries, the child worker population is around 45,000. The children, most of them from neighbouring villages, work either in small cottage units in their own villages or are brought into Sivakasi town by organised transport.

. . . Between 3 and 5 every morning, children in villages as far as 30 km away are rudely woken up by their parents, handed a small lunch packet, and bundled into buses or vans belonging to the factory owners. Each of these villages has an agent who "enrolls" children, and who ensures that the children are awake when the transport arrives in the pre-dawn darkness. Each agent gets a monthly salary of Rs 150, and parents are offered a "salary advance" of Rs 200 for each child they pledge to the factories. Late in the evening, between 6 and 9 p.m., the children are dropped back to their villages after they have put in a 12-hour day, with no relaxation periods.

An estimated 44 percent of the child workers are below the age of 15. Legally, every child has to possess a doctor's certificate clearing him or her for employment, but such certificates can always be obtained for a consideration. Girls out-

The use of child labor is widespread throughout India. (Maria Donoso Clark)

number boys in every factory, for they are considered more dexterous, working at filling match frames, making matchboxes, counting sticks, or pasting labels, while in the fireworks factories they dye newsprint with the distinctive red of the crackers, roll gunpowder, and package the final product.

Most of these children have never been to school, and childhood and play are alien concepts to them, their lives shared dangerously with chemicals and noxious fumes, dust from chemical powder and the heat of the boiler rooms. The younger children, between four and seven years, earn about Rs 2 a day for this unending work—there are no days off—and the older children earn a maximum of Rs 7 a day.

The security arrangements in every small-scale and cottage factory are elaborate. Visitors are stopped at the gate, and by the time entrance is gained into the factories, the children have been whisked away to nearby fields or hidden in the large storage sheds. Most match or fireworks units are owned by Nadar families, and each owner is a member of the Sivakasi Chamber of Match Industries (SCMI).

The children usually ignore simple illnesses, but when questioned, they tell of headaches and skin rashes. Doctors report a higher than usual incidence of tuberculosis and respiratory ailments, with 20 percent of those examined suffering from worms or other intestinal infections and 30 percent with vitamin deficiencies.

Often children are the sole support of their families, and thus school is out of the question. Of those who do attend classes, 80 percent drop out by the end of the fourth grade by which time—such is the poor quality of public education— they have learned little and soon forget even that. They grow up stunted in mind and body and become the mothers of a generation like themselves.

HELPING CHILDREN TO LEARN AND PLAY

I was told of a young man named Prabhakaran who was helping match children in an out-of-the-way Tirunelveli village and took a crowded bus south from the temple city of Madurai. . . .

Prabhakaran was about thirty years old: five-foot-five, with a trim mustache, and a smiling, direct look. He said he was a Dalit and his caste used only one name. His father was a forest guard, and this enabled him to complete high school in 1973. At first he became a forest guard but then quit.

"Our community suffers humiliation and oppression from other castes," he said. "Our girls are raped, and we can't do anything about it. You read about such things and experience some of it in your own life, and you feel you should do something for your own people. I took up social service and worked with some Indian and foreign institutions, but I found a lot of contradictions between what they preached and what they practiced. Then a British agency, Action Aid, wanted to get beyond welfare. They offered to pay me and a friend named Balakrishnan 250 rupees a month if we could develop something different.

"We went to one place and other, but they suspected we might be Naxalites or some other extremists or the secret police. Finally we came to a small village called Menak-shipuram and explained we wanted to establish a nonformal education center for children. A man said, 'Your idea is good, but I don't know if you're good men or bad men. Time will tell. If you're good men, you'll stay on forever. If you're bad, you'll be discovered.'

"It was a village of forty-three houses. We started schools in the street in the night and morning and played with the children, but they were terribly tired and fell asleep in the classroom. Besides, their parents were not motivated: they had no thirst for knowledge. We concluded we had to do something else along with education."

Balakrishnan left for other work, and in 1983 Prabhakaran moved about ten kilometers to his present village, Vahikulum, and formed the Malarchi Trust as an agency to get government grants to start health and income-generating programs. A year later a drought began and stretched for four years. He recalled the bitter years:

"There was no water or fodder for cattle, and farmers who had bought cows for three thousand rupees sold them for fifteen hundred. Later, cows were sold for only two or three hundred rupees. Thousands of people migrated to the rock quarries of Kerala; school attendance dropped by 30 percent, and the children in the match factories had to work harder than ever. People started stealing, and even the illegal arrack [country liquor] sellers had no business.

"People believed it was God's anger for their sins. They made a big image of a man called *Kodumbavi* [the Great Sinner] and dragged it through the streets, kicking it, spitting on it, and finally burning it to ashes. They believed once the great sinner was no more, there would be rain. But is was no use.

"We had to provide work so people could buy food. The government had some projects but not enough. Action Aid and Oxfam gave us money, and we deepened wells, cleared streams, and built new village ponds to store water when the drought ended. We generated 18,000 man-days of labor, with men paid ten rupees a day and women eight rupees."

"EVERYONE WANTS HIS OWN PALACE"

In the process the Malarchi Trust spread to twenty-three villages with a staff of twenty. With government and foreign funding it established a nutrition supplement program for schoolchildren, a TB detection program, child and maternity care, and a small cooperative bakery. It also organized women's groups to press for such things as better drinking water or fixing village streets.

"In this area 15 to 20 percent of Dalit families do not earn even two thousand rupees [$140] a year," Prabhakaran said. "Fewer than 10 percent earn more than seven thousand rupees [$90]. There are so many government programs, but they don't reach the poor."

"Why do the match factories hire so many children?" I asked. "Is it because their margin of profit is low?"

"No, they can hire adults and pay the full minimum wage and still do very well," he replied. "But they're greedy and find it easy to buy politicians with money for elections. The owners, the officials, and the politicians are allies against the poor. Greed is everywhere: a belief that only if you have wealth and power can you be respected. Everyone wants his own palace. In the process they lose their humanity and their respect for honesty and truth. People live a double life. They pretend to be honest, but they're dishonest. They pretend to care for others, but they don't."

One evening we visited a literacy class for children of the match factories. They said thirty-five girls and five boys from thirty-three houses left home at seven in the morning and did not return until eight at night. They said many years ago, when they were little girls, they had to wake up at three in the morning and run to catch a bus five kilometers away, but now a company bus picked up and dropped off children from several villages at a point about a kilometer away.

The girls did the same job, making boxes and pasting labels, for which they were paid by the gross. An eighteen-year-old had worked at the same task for ten years and could make forty to forty-five gross boxes a day, earning twelve to thirteen and a half rupees. A seventeen-year-old girl had worked since she was five and had achieved the same rate of production. A fifteen-year-old, who had worked since she was seven, and a thirteen-year-old, who had also started at seven, produced thirty-five to forty gross of boxes a day, earning from ten and a half to twelve rupees. One said she had two sisters, who also worked in the match factory, and four brothers, two of whom were in primary school. The three sisters were the sole support of their family.

The girls said it was the custom of the match factories for children from certain villages to specialize in one type of work, so making match boxes was the only task they had learned. They said because of this specialization, they could sit with friends and talk about common interests.

They had been coming to the after-hours class for several years but had learned little. They said they could write their names and the names of family members, do simple arithmetic, and read labels on packages and movie posters.

"Will you get married?" I asked.

"Who can tell what we will do," one replied.

"But if you do, will you stop working?" I asked.

"I will stop until my child is old enough to walk in the street and then return to work."

"What happens if you get sick?" I asked another.

"We have to take care of ourselves," she replied. "Some factories have doctors but not ours. Even if a factory has a doctor, the girls have to pay for the treatment."

I asked a third girl if they kept any of their wages for themselves.

"Maybe five or ten rupees for hairpins or a glass of tea," she replied. "Two or three times a year, when the factories are closed during festivals, we go to the cinema."

"Don't you want to do anything else?" I asked.

"We went to the match factory when we were small children," she replied. "Now it is our life."

"They have pocket money and a false sense of confidence in themselves," Prabhakaran said as we left. "We have tried many ways to break the cycle. We are now experimenting with alternative education centers to teach both literacy and alternative skills. Children now go to school where the teaching style is monotonous, and they learn almost nothing. The teacher calls them lazy and idiots. She doesn't realize she can do something to stir the children.

"We have applied to the education ministry in New Delhi and a foreign agency in Belgium for funding for a pilot project involving 150 children. It will be costly: they can't attend unless we pay a small stipend and provide a midday meal. They will learn literacy and vocational subjects, but we also want games and sports, and we want to put on plays they'll write and act themselves.

"I want to revive the dying art of drums. Once Tamil Nadu was famous for its many kinds of drums: drums played with one hand, drums played with sticks on two sides, big drums and small drums. Our traditional culture is lost. Our people have their own ways of expression, but this is being suppressed. They sing commercial songs from the cinema. The man who writes the lyrics or the man acting in the film is doing that for money. But our own songs were not for money but for ourselves. People see things in the cinema and think only that is good: our own expressions are not to be admired or appreciated.

"Our plan is to recognize the talents of children. Acting—helping them come out of themselves and giving them pleasure and courage—doesn't need money. And educational concepts can be introduced through games and art forms: reading, writing, and doing sums can be taught in a pleasing way that brings out the best in children."

Mass Education

&INTRODUCTION: More than three hundred million young Indians are under the age of fifteen and ideally would be in school. But as the last reading indicated, many children work in factories or in other forms of hard labor employment.

The Indian Constitution promises free education to all youngsters, following the idea of universal education first introduced under the British in 1864. The belief in education as a vehicle of upward social mobility has grown in popularity ever since. In 1960, about fifty million students were attending schools; by 1990, there were double that number in more than 50,000 schools. Since 1960 the number of Indian students enrolled in secondary school has increased by 400 percent. The literacy rate in 1990 stood at 50 percent for school-aged children, although the rate varied greatly by region. For example, in the southern state of Kerala, 70 percent of women are literate, while in the northern state of Rajasthan less than 30 percent can read or write. The state of Kerala recently claimed that it had achieved 100 percent literacy.

Despite this impressive expansion of public education and the dramatic gains in literacy, India's educational achievements have fallen far short of the goals set in 1947. Like other aspects of development in India, the education glass can be seen as half full or half empty.

The following selection, consisting of two parts, focuses first on the problems of implementing mass compulsory education in the absence of adequate resources and then looks at what many consider the best hope for increasing literacy in India: adult, nonformal education.[15]&

Mrs. Bhatt is a well-known social activist in Ahmedabad and a member of Parliament. She is the founder and organizer of the Self-Employed Women's Association. SEWA has organized thousands of women and children, including workers in the bidi [cigarette] industry, garment makers, and ragpickers. Many of the women and children collect scrap and junk from middle-class families, such as bags, bottles, and rags, which they recycle for sale. About a third of the members, she said, are ex-untouchables, another third Muslims, and the remainder belong to lower castes. SEWA was initially affiliated with the Textile Labour Association, one of the powerful unions in Ahmedabad, but it was expelled when, according to Bhatt, she and the union split over the issue of employment reservations [or quotas] for Harijans ["I supported the Harijans"]. Ella Bhatt is regarded as the doyen of social activists in Ahmedabad. She has successfully brought together people in the unorganized sector, people not easily organized. She has created self-help projects and attracted attention and financial support from outside agencies. She is widely regarded as an articulate spokesperson for poor women.

"Our present education system is good for nothing," she said as we began our conversation on the small patio of her modest home in Ahmedabad. "The schools do not build character nor are they able to prepare the children for self-employment. Teachers should be sympathetic to children and teach them what is relevant. But what is the situation? The teaching is poor. Sometimes the teachers are not even present, especially in the farming season. For the development of the country, social values should be given to the children in school, and that is not done."

What social values?

"Work, discipline. Not to cut trees. Communal harmony. Equality. Bringing an end to untouchability.

"If I am a poor family," she continued, "but I am paid enough, then I will not want to send my child to work. I would send the child to school. If workers had more income child labor would decrease. But one point is left out. Schools do not prepare for careers. There are vendors whose sons have degrees, but their sons do not have jobs. The educational

system has educated them to become clerks. We think that if
we go to school we should have white-collar jobs. There is no
regard for manual labor in our educational system. So these
educated sons have become an anti-social element now.

"Our primary schools are worthless. The children do not
learn. I see children in the municipal schools up to fourth
standard and still they do not know how to write."

Why are the teachers unable to teach? I asked.

"That love for the children, that need to impart knowledge
is not there. The teachers do not care. Sometimes there is
rotten food in the lunch boxes the children bring to school
and the teachers do nothing! It makes me so sad. It is not
because teachers are badly paid. They get seven hundred to
eight hundred rupees a month and the pay scales have gone
up. The teachers are part of the lower middle class. They have
an SLC pass [School Leaving Certificate] plus a diploma in
teaching that they get after two years of study. Education is
well paid now and the teachers are organized—but they do
not teach. If we don't respect them it is because we see them
doing other business than teaching."

Why do the teachers lack motivation?

"I have visited many schools and spoken to many teachers.
The teachers say that parents do not cooperate. They say that
attendance is not regular and parents do not care. I ask them,
'Why don't you go to meet the parents?' But the teacher says
to me, 'It is not my job.' So I say, 'Send a note to ask the
parent to come.' And she says to me that the child will not
take the note, or if the child does, then the parents do not
know how to read. And she tells me that the parents do not
see that their children do homework. I hear teachers say that
the parents are from the lower castes and that the children
'have no mind.'

"The teachers do not do anything outside the classroom.
The schools are like the medical system. Medicine here is
clinically based. Doctors think people should come to the clinic.
Teachers think parents should come to the classroom. They say
they have no responsibility to go to see the parent. No doubt

there are exceptions among the teachers—and among the doctors—but I am speaking of the general situation."

Are teachers from the lower castes better with the child-ren?

"No, they are not sympathetic. When low-caste children are educated in the private schools, they want to become babus [clerks]. They don't want to look back. They don't want to work with people in their own community. There are a few educated lower-caste graduates who are voicing some protest, but most do not care." . . .

Even if the schools are as bad as you say they are, I asked, wouldn't it be better if the children went to school rather than started to work at such early ages?

"These are precious years for learning their trade," she replied, "and these preparatory years would be gone if they went to school. The poor children who go to school will not complete their education, and they will not get a degree. Most probably they will drop out of school and not go to college. So if they go to school then they are suited for nothing."

Ella Bhatt's criticism that the elementary schools have failed because they do not prepare children to work reflects the sentiments of Mahatma Gandhi in articles he wrote in the 1930s on what he called "Basic Education.". . .

INDIA'S LITERACY MIRACLE

Squatting on the ground in her faded sari, a piece of paper before her, Shakuntala clenches a pencil in her chapped and overworked hand. She begins to draw squiggles. It is Malaysian, the script of Kerala State in southern India, where she lives. "We need plumbing so that we will not get sick anymore," writes Shakuntala. It is the first petition of her life, and it is addressed to the district chief.

Shakuntala is in her mid-40s. She works as a day laborer on a plantation. She has never attended school. A year ago she could neither read nor write. Now she can, even though she makes many mistakes. For the first time in her life she worked her way through a newspaper. "I did not know how big the world was," she says. "Much bigger than on television."

These children in a village classroom are part of the 100 million students enrolled in schools throughout India. (Donald Johnson)

Shakuntala took part in a program that demonstrated that miracles are possible. In just one year, the inhabitants of an entire district in India (more than 200,000 people—all between ages five and 65) learned to read and write. The town of Ernakulam in Kerala became the only place in the Third World with a literacy rate of 100 percent.

The initiators of the *Sakasharata Yagnam,* or literacy campaign, seek to demonstrate that illiteracy in the Third World can be overcome. Above all, the people of Ernakulam have shown that learning to read and write is not simply a matter of spending money, a frequent claim whenever new data on rising illiteracy come out, as they did at the United Nations Educational, Scientific and Cultural Organization (UNESCO) conference in Thailand at which 1990 was proclaimed the year of world literacy.

UNESCO's ambitious goal of teaching 1 billion illiterates around the world to read and write by the year 2000 has been set in motion. In India alone, 64 percent of the population is unable to read or write. It is no consolation to this proud nation, with its great cultural heritage, that four countries in Asia have even worse statistics: Pakistan, Nepal, Bangladesh, and Afghanistan. But India lags far behind China, Indonesia, Sri Lanka, and even Burma.

Women are the greatest victims. In the Third World, 48.9 percent of them can neither read nor write. Among men, the figure is 27.9 percent. The illiteracy figures for India are 71.1 percent of the women and 42.8 percent of the men. "If more women went to school in our country, we would have 600 million people instead of 850 million," says Sam Pitroda, who heads the national literacy program. As the level of education of Third World women rises, the child mortality rate and the birthrate decline.

"Every developmental directive is closely tied to reading and writing," Pitroda says. "Why doesn't development fare well in the countryside? Because that is where the majority of the illiterates are. Why doesn't family planning work? Because the women cannot read or write."

"Each one teach one" is the new slogan of the literacy campaign. To the chagrin of some bureaucrats, Pitroda found that nationally sponsored programs did not catch on. "We have some 4 million students at our universities and about 1.6 million pupils in classes from the ninth to the twelfth grade. If each of them teaches just one person to read and write in the course of the year, it is a beginning."

That campaign is already in progress in many parts of the country, including New Delhi. Neeraj Bali, a ninth grader who is studying with a 28-year-old laundry worker, sometimes finds it difficult to give up free time, but he believes that "it is a national disgrace for people to have to sign with their thumb print."

The government in New Delhi thinks that it will take two years to reach a minimal level of literacy, despite the great willingness to learn and the industriousness of India's illiterate people. There is the fear that many might drop out. That is why people are saying, "Be quick and rigorous." This is perhaps more plausible in Kerala than elsewhere, because of Kerala's traditions.

The people of Kerala elected a communist government in 1957. They are proud of their progressive social politics, their agrarian reform, and their health system, which is the envy of the other Indian states. The life-expectancy in Kerala of 76 years is the highest in India, as is the literacy rate of 71 percent.

The miracle of writing began in Kottayam, a town of 70,000 in Kerala, located amid tea and coffee plantations. It boasts a dozen high schools, four colleges, and one full-fledged university. Its literacy rate was 86 percent two years ago, a national record. Still, there were 2,029 illiterates—but they were taught to read and write in just 100 days by 1,024 volunteers.

Volunteers repeated the example of Kottayam in Ernakulam in an enormous campaign that involved house visits, street theater, songs, marches, and educational lectures. In Kerala, people believe that there could soon be many more Shakuntalas if only the right starting point is found.

Toward a Billion Indians

᷷INTRODUCTION: Despite India's impressive gains in agriculture and industry, more than 300 million Indians live under the poverty line, only 36 percent can read and write, and the average Indian earns less than $300 a year. The challenges of economic development are staggering, and they are made even more difficult by rapid population growth. If India's population continues to increase at its present rate, the economy will have to grow faster and faster just to stand still. The following selection examines the dynamics of India's population growth and the attempts to control it.[16]᷷

There are two radically different and often competing perspectives on the population problem in India: the national, or macro-level, perspective and the personal, micro-level perspective; the big picture and the small picture, so to speak. From the macro level, India's population seems like a juggernaut moving ahead inexorably and destructively. In 1947, at the time of independence, India had a population of 360 million. By 1999, India's population stood at 987 million, a 627 million increase since independence. India's population, second only to China's (1999: 1,254 million), is projected to reach one billion by 2000.

Each year India adds almost eighteen million to its population, the equivalent of the total population of Australia. In four years, it adds the equivalent of the population of France, and in ten years the equivalent of all of Western Europe. If India continues to grow at this rate, in eighty-five years it will have as many people as the whole world has today, 5.3 billion.

POPULATION
(IN MILLIONS)

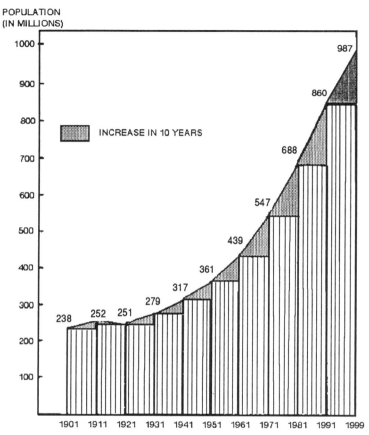

Figure 1: This graph illustrates the effects of India's recent growth rates. Notice how it parallels Figure 2.

No poor country can hope to produce schools, housing, medical care, food and employment for that many new people, especially if the goal is to improve the standard of living rather than just maintain it. At India's current population growth rate, just to provide basic education will require opening 150 new primary schools every day of the year. (At present, only sixty are opened.) It has been estimated that every baby born will cost the country at least $1,000 in social services. In short, from the macro perspective, children are economic liabilities. As one Indian magazine put it, "The self-sufficiency attained in foodgrain production is being eaten away rapidly. The pace of population growth also means generating more jobs, more houses, and more hospitals if the majority has to cross the *Garibi Rekha*—the poverty line."

THE MICRO PERSPECTIVE

From the micro perspective, however, children are economic assets. They help with housework, farm work, and provide old-age support for their parents. They are the only source of security in a world fraught with uncertainty. In the rural areas, children—especially boys—can begin working as day laborers as young as seven or eight, earning very little but more than it costs to support them. The hope of every landless peasant is to save enough money— much of it from the labor of the children—to buy a piece of land of his own. "It is the large families that get ahead,"a farmer in Karnataka said, implying that this system works. Children are also used—and misused— as workers in industry.[17]

At the micro level—from the point of view of poor parents—it is rational to have large families. Children may not guarantee a better future, but without them there is no hope. When confronted with the macro-level argument that more children means more competition for scarce jobs, more sub-dividing of land into smaller and smaller holdings, the Karnataka farmer answered: "Perhaps that is true but my sons are the ones who will get the jobs. They are more able than others; they work harder." All parents harbor such optimism for their own children, but in reality most of these Indian children will never own land, the majority will not finish primary school, and all of them will live in a country that will find it increasingly difficult to provide social services to them because of their numbers.

What can be done? One answer is to put the "good life" within the reach or at least within the aspirations of the average person. If parents can hope to provide medical and dental care for their children; if they can hope to buy them decent clothes and even toys and sports equipment, then they will not only want to provide these things. They will also realize that the more children they have the less likely it will be to provide them. Therefore, smaller families are desirable. Children under these conditions are no longer economic assets, they are liabilities.

It is precisely this calculus that has led parents in industrialized countries to opt for small families. As the saying goes, "The best contraceptive is middle-class status." But as long as India's population continues to grow at its present rate, the chances of leading hundreds of millions of people into the middle class remain slim. The Indian government realizes it cannot wait for economic development to solve its population problem, since population growth itself is one of the major drags on economic progress. Thus India has attempted to limit fertility through family planning as a means of slowing population growth and boosting economic development.

THE FAMILY PLANNING PROGRAM

Since 1951, when India became the first nation in the world to launch a family planning program, the Indian government has conducted a vigorous propaganda campaign to promote the small-family ideal. It has used every means of com- munication at its disposal: newspapers, radio, television, billboards, drama and dance performances, puppet shows, traveling clinics, and village family-planning centers. It has also made a variety of contraceptive techniques available, including sterilization and abortion. "We offer them the cafeteria approach—take what suits you best," according to Dr. S. Chandrasekhar, former Indian minister of Health and Family Planning. "A newly married man may prefer a condom. After a few years, the wife may agree to have a loop [an intrauterine device, or IUD]. Once they've had their quota of children, one or the other of them may go for a vasectomy or tubectomy [male and female sterilization operations.]"

To encourage men to have vasectomies, the government offers cash incentives and compensation for lost wages, in addition to the free operation itself. To see how the system worked, a well-known Indian writer, Dom Moraes, toured

Motivational messages—on billboards, in newspapers and on buses—are an important part of the Indian family planning program. (Embassy of India, Washington, D.C.)

India on assignment for the United Nations.

He visited Dr. D. Pai, a Bombay physician known for his energy and imaginative ways of reaching out to the people with medical care and family planning services. He once commandeered twenty buses, took out the seats, recruited a team of medical interns and vaccinated more that one million people in seventeen days. Dr. Pai observed at that time, "People don't come to you; you have to seek them out. I did that, and I beat the epidemic. So I got the name of a troubleshooter."

The Indian government then asked Dr. Pai if he would turn his attention to family planning. Dom Moraes tells the story this way: "They said to me, 'Pai, we want you to insert 100,000 loops,' as though all I had to do was lift 100,000 skirts and push them in." Dr. Pai roared with laughter. "Anyway, I organized a big exhibition on family planning. The idea was that people should become aware of what it was. Do you know where those fools mounted the exhibition? In the city museum. In fifteen days less than 2,000 people went there. So I thought, where to put this damn thing so that people will see it? It must be in an area where crowds collect. But which are the places in the city where the largest crowds collect? The answer came to me in a flash: the railway stations."

The suburban trains in Bombay, at rush hours, are packed with commuters—packed so densely that many passengers, unable to crush their way into a compartment, hang like dark fruit from the door frames and windows. Every week some fall off and are killed, but this does not act as a deterrent. The congestion and cost of the city has driven people out to the farther suburbs, and some commuters live as much as forty miles from their work. At the main railway stations, Pai was thus assured of an inexhaustible supply of potential converts. He started at Churchgate station, where one of the main suburban lines discharges thousands of commuters daily into the city.

He swished the red tape to one side, browbeat the station master into acceptance, and took over an ice cream stall, where he set up his exhibition. The exhibition was staffed by his interns, who acted as motivators. Every day thousands of people who were awaiting a train or had recently descended from one visited the stall in order to kill time. The interns tried to convince the men who already had three or four children to visit a hospital for a vasectomy. This was not very successful, at first, until Pai found out why. He talked one day to a mill worker with four children, told him that the vasectomy was simple and painless, and advised him to have the operation.

"I told him to report to the hospital the next day. He said he would and walked off. Suddenly, I had the feeling he would not come. So I called him back and said, 'Swear on your children that you will come.' He would not swear. He said, 'Sir, when a government officer asks an ordinary man like me to do something, it's best if you seem to agree. But if this operation is as simple and painless as you say, why do I have to have it in a hospital? A hospital is a place you leave feet first.' With that I suddenly knew what I must do. I told him, 'Come back to the station tomorrow. I will do the operation here, and in a few minutes you will be able to walk away.'"

The mill hand came back the next day. Pai put up screens and vasectomized him. "After that I obtained small rooms in several stations as clinics. The motivators move around on the platforms and outside the station and bring people in. The doctor does the operation in a few minutes. It is beautiful to watch. So economical, so clean. One nick, and it's done! Now we do vasectomies in several railway stations. We also do them in our mobile vans. And of course I recruited the leaders of various slum areas. The people are afraid of the leaders and do as they advise. To organize all this in the slums, man, I have risked a knife in my back time after time."

All over India, cash incentives are offered to those who are vasectomized. The sums vary from about sixty rupees in the north to twenty-three rupees in Bombay. Some industrial concerns pay additional sums of up to two hundred rupees to any of their workers who volunteers for vasectomy. The government emphasizes that this is not a bribe.

The sum paid is intended, it says, as compensation for any workdays the volunteer may lose. However, the motivator who brings a man in to be vasectomized also receives payment per head: ten rupees per man in Bombay. Quite obviously, the motivators want to produce as many men as possible. The system has been under heavy critical fire since it started.

The motivators have been accused of bringing in illiterate men who do not fully understand what is being done to them, of bringing in unmarried men and men who are virtually senile, of bringing in men who have been vasectomized and men who have been coerced in some way. Some of these accusations are probably true. "But there is no time," said Pai very seriously, when I brought the matter up. "There is really no time. Such a huge problem and so little time. I think we should now have compulsory sterilization after three children, but others disagree. It may still come to that. But so far as possible, we try and check on the patient when he comes."[18]

India has always held fast to its voluntary approach to family planning. As a democracy, it has never tried to legislate family size or impose sanctions on large families. But during the State of Emergency in 1975-77, when many civil rights were suspended, Prime Minister Indira Gandhi's son, Sanjay, led a major sterilization campaign that brought renewed and vociferous charges of deception and coercion.

When Mrs. Gandhi was defeated in 1977, not only was the sterilization campaign halted but family planning in general suffered a loss of popular support.

Since 1977 the Indian government has attempted to purge all compulsion, or appearances of compulsion, from the family planning program and to rehabilitate its image by tying it to family welfare. Besides changing the name of the Ministry of Health and Family Planning to the Ministry of Health and Family Welfare, the government has integrated family planning efforts into programs in health, nutrition, education, and especially mother and child care and women's development programs.

Financial incentives are still offered for sterilization and IUD insertions, but the incentive program has been expanded to include free insurance to those who limit or space child-bearing and social security to aged couples with only one daughter and no sons. According to a United Nations report, "The revamped family welfare campaign is based on five main principles: families should be limited to two children; the law that bars marriage for girls under age 18 should be enforced; families should not continually produce children until a son is born; all infants should be immunized in their first year; and births should be spaced at intervals of three years."[19]

How successful has India's family planning program been? The short answer is, more successful than the skeptics predicted but less successful that the optimists hoped. In 1985, the Indian government set the goal of establishing the two-child family as the norm by the year 2000. The average family size in 1999 was 3.4 children, making it extremely un-likely that the two-child target will be reached by 2000. How-ever, as the graph below indicates, progress has been made. The birth rate has declined gradually between 1971 and 1999

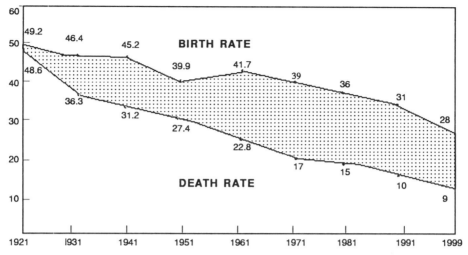

Figure 2: This graph shows the number of births and deaths each year for every 1,000 people in the Indian population. The U.S. birth rate in 1999 was fifteen, the death rate was nine.

and the growth rate has begun to slow down as well, despite the continuing drop in the death rate. (The growth rate, by natural increase, is calculated by subtracting the death rate from the birth rate and dividing that number by ten to get a percent rate. Thus, in 1999 the Indian birth rate of twenty-eight minus a death rate of nine equals nineteen, or a 1.9 percent annual growth in the population).

It should be pointed out that India's growth rate of 1.9 percent is high but not extremely high by world standards. Many Third World nations have growth rates above 2.5 percent, with the highest about 4 percent. But the size of India's population ensures that a large number of people will be added to its population each year even if its growth rate is modest. (In 1999, the U.S. birth rate was fifteen and its death rate nine.)

Another target set by the government called for a death rate of 10.4 and an infant mortality rate of eighty-seven per 1,000 live births by 1990. As the graph above shows, India has achieved its target death rate and, with an infant mortality rate of seventy-two per 1,000 in 1999, it has hit that target as well. The hope and prediction of family planning professionals is that parents will have fewer children if they perceive that those children who are born will survive. In the short term, however, keeping infants alive has the effect of increasing population size. Nevertheless, the lowering of the death rate must be seen as a significant health achievement, independent of population considerations.

Most experts agree that India will not reach its goal of reducing its population growth rate to 1.1 percent a year by 2001. That would require lowering the birth rate from thirty-one to twenty-one in ten years, more than double the drop in any previous decade. It would require increasing the percentage of couples using effective contraception from the 1990 level of 40 percent to 60 percent. Some observers feel there is not sufficient political commitment to achieve such goals. As *India Today* magazine observed:

> "Talking about family planning is like singing the requiem at a wedding party," says an MP [Member of Parliament]. Ever since the Sanjay overkill and its disastrous impact, politicians have been shying away from the subject. The dismal population scenario is largely a result of a lack of political commitment.
>
> Much of the problem is as another MP, who doesn't want to be named, explains: "If we provide a [water] tap or health centre, I could win votes. But if people themselves don't want to adopt family planning and I force them, then I'm finished."[20]

Providing people with things they do need may in fact be part of the answer. In the South Indian State of Kerala, the birth rate in 1988 was only 20.3, already below the national target level of twenty-one set for the year 2001. In 1989, Kerala's birth rate dropped to 19.8. The general explanation for this low rate is the high literacy and education levels of women in Kerala, along with good health facilities and women marrying late. (Women tend to marry later when they stay in school and when they have career aspirations.) Emphasizing education, especially among women, seems to have an independent effect on fertility and it may also make couples more receptive to family planning programs. Most important of all, it may have the effect of bringing micro-level perceptions in line with macro-level ones.

India's ultimate goal is to reach zero population growth by the year 2050 with a population of 1.3 billion. Whether that goal is reached or not, Indians will represent one in every five persons in the world by that year.

Dam Development

⁊►INTRODUCTION: Among the centerpieces for the Nehru style of development were gigantic hydro projects planned to dam India's major river systems, which would then provide millions of farmers with much needed irrigation as well as electrical power for industry. The Bakra-Nagal project in North India, built during the 1950s, was at the time one of the largest such hydro-electric projects in the world. Other such projects along the Kauvri in South India have brought both lifegiving water and electrification to millions of rural farmers. At one time, there was much discussion among planners of building the world's largest river project by linking the Ganges of the North with the river systems of the South.

These major river projects have always caused great controversy. Although undoubtedly adding greatly to industrial growth and generating many new jobs, the great river projects also displace thousands of small land holders and often disrupt the delicate balances of agricultural villages. Many villages inevitably disappear in such ventures.

One of the most controversial river projects in modern Indian history is the planned Narmada Dam project situated largely in the state of Gujarat, but running through several states across Central India. In large areas where the project will be constructed, many tribals, some of the poorest people in India, will be displaced. The Narmada project has a long history. The idea was first suggested by Sardar Patel, the first deputy prime minister of India and a loyal member of one of Gujarat's largest and most influential communities. He convinced Nehru of the value of the project and the prime minister blessed the undertaking by laying the foundation stone just two years before he died. The Narmada project was to be completed in the 1990s, but fierce opposition to the development gained strength until, by 1991, open violence over Narmada was a real possibility.

The following reading offers the arguments from both sides of the issue and provides first-hand testimony from two of the major leaders of the two sides.[21]⁊

In the sleepy hamlet of Ferkuva on the Gujarat-Madhya Pradesh border, the ingredients of an epic battle are brewing. Ranged on one side are thousands of tribals and environmental activists led by the formidable Baba Amte. Facing them is a human wall of Gujaratis and social workers determined to block their entry into Gujarat. The *casus belli* is the Narmada Dam project. And the mood in the warring camps is swinging between outright hostility and uneasy stalemate.

One side is determined that the Sardar Sarovar Project (SSP) on river Narmada in Bharuch district will go ahead. The other, spearheaded by Baba Amte, is determined to halt the Rs 6,400-crore [one crore = ten million] project—one of the biggest enterprises ever undertaken in India since Independence.

Armed with tractor-trollies full of food supplies, the Sangharsh Yatris began their march from Barwani in Madhya Pradesh on Christmas day and travelled through the Narmada Valley before arriving at the Gujarat border, where the pro-dam legions stood massed on the other side.

The rallying cries of the two opposing groups make their aims clear. Medha Patkar, who has almost single-handedly mobilised the tribals in the Narmada Valley against the project declares: "The project is socially unjustifiable, ecologically unsustainable and economically unviable."

Retaliates a pro-dam worker, equally vehemently: "They are espousing the cause of the displaced persons alone. But we are fighting for the lakhs [100,000] of drought-affected and flood-affected people in Gujarat. The dam is the only way to end the miseries of these people. It is Gujarat's lifeline."

Each side has been bent on showing the size of its infantry. As the anti-dam crowd began trudging its way to the border, the pro-dam organisations staged a massive rally on December 29 with the active support of Chief Minister Chimanbhai Patel and the Minister for Narmada Development, Babubhai Patel.

Ferkuva was swamped by the 80,000 people who rallied to the "save the dam" cry. Chimanbhai told the cheering crowd: "I want the Baba to know that the people of Gujarat and their government are united. Their resolve is as firm to-day as it was during the lifetime of the Mahatma and the Sardar."

The historical allusions reveal the messy background to the *cause celebré*. First conceived in 1946 by Sardar Vallabhbhai Patel, the foundation-stone was laid by Pandit Jawaharlal Nehru in the early '60s. Controversy dogged the project from day one and has lasted decades: from the height of the dam to which state would be responsible for the farmers and tribals displaced by its creation.

So it's an issue that people in the area have grown up with and have fixed opinions on. The war of words between the two camps on the border became shriller on New Year's day when the pro-Narmada ranks moved closer to the spot where the anti-Narmada ranks were camped. Loudspeakers—or just sheer lung power—blared out angry slogans across the divide. Chunibhai Vaidya, from the pro-dam side, made an incursion into enemy territory to announce that it was unthinkable that the Government might review the project.

At the heart of the whole dispute is the fate of the people—mainly tribals—who will be displaced. Baba Amte says that he is opposed in principle to all government projects of this size. And he intends to return the Padmashri and Padma Vibhushan [government honors] which he was awarded for his social work as a protest against the way the Patel Ministry has treated his anti-dam followers.

The main complaint of the anti-dam organisations is that it will be impossible to rehabilitate all the people who will be displaced. In the Nimad region of Madhya Pradesh—where the agitation has snowballed—nearly one lakh people, mainly Adivasis, will be displaced.

Second, they say the project will be a financial disaster. Costs are likely to escalate to a dizzying Rs 11,000 crore. And thirdly, the dam waters will cover only 10 percent of the drought-affected regions.

Their agitation intends to focus on the following:

- mobilising the people who will be displaced;
- putting pressure on the Environment Ministry to withdraw its approval;
- persuading the World Bank to stop aid to the project through Japan, the World Bank's second biggest donor.

The campaign has already led to one World Bank expert speaking out against the project and calling for aid to be suspended "until the Gujarat Government corrects the various deficiencies which exist with regard to the displaced people."

On the other side of the fence are the supporters of the dam who are enraged by the obstacles they feel are being put in the way of Gujarat's development. Their memories are permanently scarred by the tragedy of the three-year-long drought, which ravaged the state in 1984-87. Rs 1,500 crore had to be spent on relief operations; Rs 5,000 crore worth of agricultural production was lost; and several lakh of cattle died like flies and deprived farmers and landless labourers in the state of their livelihood.

The poor, as always, bore the brunt of the devastation. Says Chunibhai Vaidya, a prominent pro-dam activist: "The people and government of Gujarat are united on this issue. The reports that only rich farmers and industrialists will benefit from the dam being built are akin to the propaganda put out by Goebbels."

The pro-dam camp contains quite a few social workers who initially opposed the project tooth and nail. Prominent campaigners such as Anil Patel changed their minds when the former government of Amarsinh Chaudhary announced a fresh rehabilitation package for displaced people in 1987. Now Anil Patel says: "The package is the most generous we can expect. If those fighting for the tribals really want to help them, they should help the Government implement the rehabilitation programme."

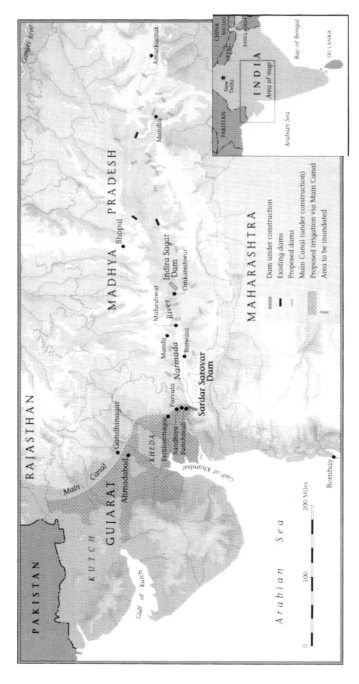

From Amarkantak (far right) the Narmanda flows west 800 miles to the Gulf of Khambat. The Sardar Sarovar dam is creating a huge reservoir to generate electricity and supply water for irrigation. (Copyright © Bowring Cartographic)

The anti-dam activists say they are prepared to talk to the state Government provided it halts construction of the river bed. This is unlikely even to be considered. Work on the project—awe-inspired in its scale—is hurtling along at breakneck speed. Each statistic connected with the dam is very impressive. An average of 5,600 cubic metres of construction work is carried out every day. And this is likely to go up to 7,000 cubic metres. A giant cable trolley costing Rs 22 crore was recently installed to speed up the work. The towers of the trolley are 110 metres high, taller than the Qutab Minar.

Labourers and engineers work in three shifts 24 hours a day. Each shift has 800 workers. At night, flood lights are used. Over 200 trucks work round-the-clock carrying cement and gravel. Every day the project swallows up about Rs 1 crore.

Projects of this scale develop a momentum of their own. This one is already so far underway, that it's hard to imagine its opponents will succeed in calling it off. With the Government's resolve to go ahead, and large sections of public opinion backing it, the dam's opponents will find the going tough. So the stage in the hamlet of Ferkuva is set for the battle and the cast of thousands is ready, but the only thing really moving in the conflict is the police, scurrying between the two sides to ensure the stalemate doesn't escalate to all-out war.

BABA AMTE: "I'M READY TO DIE"

Baba Amte, 70, spoke to Senior Correspondent Uday Mahurkar last fortnight about his determination to oppose the project. Excerpts:

Q. What made you take up cudgels against the SSP?

A. I am basically against all big dams as they are symbols of development that enrich some at the cost of others. I am for development with a human face.

Q. Gujaratis charge you with brainwashing the Adivasis [untouchables] and pitting them against the other.

A. The allegation is unfounded. I would rather die than see such a confrontation. I am trying to remove the feeling of alienation amongst the Adivasis. During my Bharat Jodo Yatra [Pilgrimage for Indian Unity] I found they feel more alienated than even the Sikhs.

Q. Will you win this battle?

A. Our struggle has already passed a death warrant against all such giant projects in future. The people who are going to be displaced by the SSP are determined to fight till the end.

Q. What if the Government goes ahead with the construction work?

A. The fight will go on. I am prepared to die for this cause. And my death will achieve what my life couldn't. I will organise drown-and-die squads of the oustees who will take a pledge to drown themselves in the Narmada.

Q. Isn't a solution possible?

A. Every national problem has a national solution. We want a dialogue on the project's review. But first the cutting of trees in the forest must stop. So should the shifting of oustees and the construction work.

Q. What is Gujarat's stand?

A. They are willing to talk only on the rehabilitation issue.

Q. You have alleged that there has been large-scale corruption in the SSP's construction work.

A. All building contractors fill the coffers of political parties. We want the authorities to investigate the assets of the owners of Jaiprakash Associates, the dam constructors.

Q. Is it practical for you to call for a halt on the project with Rs 1,000 crore has already been spent on it?

A. Going by the fact that its cost would escalate to over Rs 11,000 crore by the time it is completed, it is only 1 per cent [sic] of the total amount. It is a small price to pay for an issue that concerns thousands of people.

BABUBHAI JASHBHAI PATEL: "THEY HAVE CLOSED MINDS"

One of the strongest supporters of the Sardar Sarovar Project, Babubhai Jashbhai Patel, 80, after taking over as minister for Narmada development, sped up the pace of work on the project. Last fortnight he spoke to Uday Mahurkar. Excerpts:

Q. Is an agreement with the anti-dam activists possible?

A. Yes, if the demand is limited to the question of oustees. Lowering the dam's height by even an inch will prevent adequate water supply to the arid zone of the project area.

Q. Activists claim there isn't enough land for rehabilitation.

A. Five acres of land is being given even to the landless amongst the oustees. We have enough land to rehabilitate all.

Q. Activists also allege that just 10 per cent of the drought-prone areas of Gujarat will be covered.

A. Of the total 19 lakh hectares to be irrigated, 13 lakh is in these areas and Rajasthan. Of the 4,720 villages, which are to get drinking water, 2,568 are in Gujarat.

Q. What if the people of Madhya Pradesh and Maharashtra refuse to leave?

A. That is a hypothetical question. Still, our rehabilitation package is so attractive that they will be tempted to accept it.

Q. Is it true that the clearance granted by the Ministry of Environment to the SSP in 1987 was conditional?

A. This is untrue. The only condition put by the Ministry of Environment was that the environmental safeguard measures are planned and implemented *pari passu* with the progress of work on the project. And we are fully abiding by it.

Q. Why have the activists and Baba Amte taken such a hard line?

A. They have a closed mind. But to be fair to them, their apprehensions are mainly based on the poor record on the rehabilitation front.

Q. What is the way out of this stalemate?

A. All of Gujarat is one on the dam issue. The activists are concerned about the problems of one lakh oustees alone. But we are concerned about millions of people pining for water and the 7.5 million people—mostly Adivasis—affected by floods in the Narmada. The only way out is that they stop brainwashing the illiterate and help us rehabilitate them.

The Bhopal Tragedy

🙢INTRODUCTION: The argument over foreign participation in the Indian economy has raged since independence. Should India, like Thailand, throw itself open to multinational corporations so that jobs and capital would immediately flow into the country? Or should, as Nehru argued, India control its own economic destiny and become self-sufficient, even if that decision meant slower growth? From the perspective of the Western industrialized nations, investing in Third World nations means good economic sense. Production costs, particularly labor costs, are much cheaper in Third World countries and safety and other government- imposed regulations tend to be far less strict.

India's policy on foreign investment was, until recently, to insist that India control 51 percent of the enterprise, thus making all foreign companies subject to government regulation. One of the major exceptions to this rule, and one of the most successful American joint ventures in India, was Union Carbide. The multinational company first established itself in India to produce batteries, and later, with the onset of the Green Revolution, began to produce pesticides. By 1984, seven years after Union Carbide's largest pesticide plant was opened in Bhopal in Central India, the factory was producing 2,500 tons of pesticides annually.

However, this success story took a tragic turn on December 2, 1984, when poisonous gas began leaking from the Bhopal plant.

The sleeping city of Bhopal was totally unprepared for the events that followed the first gas leak. By the next morning, much of the world learned of one of the worst industrial accidents in history. Within hours of the explosion at Bhopal, which released forty tons of toxic gas, some 3,000 people lay dead. Hundreds of thousands more were dying or seriously injured and countless more would not realize the consequences of their exposure to the deadly wind until years after

324

the tragedy. Although the official government estimate of the total casualties was about 2,000 people, Alfred de Grazia in *A Cloud Over Bhopal* suggests that 3,000 were killed, 10,000 seriously disabled, 20,000 significantly disabled, and 180,000 affected in some way by the poison. To complicate the relief efforts, doctors could not find out what kind of gas had leaked, and thus were handicapped in providing adequate treatment.[22]

As the Bhopal tragedy developed, so too did the debate over the merits of foreign investment and the relationship between the industrial and Third World nations. It is estimated that as much as 80 percent of the population of Bhopal were severely affected by the gas leak. The following accounts of the accident are taken from a collection of interviews with people who actually experienced the mass destruction of human life.[23]

BANO BI, AGE 35

THE NIGHT THE gas leaked, I was sewing clothes sitting next to the door. It was around midnight. The children's father had just returned from a poetry concert. He came in and asked me, "what are you burning that makes me choke?" And then it became quite unbearable. The children sleeping inside began to cough. I spread a mat outside and made the children sit on it. Outside we started coughing even more violently and became breathless. Then our landlord and my husband went out to see what was happening. They found out that some gas had leaked. Outside there were people shouting, "Run, run, run for your lives."

We left our door open and began to run. We reached the Bharat Talkies crossing, where my husband jumped into a truck full of people going to Raisen and I jumped into one going towards Obaidullahganj. It was early morning when we reached Obaidullahganj. The calls for the morning prayers were on. As we got down, there were people asking us to get medicines put on our eyes and to get injections. Some people came and said they had made tea for us and we could have tea and need not pay any money.

Meanwhile, some doctors came there. They said the people who are seriously ill had to be taken to the hospital. Two doctors came to me and said that I had to be taken to the hospital. I told my children to come with me to the hospital and bade them to stay at the hospital gate till I came out of the hospital. I was kept inside for a long time and the children were getting worried. Then Bhairon Singh, a Hindu who used to work with my husband, spotted the children. He too had run away with his family and had come to the hospital for treatment. The children told him that I was in the hospital since morning and described to him the kind of clothes I was wearing.

Bhairon Singh went in to the hospital and found me among the piles of the dead. He then put me on a bench and ran around to get me oxygen. The doctors would put the oxygen mask on me for two minutes and then pass it on to someone else who was in as much agony as I was. The oxygen made me feel a little better. The children were crying for their father so Bhairon told them that he was admitted to a hospital in Raisen. When I was being brought back to Bhopal on a truck, we heard people saying that the gas tank has burst again. So we came back and went beyond Obaidullahganj to Budhni, where I was in the hospital for three days.

I did not have even a five paisa coin on me. Bhairon Singh spent his money on our food. He even hired a taxi to take me back to Bhopal to my brother's place. My husband also had come back by then. He was in a terrible condition. His body would get stiff and he had difficulty in breathing. At times, we could give up hopes of his survival. My brother took him to a hospital. I said that I would stay at the hospital to look after my husband. I still had a bandage over my eyes. When the doctors at the hospital saw me, they said "why don't you get admitted yourself, you are in such a bad state." I told them that I was alright. I was so absorbed with the sufferings of my children and my husband that I wasn't aware of my own condition. But the doctors got me admitted and since there were no empty beds, I shared the same bed with my husband in the hospital. We were in that hospital for one and a half months.

After coming back from the hospital, my husband was in such a state that he would rarely stay at home for more than two days. He used to be in the Jawahar Lal Nehru Hospital most of the time. Apart from all the medicines that he used to take at the hospital, he got medicines like Deriphylline and Decadron from the store. He remained in that condition after the gas disaster. I used to take him to the hospital and when I went for the Sangathan [organization] meetings, the children took him to the hospital. He was later admitted to the MIC [the chemical, methyl iso-cyanate] ward and he never came back from there. He died in the MIC ward.

My husband used to carry sacks of grain at the warehouse. He used to load and unload railway wagons. After the gas, he could not do any work. Sometimes, his friends used to take him with them and he used to just sit there. His friends gave him 5-10 rupees and we survived on that.

We were in a helpless situation. I had no job and the children were too young to work. We survived on help from our neighbors and other people in the community. My husband had severe breathing problems and he used to get into bouts of coughing. When he became weak, he had fever all the time. He was always treated for gas related problems. He was never treated for tuberculosis. And yet, in this post-mortem report, they mentioned that he died due to tuberculosis. He was medically examined for compensation but they never told us in which category he was put. And now they tell me that his death was not due to gas exposure, that I can not get the relief of Rs. 10,000 which is given to the relatives of the dead.

I have pain in my chest and I get breathless when I walk. The doctors told me that I need to be operated on for ulcers in my stomach. They told me it would cost Rs. 10,000. I do not have so much money. All the jewellry that I had has been sold. I have not paid the landlord for the last six years and he harasses me. How can I go for the operation? Also, I am afraid that if I die during the operation, there would be no one to look after my children.

I believe that even if we have to starve, we must get the guilty officials of Union Carbide punished. They have killed someone's brother, someone's husband, someone's mother, someone's sister- how many tears can Union Carbide wipe? We will get Union Carbide punished. Till my last breath, I will not leave them [be].

[Shahazadi Bahar, below, reflects on her experiences and how she became an active member in the Bhopal Gas Peedit Mahila Udyog Sangathan, or Bhopal Gas Affected Women Workers Organization, formed to help rehabilitate victims.]

SHAHAZADI BAHAR, AGE 35

. . . The world is very selfish. I, too, joined the Sangathan with some selfish motive. I thought I could get some sewing job through the Sangathan. But though I have not been benefitted, there are others who have. Quite a few people have got monetary relief of Rs 1000, Rs 3000 and Rs 750 per month. And now the provision of interim relief of Rs 200 per month per person is a big victory for the Sangathan. This has brought in a new hope and a new determination. We are certain that we will win this battle.

The Bhopal victims are entitled to compensation. We need hospitals, medicines, jobs, clean air and water. We have to have medical treatment centers in the community itself. The bigger things are, the more they create problems. Hamidia hospital is so big but we can not get treatment there, only those with money are treated properly. We need jobs that do not need hard physical work. I get breathless when I walk and can not see properly. Two of my daughters are being treated for tuberculosis.

They should not have allowed Union Carbide to set up its factory. When these companies want to set up some factory, they mention some product in the agreement (with the government) and they start producing something else. Then the people in the neighborhood do not get to know what is being produced. Workers in the factory are forbidden to speak to people in the community. Such factories should not be allowed in the first place. And even if they are allowed to be set up, the neighboring community must be consulted.

Wall sign outside the Union Carbide plant in Bhopal associates the gas leak with the atomic bombing of Hiroshima. The lettering "CPI(M)" on the right refers to the Communist Party of India (Marxist). (Donald Johnson)

The officials of Union Carbide should be given the severest punishment. If someone kills just one person, he is put in jail for 20 years. And here the Carbide officials have not been put behind bars for 20 minutes. They should be hanged. I am certain that the Sangathan will win the battle. The struggle for truth will be a success. Truth always wins, it only takes a little longer.

[Another active member of the Sangathan, Abdul Jabbar, discusses his role as convener of the organization and his opinions on what has been done to help the victims of Bhopal.]

ABDUL JABBAR, AGE 36

I am the convener of the Bhopal Gas Peedit Mahila Udyog Sangathan. I am a gas victim myself, my father died because of the gas. We in the Sangathan are fighting against a killer multinational and an apathetic government. Union Carbide is trying its best to evade accountability for the genocide it has committed. It is trying to wriggle out of the situation by using its wealth and its political power. The new government at the Centre seems to have taken a strong stand against Union Carbide. But the government has yet to take effective action for medical treatment of the gas victims. . . .

People outside Bhopal seem to have forgotten the gas disaster. Earlier a lot of concern was expressed for the Bhopal victims but now that seems to have died down. Even today hundreds of thousands of the gas affected people continue to suffer from gas-related illnesses and people are still dying painful deaths. Yet most people seem to believe that the Bhopal issue is over. This is indeed unfortunate.

✒POSTSCRIPT: In the last interview, Abdul Jabbar stated that "People outside Bhopal seem to have forgotten the gas disaster." What transpired in the Indian and American courts between 1984 and 1990 would seem to bear out the truth of Jabbar's statement. After the gas cloud had blown over, investigations began and thousands of people claimed billions of dollars in damages. The Indian government agreed to pay emergency relief to victims. However, since most victims had trouble proving their claims, the government was reluctant to pay. American lawyers flew to Bhopal to line up clients and some urged the poor homeless victims to keep a log of incoming and outgoing calls on their non-existent telephones. Lawyers filed claims in Indian and American courts and the subsequent legal confusion resulted in little money being paid to any victims.

Union Carbide, meanwhile, hired hundreds of "communications specialists" to counteract the growing hostility it was encountering all around the world. Union Carbide resisted the pressure from mounting court cases and public opinion to offer just compensation to the Bhopal victims. The company also stonewalled all requests for plant manuals and official transcripts relating to the disaster and continued to disavow any responsibility in the explosion. In an effort to avoid bankruptcy and to avert a hostile take-over bid, it sold off its major assets and distributed the gains to its shareholders. The company then took out a $2.5 billion loan and sold its Eveready battery division and its consumer products division.

As the maze of private and group law suits grew, the Indian Government insisted that it alone had the responsibility to bring the case against Union Carbide and the government gradually assumed sole control of the legal proceedings. Union Carbide was quite happy to deal solely with the Indian government rather than with the thousands of separate individuals. For several years, several Indian courts argued over jurisdiction for the case. Finally, on February 14, 1989, the Supreme Court of India handed down its official decision, one that had already been worked out between Union Carbide and the Indian Government. For the worst human disaster since the atomic bomb was dropped on Nagasaki, Union Carbide was to pay $470 million in compensation. In comparison, Johns Manville, after a long court battle, paid out some $2.5 billion to victims of its asbestos poisoning, a settlement that drove the company into bankruptcy. In another compensation case, the relatives of the more than 300 victims of a 1984 Air India crash were paid about $85,000 for each fatality.

Union Carbide's profits for 1988 stood at $720 million compared to $325 million for 1984, the year of the disaster. When news of the settlement reached the United States, Union Carbide shares went up two dollars on the New York Stock Exchange.

When the V. P. Singh Government took office in the winter of 1990, it moved swiftly to investigate the Supreme Court settlement of 1989. Since a single judge of the Court had handed down the ruling, the Singh government asked that the full Court hear the Bhopal case and that all Supreme Court judges be involved in the final settlement. The review dragged on for two years until in September, 1991, the Supreme Court of India finally upheld its 1989 decision, but voted to keep open criminal charges against Union Carbide officials who may have been responsible for the tragedy.

However, the innocent victims of the disaster still have received little, if any, compensation.

A Turnabout on Development

INTRODUCTION: As the new Congress government again assumed leadership in June, 1991, with the aging P. V. Narasimha Rao as the new prime minister, even the facade of economic prosperity during the 1980s was at an end. Facing India's worst balance-of-payments crisis in its history, with a 14 percent inflation rate, scarce foreign reserves, and a rising debt of $70 billion, the Rao government faced at the same time older problems, such as continuing poverty and sluggish growth. The country once again had to consider the old question in Indian development—how much free enterprise and how much central government planning? Should the commitment to a planned economy made by Nehru and continued by his daughter Indira be kept? Or should India, like many former socialist countries, especially the Soviet Union, open its system to greater market capitalism? In June of 1991, with the appointment of Manmohan Singh, an international economist, as minister of finance, the new government gave its answer. The following is adapted from news reports of the new finance minister's first major press conference, where he announced the new Indian policy toward economic development.[24]

Manmohan Singh, the new Indian finance minister, and a strong advocate of the free market system, announced on July 5: "I have the prime minister's mandate to think big," and "We are now in a different ball game." He went on to add that, ". . . the need of the hour is strict fiscal discipline, curbing wasteful expenditure and freeing the economy from the shackles of unnecessary control."[25] Such sentiments by an Indian finance minister would have been intolerable under Nehru or Ms. Gandhi during the period where the West, espe-

332

cially the United States, was looked upon as a new imperial threat. Singh went on to suggest that India now had to open its doors to Asia and the West. To achieve modernization of the economy, the finance minister spoke of streamlining India's do-nothing bureaucracy, reducing government subsidies to inefficient industries, promoting foreign trade and generally moving away from the old socialist model for development begun by Nehru in the 1950s.

Manmohan Singh's appraisal of India's present economic climate mentioned the familiar list of deeply rooted problems within Indian society which must be dealt with if the economy is to begin to match the growth rate of South Korea and Taiwan in this century. In his July press conference, he recounted the familiar list of obstacles that still lie in the path of development. The lack of public services, great poverty, persistent illiteracy, gigantic bureaucracies, caste and "blurred ideology" have left India, according to the finance minister, "almost locked in a cycle of economic despair."

Yet, even with these problems, India, Mr. Singh argued, has: ". . . tremendous potential, a country of 850 million people, a vast domestic internal market. We have a tremendous reservoir of managerial, entrepreneurial and technological skills and our people, when they compete abroad, are second to none whether it's in terms of academic institutions or in terms of making money in the U.S. or U.K. Yet I found India has become increasingly marginalized. There must be a deep examination of what has gone wrong. Why is it that South Korea is talked about? In 1960, South Korea had the same per capita income as India. Today, South Korea's income is 10 times India's."[26]

With the Congress Party victory in the 1991 elections, for the first time in India's history as a free nation, a significant debate had been opened on the very philosophy and policies that had been hallmarks of the Indian economy since 1948. Ironically, the very Congress Party which had led the nation to freedom and had governed the nation for most of its history as an independent nation, might now be launching a second revolution by implementing in the very nation which had developed the concept of "mixed economy" a democratic change leading toward a more open, free market, capitalist economy.

In another testimony, Karen Elliott House, international president of Dow Jones, wrote in 1995:

> While democratic systems like India's or the U.S.'s frequently seem less decisive and act more slowly than authoritarian ones, when policies are vetted and voted they have a durability that authoritanianism's arbitrary moves can't match. . . . What India has to recommend it [over China] is a future based on longer trends, deeper traditions and more profound tensile strengths.[27]

❧POSTSCRIPT: On February 28, 1992, Finance Minister Manmohan Singh presented the 1992-1993 budget to the Indian Parliament, and true to his word, proposed changes that reinforced the economic changes he had initiated six months earlier: cutting of government subsidies, privatizing state-owned enterprises, expanding the stock market, reducing the top tax rate on personal incomes from 62 to 52 per cent, and opening the Indian economy to foreign investments.

The World Bank, which lent India $4.5 billion in 1991 and another $2.7 billion in 1992, said "the Budget reaffirms that India is continuing broad-based and, in several areas, far-reaching structural reforms." The *New York Times* put the budget story on page one under the headline: "A Revolution Transforms India: Socialism's Out, Free Market In."

However, opposition parties and many groups in India's vibrant voluntary sector accused Singh of caving in to World Bank and International Monetary Fund pressure. The IMF in particular had suggested a number of "structural adjustments" as the condition for further loans. Much of the resistance to these policy changes has centered on the heavy additional burden that they would place on the poor and on the shortcomings of the market economy in meeting vital social and environmental needs. ❧

A Future Without Shock

෯INTRODUCTION: The meaning of India's "Living Tradition" continues to be hotly debated by Indians of all walks of life. As India enters its sixth decade of independence and faces a new millennium, many thoughtful observers are offering their analyses and prescriptions for the nation they would like to see.

One such observer is Shashi Tharoor, a distinguished diplomat, prize-winning novelist, and friendly—but incisive—critic of his own country. Tharoor concludes his personal history of India since independence by offering his views on what India has been, what problems confront it; and how the world's largest democracy might become more humane while honoring its rich traditions of pluralism and respect for all people.[28]෯

. . . On the sixth of December 1992, howling mobs of Hindu extremists tore down a disused mosque in India's northern heartland. In the frenzy that followed that wanton act of destruction, the streets of sixty-five cities and towns erupted; two thousand were killed in rioting, several tens of thousands injured, billions of dollars worth of property destroyed. Barely had calm and order been restored with the city of Bombay, *urbs prima in Indis*, the country's thriving commercial capital, blazed again in an orgy of organized violence against its Muslim minority. When that too was put down—but only after hundreds more lives were lost, thousands more livelihoods shattered—the next act in the tragedy followed. A series of thirteen bombs exploded across the city in a well-planned and orchestrated terrorist assault on Bombay's nerve centers, including its newly computerized Stock Exchange.

335

When another huge explosion rocked Calcutta days later, and the United States urged its citizens to cancel planned trips to New Delhi, the questions began to be asked: "Is it all over for India? Can India ever recover from this?"

Of course the answers were no and yes, but outsiders cannot be blamed for asking existential questions about a country that so recently had been seen as poised for takeoff. The factors that point to India's potential—its size, its human resources (particularly a skilled, educable and inexpensive workforce), its burgeoning middle-class market, its thriving democracy—also points to its pitfalls. Was the country simply too vast, too riven by differences, too torn apart by ancient and incomprehensible hatreds, to be taken in the direction that Malaysia, Indonesia, and now even China were going?

India can recover from the physical assaults against it. It is a land of great resilience that has learned, over arduous millennia, to cope with tragedy. Within twenty-four house of the Stock Exchange bombing, Bombay's traders were back on the floor, their burned-out computers forgotten, doing what they used to before technology changed their styles. Bombs alone cannot destroy India, because Indians will pick their way through the rubble and carry on as they have done throughout history.

But what *can* destroy India is a change in the spirit of its people, away from the pluralism and coexistence that has been our greatest strength. Equally, there are vital areas of life, political and economic, in which India cannot afford *not* to change. . . .

India has some serious problems. Three vital border states, Kashmir, Assam, and Punjab, have suffered secessionist ferment in the 1990s and though Punjab seems to have turned the corner, violence has become endemic in the country, with bomb blasts (and their accompanying tragic toll) a frequent occurrence even in the capital. Until T. N. Seshan astonished the country and the world with his conduct of the 1996 elections, it seems that amid assaults, intimidation, and "booth-capturing" (ballot-stuffing by thuggery), we were unable to exercise our democratic rights without spilling blood. And as if we did not have enough violence of our own, terrorism is also imported: Rajiv Gandhi's killing in an otherwise tranquil Tamil Nadu state occurred at the hands of Sri Lankan "Tamil Tigers" who had crossed the Palk Strait, bringing their murderous campaign for a separate homeland onto Indian soil.

Corruption, violence, sectarianism, the criminalization of politics, and widespread social tension all mounted during a period when a degree of economic liberalization opened up a new entrepreneurial ferment. A new consumer culture was born amid a population of whom 65 percent live below a tragically low poverty line and 25 percent earn less than twenty-five dollars a month. As the visible consumption of color TV sets, VCRs, and automobiles increased, there was more for the have-nots to aspire to, and more for the hungry and frustrated to resent. The competitive ferment has erupted through all the fissures in Indian society—farmers and peasants raging against the cities, Hindus bitterly protesting the "pampering" of the Muslims, Assamese revolting against being reduced (by Bangladeshi immigrants, Calcutta capitalists, and Delhi bureaucrat alike) to second-class citizens in their own state. A combination of India's own economic choices and external factors has left the country with a colossal economic challenge, with chronic fiscal deficits, an increasingly disastrous balance of payments, a deficient infrastructure, and mounting unemployment and inflation.

The social ferment engendered by economic change is also a key factor in the communal violence following the Hindutva resurgence of the 1990s. The youths who smashed the Babri Masjid wore the shirts and trousers of lower-middle-class urban youth, men whose opportunities have not matched their expectations, and who are taking out their resentment on the visible Other. Various sections of Hindu society are seeing their status and privileges threatened by bewildering processes of change: affirmative-action programs for Dalits and "backward classes," trade liberalization, economic reforms that have brought foreign employers into the country, remittances from Gulf labor that have made nouveaux riches out of their Muslim neighbors. A worldview resting on timeless assumptions has been jolted by the realization that you can't take anything for granted any more. . . .

The challenge of India democracy is to meet the basic material needs of all Indians while accommodating their diverse aspirations within the national dream. Economic policies are central to political prospects. . . .

The economic reforms ushered in since 1991—and whose continuation under an avowedly left-of-center United Front (UF) government in 1996 suggests that they are indeed irreversible—have been steps in the right direction. But the progress made so far, with the hesitancy characteristic of a government looking over its electoral shoulder, has been limited largely to the removal of restrictions on investment, a partial deregulation of industry, and the easing of some controls on trade and foreign exchange. Much more needs to be done to attract investment in labor-intensive enterprises, to channel foreign and private-sector money into infrastructure development (our roads are an abomination, our national highways little better than country paths), to liberate existing small-scale industries from crippling bureaucratic restrictions and promote the establishment of additional ones, to reduce the discretionary power of officialdom over the economic activity, and to eliminate the influence of the criminal underworld. The speculators and racketeers on the make who have inevitably cashed in on the early stages of liberalization are an unnecessary evil and must be curbed. . . . Deregulation of the economy must, paradoxically, be accompanied by more effective regulation of the way in which the deregulated economy works.

Above all, more Indians must develop a stake in the reforms. Economic change must reach the ordinary Indian; it must, as it has done in Malaysia and Indonesia, result in a visible improvement in the standard of living of the overwhelming majority of the people, including the poorest of the poor. This means that liberalization must produce not only

shinier foreign cars for the affluent, but jobs for the unemployed, food for the hungry, and spending money in the
hands of the needy. Otherwise the political support for
economic reforms will melt away. The market will hold no
magic for those who cannot afford to enter the marketplace.
Conversely, if liberalization comes to mean the liberating of
the creative energies of the Indian people, involving them in
the grand adventure that development can become, it will
have the effect not merely of producing growth and
prosperity but of giving Indians of all classes and backgrounds
a psychological stake in the new India—an India that they see
as serving their interests.

This could be the key that opens the door to more
generalized prosperity for Indians as a whole. The Indian
businessman and writer Gurcharan Das argues that "even if
we do nothing else but merely ensure that we don't close the
economy—don't reverse the reforms we have made—and improve the quality and quantity of education, the momentum
of the global economy will carry us on its shoulders." Self-
reliance as an end in itself is increasingly irrelevant for economics in today's interdependent world; but individual
self-reliance in a free and fair economic environment could
yet transform the lives of India's people. . . .

We are not by nature a secular people—religion plays too
large a part in our daily lives for that—but Indian secularism
should mean letting every religion flourish, rather than
privileging one above the rest, while ensuring that the tradition of dharma infuses both public policy and private conduct. After all, there are too many diversities in our land for
any one version of reality to be imposed on all of us. Hinduism is a civilization, not a dogma. Worse, the version
propagated by the proponents of Hindutva resembles nothing
so much as the arguments for the creation of Pakistan, of
which Indian nationalism is the living repudiation. Hindu
resurgence is the mirror image of the Muslim communalism
of 1947; its rhetoric echoes the bigotry that India was
constructed to reject. Its triumph would mark the end of

India, and that, I am convinced, Indians will not let happen.

And finally, yes, we can drink Coca-Cola without becoming Coca-colonized. I do not believe that Indians will become any less Indian if, in Mahatma Gandhi's metaphor, we open the doors and window of our country and let foreign winds blow through our house. Our popular culture has proved resilient enough to complete successfully with MTV and McDonald's; there is probably a greater prospect of our music and movies corrupting foreign youth, especially in other Asian and African countries and among subcontinental expatriate communities in the developed world, than of the reverse. Besides, the strength of "Indianness" has always lain in its ability to absorb foreign influences and to transform them by a peculiarly Indian alchemy into something that belongs naturally on the soil of India. The language in which this book is being published in India is just one example of this.

The independent generation, newly freed of the incubus of colonialism, was deeply mistrustful of the outside world. After all, the British had come to trade, and stayed on to rule; foreign investors were therefore seen as the thin end of a neo-imperialist wedge. The result was stagnation and under-employment, as we turned away investments that would have created jobs and strengthened infrastructure, while we tried to divide an ever-shrinking economic pie. (I have often wondered how much of our political troubles can be laid at the door or our economic choices. Youth and students without economic prospects in a rigidly controlled economy were ready material for agitations and militant movements; had we opened up the economy earlier, they might have been recruited by MNCs [multinational corporations] rather than by terrorist gangs.) Today even Communist China has learned to transcend history, to put the past in its place and open the doors to the future. India's youth have no colonial hang-ups to hobble them; they can look with confidence, not fear, at what the outside world has to offer them.

I began . . . by recalling my own cynicism as an adolescent in the India of 1975. Which way will India's youth turn? In resolving these great debates of our time, their challenge is not only to develop, and take pride in, the "sense of belonging" whose absence I bemoaned as a nineteen-year-old. It is also to sustain an India open to the contention of ideas and interests within it, unafraid of the process of the products of the outside world, wedded to the pluralism that is India's greatest strength, and determined to liberate and fulfill the creative energies of its people. Such an India can make the twenty-first century her own. Back in 1975, I ended my article with the words, "Perhaps our citizens of tomorrow with be of a different breed." Perhaps they already are.

SOURCES

Part One: THE HINDU CYCLE OF LIFE

1. Indira Gandhi, "India and the World," *Foreign Affairs* 51 (October 1972), pp. 65-66.

2. Song 89, *Women's Folk-Dongs of Rajputana,* complied by L. Winifred Bryce (New Delhi: Publications Division, Ministry of Information and Broadcasting, 1964). Reprinted by permission.

3. Excerpt from Samtha Rama Rau, "Families Are Different in India," *The Reader's Digest* (August 1965) by The Reader's Digest Association, Inc. Used with permission.

4. Shorbha Alexander with Sushsweta Ghosh, "Family: Joint, Nuclear, or Single," *Times of India: Centennial Edition* (August 15, 1988), pp. 68-69.

5. By Donald J. Johnson.

6. Adapted from Swami Chinmayananda and Kimari Bharathi Naik, *Bala Ramyanam* (Madras: Chinmaya Publications Trust, n.d.), pp. 21-27.

7. From Taya Zinkin, *Challenges in India* (New York: Walker and Company, 1966), p. 187.

8. Ravi Shankar, *My Music, My Life* (New York: Simon & Schuster, 1968). Copyright 1968 by Kinnara School of Indian Music, Inc. Reprinted by permission of publisher.

9. *Ibid.*

10. Prakash Tandon, *Punjabi Century 1857-1947* (Berkeley: University

of California Press, 1968), pp. 52-55.

11. From Ved Mehta, *Face to Face* (Boston: Little, Brown and Company 1957 by Ved Mehta) by permission of Little, Brown in association with the Atlantic Monthly Press.

12. R.K. Narayan, *The Bachelor of Arts* (East Lansing: Michigan State University Press, 1954). Reprinted by permisssion of William Morris Agency, Inc. Copyright © 1954 by R. K. Narayan and Michigan State University Press.

13. Mehta, *Face to Face, op. cit.*

14. Ainslie T. Embree, *The Hindu Tradition* (New York: The Modern Library, 1966), p. 89.

15. Reprinted by permission of Hawthorne Books, Inc. from Krishnalal Shidharani, *My India, My America.* Copyright © 1941 by Krishmalal Shidharani.

16. Dhan Gopal Mukerji, *My Brother's Face* (New York: Dutton, 1924), pp. 128-32.

17. Ved Mehta, *Walking the Indian Streets* (Boston: Little, Brown and Company, 1959), pp. 123-29. Reprinted by permission of author.

18. Embree, *The Hindu Tradition, op. cit.*, pp. 79-80.

19. By Donald Johnson.

20. Harold Isaacs, *India's Ex-Untouchables* (New York: John Day, 1965). Available in a Harper & Row Paperback, 1974. Reprinted with permission of author.

21. Pajkaj Pachauri, *India Today* (September 30, 1990), pp. 30-31. Used by permission of Living Media (India) Ltd.

22. Nonitra Kalra, *India Today* (October 15, 1990), pp. 15-16. Used by permission of Living Media (India) Ltd.

23. *India Today* (October 15, 1990), pp. 17-18. Used by permission of Living Media (India) Ltd.

24. Kapil Vatsyayana, *The Kama Sutra* (New York: Castle Books, 1963), pp. 58-61.

25. Adapted from "The New Sensuality," *Illustrated Weekly of India* (April 30, 1989). Used by permission.

26. Adapted by Donald and Jean Johnson from R. Shamasastry, trans. *Kautilya's Arthasastra* (New Delhi: Asia Publishing House, 1933);

and from Heinrich Zimmer, *Philosophies of India,* Joseph Campbell, ed. (Princeton: Princeton University Press, 1974), pp. 114-15. Used by permission of publisher.

27. Zimmer, *Philosophies, op. cit.,* pp. 120-23.

28. Canarese folk-song. "The Nearness of Death," from Charles E. Cover, *The Folk-songs of Southern India* (Madras: South India Saiva Siddhanta Works Publishing Society, 1959), p. 18.

29. From Ann Stanford, trans., *The Bhagavad Gita* (New York: The Seabury Press), 1970, 2:27. Copyright © 1970 by Herder & Herder, Inc. Used by permission of publisher.

30. Louis Renon, *Hinduism* (New York: George Braziller, 1961), p. 129.

31. Swami Nikhilanarda, *The Upanishads* (New York: Harper & Row, 1964), p. 321.

32. Barbara Stoler Miller, *Bhartrihari: Poems* (New York: Columbia University Press, 1967), p. 46.

33. Swami Ramakrishna, trans. by "M," *The Gospel of Rāmalarishna* (New York: Vedenta Society, 1947).

34. Stanford, trans., *Bhagavad Gita, op, cit.,* 9:19, 10:8, 32, 36, 4, 5, 39.

35. Juan Mascars, *The Upanishads* (Baltimore: Penguin Books, 1965), pp. 117-118.

36. Miller, *Bhartrihari, op cit.,* p. 137.

37. "Laws of Manu," Chapter VI:2-3, in William H. McNeil and Jean W. Sedlar, *Classical India* (New York: Oxford University Press, 1969), pp. 144-45.

38. Sister Nivedita, *Cradle Tales of Hinduism* (Calcutta: Advaita Ashrama, 1969), p. 243.

39. Reprinted by permission of William Morrow and Company, Inc. from Paul Scott, *The Jewel in the Crown.* Copyright © 1966 by Paul Scott.

40. From Arthur Basham, *The Wonder That Was India* (New York: Grove Press, 1959), p. 326.

41. Stanford, trans, *Bhagavad Gita, op. cit.,* 2:11, 27, 31-38; 3:35; pp. 14-31.

42. *Ibid.,* 2:47-48.

43. *Ibid.*, 2:51.

44. *Ibid.*, 9:32.

45. "She [Radha] Speaks," in Edward C. Dimock, Jr. and Denise Leverton, *In Praise of Krishna* (New York: Anchor Books, Doubleday Company, 1967), p. 58. Reprinted by permission of publisher.

46. Mahatma Gandhi, quoted in Krishnalal Shridharani, *The Mahatma and the World* (New York: Duell, Sloan and Pearce, 1949), p. xiii.

47. By Jean E. Johnson.

48. Prakash Tandon, *Punjabi Century 1857-1947* (Berkeley: University of California Press, 1968), pp. 148-52. Originally published by the University of California Press; reprinted by permission of the Regents of the University of California.

Part Two: THE HISTORIC TRADITION

1. Mark Twain, *Following the Equator* (New York: Harper & Brothers, 1899), p. 26.

2. *The Statesman,* January 21, 1954.

3. Jawaharial Nehru, *The Discovery of India* (Bombay: Asia Publishing House, 1961), pp. 50-53. Reprinted by permission of the Jawaharlal Nehru Memorial Fund.

4. Jawaharial Nehru, *Glimpses of World History* (Bombay: Asia Publishing House, 1962), pp. 9-13. Reprinted by permission of the Jawaharlal Nehru Memorial Fund.

5. Written by the authors, based on selections from N. A. and Richard McKean, eds., *The Edicts of Ashoka* (Chicago: The University of Chicago Press, 1978), pp. 25-31. Quoted selections reprinted by permission of publisher.

6. H.G. Wells, *The Outline of History* (New York: MacMillan, 1926).

7. James Legge, ed., *A Record of Buddhist Kingdoms* (New York: Dover Publications, 1965), pp. 44-47. Used by permission of publisher.

8. Nehru, *Glimpses of World History, op. cit.*

9. Adapted from Percival Spear, *The Nabobs* (London: Oxford University Press, 1963), pp. 53-57. Used by permission of publisher.

10. Munro letter to Lord Canning, in Gleig, ed., *Thomas Munro*, Vol. II, p. 57. Quoted in Michael Edwardes, *A History of India from the Earliest Times to the Present* (New York: Farrar, Straus and Cudahy, 1961), pp. 261-64. Used by permission of the publisher.

11. Edwardes, *A History of India, op. cit.* (See note 10.)

12. R. K. Narayan, *Swami and Friends* and *The Bachelor of Arts* (East Lansing: Michigan State University Press, 1954), pp. 5-6. Reprinted by permission of William Morris Agency, Inc. Copyright 1954 by R. K. Narayan and Michigan State University Press. (*Swami and Friends* is available in a Fawcett Premier Edition.)

13. Dhan Gopal Mukerji, *My Brother's Face* (Calcutta: Asia Publishing House, 1945), pp. 164-66.

14. Quoted in L. S. S. O'Malley, *Modern India and the West* (London: Oxford University Press, 1941), from Bishop J. M. Thobuon, *India and Malaysia* (1893).

15. From Leften S. Stavianos, et al., *A Global History of Man* (Boston: Allyn and Bacon, 1962, 1966), pp. 535-57. Copyright © 1962 and 1966 by Allyn and Bacon, Inc. Reprinted by permission of publisher.

16. *Social Studies, a Textbook for Secondary Schools* (New Delhi: The National Council of Educational Research & Training, 1969), pp. 282-83.

17. Rudyard Kipling, "The White Man's Burden," *Rudyard Kipling's Verse Inclusive Edition 1885-1926* (Garden City: Doubleday, Doran & Company, 1929), pp. 373-79.

18. Nirad Chaudhuri, *The Autobiography of an Unknown Indian* (Berkeley: University of California Press, 1968), pp. 113-19.

19. Jawaharial Nehru, *Discovery of India* (Garden City, NY: Anchor Books, Doubleday & Company, 1959), pp. 274-75. Reprinted by permission of publisher.

20. Reprinted by permission of Hawthorn Books, Inc., from Krishnalal Shridharani, *The Mahatma and the World.* Copyright 1946 by Krishnalal Shridharani.

21. Webb Miller, *I Found No Peace* (New York: Simon & Schuster, 1936). Copyright © by Webb Miller. Reprinted by permission of publisher.

22. Negley Farson, *We Cover the World*, Eugene Lyons, ed. (New York: Harcourt Brace Javanovich, 1937), pp. 142-43.

23. Khushwant Singh, "Why Hindus and Muslims Speak Hate," *New York Times Magazine* (September 19, 1965). Copyright © 1965 by the New York Times Company. Reprinted by permission.

24. *India Today* (December 31, 1990), pp. 42-46, as reported by Dilip Awoasthi, Aloktiwari, Farzand Ahmed, Ramesh Menon, and Uday Mahurkar. Used by permission of Living Media (India) Ltd.

25. Scott Carrier, "A Himalayan Hell," *Esquire* (January 1999), pp. 50-55. Excerpts reprinted by permission of Anderson/Grinberg Literary Management, Inc.

Part Three: AN OLD CIVILIZATION BUILDS A NEW NATION

1. "The Ballot in Rural India," *The Saturday Statesman,* June 29, 1991, p. 6.

2. Ved Mehta, *The New India* (New York: Penguin Books, 1978), pp. 162-63.

3. Adapted from Tara Zinkin, *India* (New York: Oxford University Press, 1964), p. 11-13.

4. R. G. K., " Wanted: A Revolution in Education," *The Illustrated Weekly of India* (February 11, 1973), p. 11. Reprinted with permission.

5. R. G. K. Narayan, "Fifteen Years," in *Next Sunday* (Bombay: Pearl Publications, 1960), pp. 14-17. Copyright © R. G. K. Narayan.

6. Dhan Gopal Mukerji, *My Brother's Face* (Calcutta: Asia Publishing House, 1945).

7. Kuldip Nayar and Khushwant Singh, *The Tragedy of the Punjab: Operation Bluestar and After* (Delhi: Vision Books, 1981), pp. 19-21.

8. "Liberating the Golden Temple," *India Today* (November 30, 1984). Used by permission of Living Media (India) Ltd.

9. *Ibid.*

10. *Ibid.*

11. Adapted from *Jawaharlal Nehru's Speeches, 1949* (New Delhi: Publications Division, Government of India), pp. 93-96.

12. Adapted from M. K. Gandhi, *India of My Dreams,* compiled by P. K.

Prabhu (Bombay: Hind Kutubs Ltd. Publishers, 1947), pp. 22-29; and M. K. Gandhi, *Village Swaraj*, compiled by H. M. Vyas (Ahmedabad: Navjivan Publishing House, 1962), pp. 13-18.

13. Ramindar Singh and Raj Chengappa, "Day of the Farmer," *India Today* (December 31, 1985), pp. 75-78. Used by permission of Living Media (India) Ltd.

14. Adapted from "The Little Match Girls," in Arthur Bonner, *Averting the Apocalypse: Social Movements in India Today* (Durham, NC: Duke University Press, 1990), pp. 323-28, Copyright © 1990. Reprinted by permission of the publisher; and Sivakasi, "Exploiting the Young," *India Today* (January 15, 1983), pp. 96-100. Used by permission of Living Media (India) Ltd.

15. Myron Weiner, *The Child and the State in India* (Princeton: Princeton University Press, 1991), pp. 56-61. Reprinted by permission of publisher; and Babriele Vensky, "India's Literacy Miracle," *World Press Review* and *Die Ziet*, Hamburg (September 1990), p. 66.

16. By Leon E. Clark.

17. See Bonner, "The Little Match Girls," *op. cit.*

18. Dom Morales, *A Matter of People* (New York: Praeger Publishers, 1974), pp. 22-24.

19. *World Population Politics*, Vol. 2. (New York: United Nations, 1989), p. 64.

20. *India Today* (October 31, 1988). Used by permission of Living Media (India) Ltd.

21. Uday Mahukar, "Battle Royal," *India Today* (January 31, 1991), pp. 66-68. Used by permission of Living Media (India) Ltd.

22. Alfred de Grazia, *A Cloud Over Bhopal* (Bombay: The Kalos Foundation, 1985), p. 15.

23. Bhopal Group for Information and Action, B-2/302 Sheetal Marg, Berasia Road, Bhopal 462 001, India, March 12, 1990, pp. 3-12; and *Voices from Bhopal* (Bhopal: The Group, 1990), pp. 3-4, 11, 16-17.

24. Adapted by Donald E. Johnson from Sudeep Chakravarti, "The Bold Gamble," *India Today* (July 31, 1991), pp. 10-13. Used by permission of Living Media (India) Ltd.

25. Quoted in *Times of India*, July 6, 1991.

26. From the *New York Times,* July 8, 1991.

27. From *The Wall Street Journal,* January 1995.

28. Sashi Tharoor, *India: From Midnight to the Millenium* (New York: Harper Perennial, 1997), pp. 323-29, 360-62.

INDEX